IRELAND
THE STRUGGLE
FOR POWER

IRELAND
THE STRUGGLE
FOR POWER

FROM THE DARK AGES TO THE JACOBITES

JEFFREY JAMES

AMBERLEY

For Una

First published 2017

Amberley Publishing
The Hill, Stroud
Gloucestershire, GL5 4EP

www.amberley-books.com

Copyright © Jeffrey James, 2017

The right of Jeffrey James to be identified as
the Author of this work has been asserted in
accordance with the Copyrights, Designs and
Patents Act 1988.

ISBN 978 1 4456 6246 6 (hardback)
ISBN 978 1 4456 6247 3 (ebook)

British Library Cataloguing in Publication Data.
A catalogue record for this book is available
from the British Library.

Typesetting and Origination by Amberley
Publishing.
Printed in the UK.

CONTENTS

River systems, towns and early political divisions

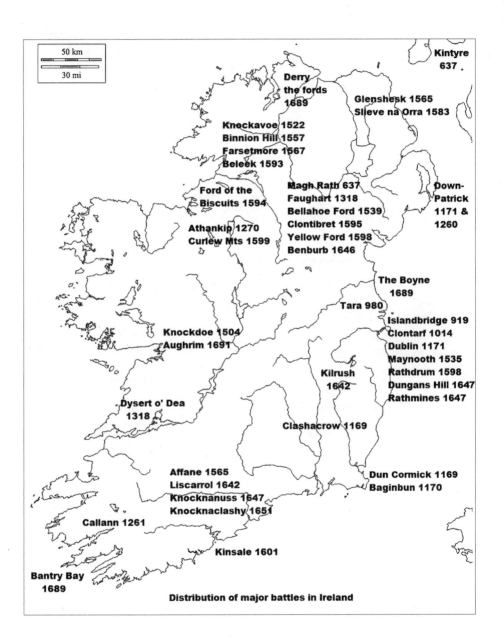

50 km
30 mi

Kintyre 637

Derry the fords 1689

Glenshesk 1565
Slieve na Orra 1583

Knockavoe 1522
Binnion Hill 1557
Farsetmore 1567
Beleek 1593

Ford of the Biscuits 1594

Magh Rath 637
Faughart 1318
Bellahoe Ford 1539
Clontibret 1595
Yellow Ford 1598
Benburb 1646

Down-Patrick 1171 & 1260

Athankip 1270
Curlew Mts 1599

The Boyne 1689

Tara 980

Islandbridge 919
Clontarf 1014
Dublin 1171
Maynooth 1535
Rathdrum 1598
Dungans Hill 1647
Rathmines 1647

Knockdoe 1504
Aughrim 1691

Kilrush 1642

Dysert o' Dea 1318

Clashacrow 1169

Affane 1565
Liscarrol 1642
Knocknanuss 1647
Knocknaclashy 1651

Dun Cormick 1169
Baginbun 1170

Callann 1261

Kinsale 1601

Bantry Bay 1689

Distribution of major battles in Ireland

50 km

30 mi

MacDonald

McDonnell

O'Donnell

Clandeboy

O'Neill of
Tyrone

McSweeny

Earldom
of
Ulster

O'Devlin

Maguire

O'Hanlon

O'Rourke

Mac-
William

O'Dowd

O'Connor

Magennis

O'Hara

MacDonagh

O'Reilly

Mayo Burke

Faly

The

O'Malley

O'Gara

O'Molloy

English

O'Dempsey

Clanrickard
Burke

O'Flaherty

Pale

O'Carrol

O'Kelly

O'Lochlann

O'Kennedy

O'Toole

O'Brien

O'More

MacMahon

Mac-
Murrough

Earldom
of
Ormond

MacNamara

O'Byrne

Burke

Cavanagh

Le Poer

Earldom
of
Thomond

Barry

MacCarthy

O'Sullivan

Lordships and major family groupings c. 1500

8

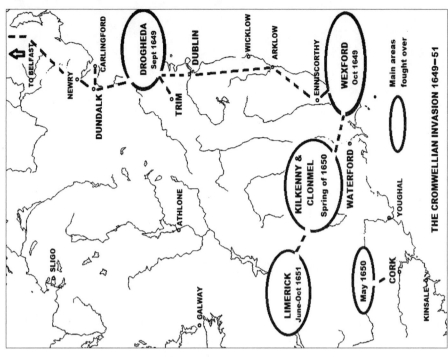

THE CROMWELLIAN INVASION 1649–51

DROGHEDA
Sept 1649

WEXFORD
Oct 1649

KILKENNY &
CLONMEL
Spring of 1650

LIMERICK
June–Oct 1651

May 1650

Main areas
fought over

TO BELFAST
NEWRY
CARLINGFORD
DUNDALK
TRIM
DUBLIN
WICKLOW
ARKLOW
ENNISCORTHY
WATERFORD
YOUGHAL
CORK
KINSALE
GALWAY
ATHLONE
SLIGO

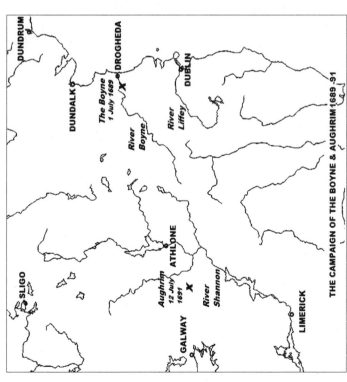

THE CAMPAIGN OF THE BOYNE & AUGHRIM 1689–91

DUNDRUM
DUNDALK
DROGHEDA
The Boyne
1 July 1689
DUBLIN
River
Boyne
River
Liffey
ATHLONE
Aughrim
12 July
1691
River
Shannon
SLIGO
GALWAY
LIMERICK

9

Gentlemen, you may soon have the alternative to live as slaves or die as free men.

Daniel O'Connell, Mallow, co. Cork, June 1843

I

HEROIC ECHOES

Roman general Agricola may have contemplated invading Ireland toward the end of the first century AD. His companion, the historian Tacitus, wrote how he frequently heard the general assert that a single legion and a few auxiliaries would suffice to conquer Ireland and keep its people under subjugation. Tacitus accurately described Ireland as an island smaller than Britain but larger than the islands of the Mediterranean. He may have been drawing on information from the Britons, as well as from maps made by early travellers. Eratosthenes' world map, *c.* 220 BC, shows the island of Ierne positioned above a larger Brettanie. Marcus Agrippa's map of the world, *c.* AD 20, fails to name Ireland, but still shows it, this time lying below Britannia. Tacitus assessed the island's inhabitants as being little different from the Britons and claimed Agricola saw propaganda value in subjugating them to Roman rule. The general claimed that the conquest of Ireland would restrain the Britons by awing them with the prospect of Roman arms all around them, 'banishing liberty from their sight'. Nothing in the end came of Agricola's deliberations. Later Irish chroniclers claimed the fame of their fighting men deterred the Roman warlord, but the Romans had not baulked when confronting similarly fierce opposition in Scotland – namely a confederation of tribes collectively known as the Caledonii, ruddy-haired and large-limbed men, among them the fierce Vacomagi and Taexali tribes. Had Agricola reached

Ireland he would have faced a similar enemy, adept at luring bodies of troops deeper and deeper into uncharted, marshy and heavily wooded territory. In the foothills of the Scottish Highlands, the Romans could rarely pin down such foes, who were capable of launching surprise attacks one moment and disappearing into the shadows the next. On one occasion only the fortuitous arrival of supporting cavalry prevented the destruction of Agricola's Spanish legionaries. Attacked under cover of night, they were for a time forced to fight back to back in the dark.

In AD 83, the Caledonii confronted their aggressors in the open. Trapped by a marauding Roman fleet and an advancing Roman army, starvation or enslavement beckoned – eventualities feared by the Caledonii more than death in battle. A speech made by the Caledonian leader Calgacus to his warriors stressed that they yet remained free and untouched by servitude. He added that they must fight, warning that the only alternative to fighting was to accept the devastation which the Romans called peace: a cycle of enslavement, tribute and submission. He said of the Romans, 'To ravage, to slaughter, to usurp under false titles, they will call empire, and, where they make a desert, they will call it peace.' At the battle which followed – Mons Graupius, fought somewhere in north-east Scotland – Roman auxiliaries carried the day, assisted by their cavalry. Agricola held his legions back in reserve. Tacitus alleged the Romans slaughtered thousands of the enemy for the loss of just 360 men. A description of the Celts as forming up 'openly, without forethought' helps explain Calgacus' crushing defeat, but of more import was the materiel and military superiority of the Romans: better weaponry, greater discipline and superior tactical awareness.

Sometime earlier than Mons Graupius, Agricola's army had crossed an unidentified stretch of water and defeated peoples unknown to the Romans until then. These were probably tribes hailing from Galloway and Ayrshire in the wilds of south-west Scotland, not the Irish as has sometimes been claimed. Agricola had with him at his side an Irish king named Tuathal Techtmar. Reflecting a theme that would reoccur throughout early Irish history, Tuathal had been temporarily exiled from Ireland by a rival. He sought Roman backing to regain his territories, not in the form of Roman soldiers or auxiliaries but in weaponry and supplies; this was in return for important trading rights, raw materials and Tuathal's promise to work to prevent Irish attacks on Roman Britain. Roman and Romano-British artefacts found in Leinster, notably at a fortified site north of Dublin and on Lambay Island, confirm a brisk trade interaction.

Agricola actively looked for allies like Tuathal to act in Rome's best interests in Ireland. According to Tacitus, 'it was the long-established practice of the Romans to make local kings the instrument of servitude.' As to why the Roman military neglected to occupy Ireland, they probably had enough to do protecting Britain. As in the Highlands of Scotland and the lands east of the Rhine, payback for such a risky venture was unlikely. Rome could not hope to gather sufficient taxes from under-developed societies to make long-term occupation viable. Southern Britain and Gaul on the other hand had much larger, thriving communities. Ireland's geographic remoteness and relative lack of sophistication therefore saved it from the attentions of Rome's legions. There was no Roman pattern of military occupation, road building and urbanisation. The country remained a patchwork of rival tribes without centralised control.

Like their Continental and British cousins, the Irish were head-hunters. When one ruler triumphed in battle over another, he cut off his victim's head and paraded it to prove his rival had been defeated and no longer lived. Greek geographer Strabo said, 'When the Celts depart from battle, they hang the heads of their enemies from the necks of their horses, and when they bring them home they nail the spectacle to the entrance of their houses.' Welsh and Scandinavian sagas from a later period also make reference to head-hunting. One bardic account tells of the Earl of Orkney dying from blood poisoning caused by an infected tooth from the jaw of a decapitated head hanging from his saddle. Open wounds on his leg must have brushed up against the mouth of his grim trophy. Other evidence of the practice comes from a Gallic carving showing a severed head dangling from a horse's neck; another illustrates a rider trampling over five lopped-off heads. Strabo thought the Irish even more savage than other Celts. He claimed that as well as hunting for heads they practiced human sacrifice, ate their dead and practiced incest. Such scare stories may have been written to serve as titillating propaganda for a Roman audience, a demonising of the *Other* characteristic of all aggressive, colonising powers.

Rather than heads, the unit of value in Ireland was a female slave, worth three cows. Codified in the fifth century, Irish Brehon law details how leaders apportioned land between themselves and others. A cooperative system prevailed, including common ownership, with provision made for the sick, old and disabled. Warfare often resulted from feuding following disputes over ownership of land, livestock and slaves. A warrior elite protected clan heartlands within which women might sometimes gain parity with men; one such example is Maeve of Connaught, a first-century female chieftain. A legendary tale known as the Cattle Raid of Cooley tells of maeve making war on her neighbours to gain possession of a bull, the ownership of which would put her on a par materially with her husband, the high-king. Maeve is said to have traded both her body and land to get the bull, promising a warrior named Daire territories to match his own, plus a chariot valued at thirty-seven bond-maidens, and 'my own open thighs' too, should he carry off the prize. An anecdotal story tells of a third-century Roman empress criticising the free-spirited Celtic women; her companion, a British queen, replied with contempt, 'We may consort openly with our menfolk, but, unlike Roman women, we do not allow ourselves to be debauched by them in private.'

Irish chieftains emerged from within a loose extended family on the basis of suitability. Status as a warrior was a primary consideration. Those overlooked often contested the chieftainship, and this led to fierce internecine conflict. Fighting men attached themselves to the households of leaders in return for sustenance and a share of the plunder. They became members of permanently established war-bands, employed to confront small-scale enemy raids and enforce their chieftain's rule. Leaders in wartime might be expected to provide upwards of 500 men for military service. Battles occurred in places where lines of communication were interrupted by natural obstacles, such as at river crossings or defiles. A high proportion probably took place along Ireland's eastern seaboard. Death in battle for fighting men was the norm. During this heroic age no prestige could be accrued from dying in bed. A member of a leader's bodyguard rarely survived his master's (or mistress') death in battle, since it would have been viewed as dishonourable to have done so. Chieftains carried swords and shields and often fought in single combat against noble opponents. Spears were cast like javelins or employed to stab an opponent when in close combat. Slingers are also mentioned as being used at these fights. Piercing slingshot added to the terror of coming under attack. Missiles uncovered at Burnswark Hill in Scotland have been described when tested as 'whistling' at very high speeds toward their targets, with the potential to kill or maim. Battles were brutal but short-lived, akin to slogging matches, devoid of elaborate tactics associated with better-drilled Romans.

Light wicker chariots were also a feature of Celtic warfare. Their first appearance in combat is said to have shaken the Romans. Julius Caesar wrote, 'The chariots of the Britons begin the fighting by charging over the battlefield; from them they hurl their javelins, although the noise of the wheels and chariot teams are enough in themselves to throw an enemy into panic.' Warriors acrobatically jumped from advancing vehicles, launching their spears before being whisked away. Both the Iceni warrior queen Boudicca and Ireland's Queen Maeve are associated with chariots in literature, as is the legendary hero Manannan. The latter, who gave his name to the Isle of Man, is reputed to have held the reins of two supernatural horses when pulling the chariot upon which he led his defeated people to the underworld, an echo, perhaps, of wars for control of Ireland dating back into prehistory. Another legendary hero who is said to have possessed a chariot is Cúchulainn. Claimed to have been scythed in the manner of the ancient Persians and Syrians, his chariot was also adorned with 'iron sickles, thin blades, hooks and hard spikes', capable of careering through a mass of soldiery, 'lacerating bones and bodies'. No archaeological evidence has ever turned up to support such a claim, so the existence of chariots such as this in the British Isles remains unconfirmed.

Better attested than scythed chariots is the fact that the famous Hill of Tara, the crowning place of Ireland's high-kings, remained until quite late on an important military and religious centre for the Irish. Dominating the low-lying grasslands of Meath, Tara has always struck a chord with writers and poets. The hill-top locale, with its breathtaking views, is a captivating place, especially when the setting sun casts in shadow the rich pasturelands that spread westward toward distant mountains. Tara retains its emotional pull into modern times: one has only think of Scarlett O'Hara's cotton plantation in Margaret Mitchell's *Gone with the Wind*, set during the American Civil War, in which the very name becomes a siren call to hearth and home in troubled times. Tara's famous halls would have been built of wood or wattle and daub. None now remain. A twelfth-century document, the *Dindshenchas*, tells of Tara's halls having numerous doors, able to accommodate 'the choice part of the men of Ireland' as well as a thousand soldiers. Upon the hill's summit now stand grassy humps and hollows, ancient monuments linked in legend to Ireland's high-kings. Some of these earthworks date back more than 4,000 years. Excavations in the 1950s of one site, known as 'the mound of the hostages', turned up a large number of Middle Bronze Age burials. Artefacts were intermingled with cremated remains, among them a magnificent but badly burned stone battle-axe. Around the neck of an uncremated teenage boy lay beads of a necklace made from bronze, amber and jet. Also found with him were a bronze knife and a pointed spike, thought to be an awl. Three chambers housed remains. Upwards of 250 interments took place there, organised into layers.

The largest monument in terms of acreage at Tara is the great banqueting hall, now comprising just two 750-foot parallel banks of earth astride a sunken area 90 feet across. The author of the *Dindshenchas* dwelt on twin themes: the transience of life and the greatness of the hall's owner, high-king Cormac mac Airt, who he likened to the biblical Solomon: 'Since Solomon, who was better than all progenies together? What offspring that would match Cormac hath the earth devoured, O God?'

Despite the build-up Cormac met a banal death, choking on a fish bone. Other mythical Irish warriors of old met their ends more memorably. Conn 'of the hundred battles', born at Tara, who gave his name to Connaught, was killed by disguised assassins. The aforementioned Cúchulainn – said in folklore to have been a hyperactive warrior, liable in a frenzy to slay friends and foe alike, and credited with single-handedly defending Ulster from the might of Queen Maeve of Connaught – was supposedly struck down by a magical spear. Mortally wounded, he tied himself to a standing-stone at Clochafarmore, co. Louth. His enemies kept their distance until a raven flew down and rested on his shoulder; only then did his assailants approach the corpse. Queen Maeve is said to have died when struck by a slingshot cast at her while she bathed in a lake. She is now reputed to lie beneath a 35-foot-high heap of stones at Knocknarea, co. Sligo. Niall of the Nine Hostages, the progenitor of a long line of future O'Neill kings, fell in battle while bravely leading a raid on Britain. Another legendary hero, Finn McCool, is said to avoided death altogether. He once destroyed a demon that lulled the hilltop residents of Tara to sleep. Through the application of self-inflicted pain, the stubborn Finn remained awake and surprised and killed the intruder. He now makes up for his long, painful vigil by sleeping through the centuries in a cave, surrounded by the men of his bodyguard, the Fianna. Like King Arthur, he will reawaken at the time of Ireland's greatest need.

In 1925, the Fianna gave their name to the Irish Republican party, Fianna Fail. The party sought, in the words of Eamon de Valera's biographer, Ronan Fanning, 'to evoke heroic echoes from the past in its bid to secure the independence of a united Ireland'. There are few real heroes in this narrative, other than those who suffered under the yoke of oppressors and sometimes fought back, but Finn's spirit seeks to intrude nonetheless.

The warlord Conn's alleged hundred battles, fought during a long reign spanning the years AD 122–157, underscore the premise that civil warfare in Ireland during early times was very much a way of life for the ruling classes. Society had become increasingly hierarchical and resources were plentiful enough for a small warrior class to exist free from agricultural duties. The life of Cormac mac Airt, whose death occurred in the year 267, bears witness to this. Not only did he subdue the north and west of Ireland, he also gained control over Leinster and invaded and later allied himself with Munster. He then led a series of destructive attacks on Roman Britain. To do this he would have needed several well-organised and militarily resourced war-bands. So too would have the fifth-century Niall of the Nine Hostages, who so sorely harmed Britain that his victims sought military support from the Continent, paving the way for the Anglo-Saxon conquest of Britain.

The Irish were skilled seafarers. Their small, skin-covered boats were well suited to penetrate riverine inlets and surprise British coastal communities. The sixth-century British monk and historian Gildas recorded how 'there emerged from the coracles that carried them across the sea-valleys the foul hordes of Scots [Irish] and Picts, like dark throngs of worms who wriggle out of narrow fissures in the rock when the sun is high'. Niall gained his nickname from allegedly holding captive five hostages from Ireland, one from each province, plus four from Britain. If true, his kingship must have been extensive and his threat to Britain very real. Contemporaries described him as 'the king of the western world'.

Dramatic recalls of troops from the Continent to Britain occurred even earlier than Niall's time. The poet Claudian, who died around the turn of the fifth century, speaks of soldiers hurriedly sent to Britain by the Roman general Stilicho during the reign of Theodosius the Great (d. AD 395). In the year 367, the Saxons, Picts and Irish managed, by coincidence or design, to synchronise their attacks on Britain and cause enormous damage. It was therefore as an aggressor that Ireland first emerged into the recorded mainstream of European history, this caused perhaps by an increase in the population of Ireland, sometimes explained by improved weather conditions and innovations in farming methods. Pressure on land made eastward migration an attractive proposition for the Irish. Coin hoards in Wales, Lancashire and Cumbria attest to increased insecurity among the local populace in western Britain due to incursions from Ireland. Supporting such a claim is a renewed Roman military preparedness in the west, dated to the third and fourth centuries. The effectiveness of these Roman counter-measures may have forced Irish migrants to concentrate their settlement endeavours further to the north, beyond Hadrian's Wall. Here they created a bridgehead in Argyll, centred on the great fortress of Dunadd, near Kilmartin.

Surrounded by a bog known as the Great Moss, the stronghold at Dunadd could only be accessed from the sea. Distribution of prehistoric remains in the region indicates a long history of contact between north-east Ireland and western Scotland. It was perhaps from here that hunter-gatherers first set out to exploit Ireland during post-glacial times, journeying in the summer months in skin boats to hunt red deer, roe deer and wild boar. Indicators of human activity in the Inner Hebrides, such as stone tools found on the east coast of the Isle of Islay, date to around 12,000 years ago. Early pioneers faced a densely forested land and an interior accessible only across lakes and down rivers. Much of the north, south and west of Ireland is mountainous and much of the interior was then a bog. DNA evidence indicates there to have been almost continuous east–west migration across Europe in far-off times: bones uncovered near Belfast of a woman who live over 5,000 years ago were discovered to have genetic sequences traceable to the Middle East, and three Irishmen who lived around 4,000 years ago had ancestry traceable back to the Pontic-Caspian steppes, a region of extensive flat grassland extending from the Danube to the Urals. From earliest times, therefore, Dunadd may have been an important stronghold and staging post. It would become the site where future kings of what became known as Scottic Dalriada were inaugurated. The River Bann in Ulster delineated Dalriada's royal remit to the west and 'the mountains of the spine of Britain', and the Drumalban range (today the eastern boundary of modern-day Argyllshire) bounded the kingdom to the east. The fourteenth-century Irish warlord Domnall O'Brien stated, 'The kings of lesser Scotia drew the source of their blood from our greater Scotia.' Churchmen called the inhabitants of Argyll the Irish of Britain. The Anglo-Saxon historian Bede meant the same thing when he referred to the Dalriadans as 'the Scots in Britain'.

King Gabhran of Dalriada appears to have been the first of a line of Irish kings to confront serious opposition from eastern Scotland. He died in battle in the year 559 after suffering a defeat against the son of Maelchon, a Pictish king from the lands beyond Drumalban. Gabhran's son Aedan also met with defeat at Pictish hands, most famously at the Battle of Circinn around 597, probably fought well to the east of Kintyre in modern-day Angus. Aedan was a belligerent man, known to Welsh poets as Aedan 'the treacherous', famous for his wide-ranging plundering expeditions, including one to the Orkneys and another to the Isle of Man. In later life Aedan looked southward to achieve his ambitions. Here a new threat had emerged, the Anglian kingdom of Bernicia, centred on Bamburgh in modern-day Northumberland. At the now long-lost Degsa's Stone (Degsastan) in 603 Aedan suffered another crushing defeat, this time at the hands of an Anglo-Saxon king named Aethelfrith, a monarch described by Bede as 'brave and most eager for glory'. Aedan's army was cut to pieces; Bede claimed the defeat at Degsa's Stone deterred southward ambitions by the Irish for a generation or more. Aedan's youngest son, Eochaid 'the yellow haired', added to the dynasty's reach by extending his influence eastward into modern-day Perth and Kinross. By the year 627 he was being referred to as Rex Pictorum. Nicknames like 'the yellow-haired' were commonly used to describe and better identify the various kings of old. Other examples are 'the great', 'the proud', 'the white', 'the bearded', 'the boneless', 'of the gapped spear', 'the red', 'the cock', 'the flat-nosed' and 'the son of the yellow bitch'; the latter presumably an insulting reference to the king in question's mother. Our hero Finn McCool was known as 'the white haired'.

Two powerful Irish kings with distinctive epithets teamed up in the year 637 to confront the powerful Domnall mac Aodha

O'Neill, the newly made, perhaps self-styled, Irish high-king. They were Congal 'the half-blind' and Domnall Brec 'the freckled', of Dalriada. Congal's half-blindness was, allegedly, the result of a bee sting that had caused a serious infection of the eye and surrounding socket. His disfigurement may have disbarred him from the high-kingship. Candidates with deformities were generally not allowed to hold high office in Gaelic society. An argument about this was likely the cause of the quarrel with the ambitious Domnall mac Aodha.

The resulting Battle of Magh Rath did not simply pit Irishmen against Irishmen. As well as his Dalriadans, Congal's ally, Domnall Brec, brought to the battlefield Picts, Anglo-Saxons and Welshmen. Congal's forces included his own army, plus others hostile to Domnall mac Aodha. Styling himself high-king of Tara, the latter called up men from all over Ireland. All save the men of Connaught were represented at what must have been the biggest battle fought on Irish soil up until this time. A druid named Dubdiad likened Domnall mac Aodha's army to the 'most powerful tides of the seas' and warned Congal and Domnall Brec against opposing it. Undeterred, Congal accepted battle. His rallying cry called for the splendid soldiers of Erin – 'high-minded kerns of fame' – to cluster round him, the true king. Bards later remembered how mightily his battalions advanced across the flooded ford of Ornam with banners bravely held aloft: one displayed a yellow lion; another a potent symbol of plunder, perhaps a bull. Referred to in the annals as the plains of Magh Comair, the location of the fighting was a stretch of rolling pastureland located a mile or so north-east of the modern-day town of Newry, co. Down. Domnall mac Aodha's mighty surge was at first countered. The fighting might have become protracted had not a Welsh king named Conan fallen victim to an enemy blade. His death turned the day in Domnall mac Aodha's favour. Domnall Brec's Welsh allies immediately became discouraged. Congal's death soon followed. Fleeing Dalriadans, Scots and Welsh attempted to regain their boats, but many were cut down. Not only was the high-kingship firmly back in the hands of the dominant O'Neill, Dalriada's regal link with eastern Ulster was also severed. The province of Argyll was cast adrift politically from the north of Ireland, something foreseen by the great Irish pilgrim of Christ St Columba, who had warned that Aedan mac Gabhran's descendants might one day lose 'the sceptre of this kingdom'.

Magh Rath firmly re-established Domnall mac Aodha and Clan O'Neill as the rulers in the north of Ireland, and confirmed the former's right to the high-kingship. A sea battle fought the same day as Magh Rath, off the Mull of Kintyre, was also won by Domnall mac Aodha's forces. Four or five years later, at the Battle of Strathcarron, near Falkirk, the still expansionist-minded Domnall Brec died fighting the Strathclyde Welsh. The author of the Y *Gododdin* lamented how 'great sturdy men came at dawn and gave the battle shout ... and ravens gnawed at the head of Domnall Brec'.

That druids attended on Congal immediately prior to the Battle of Magh Rath poses the question as to whether or not the protagonists were Christianised. Christianity had certainly reached Gaul by the end of the first century. At first, Christians had been a persecuted sect. Not until Emperor Constantine's conversion to the faith and the so-called Edict of Milan a year later, in 313, did the religion become legitimatised within the empire. Very little is known of the early progression of early Christianity into the British Isles; few literary or archaeological relics have survived. St Patrick spoke of himself as evangelizing heathen Ireland but missions may have arrived in Ireland from Rome decades earlier than his – as early perhaps as the last decades of the fourth century. Pope Celestine I's order to a missionary priest named Palladius to minister to the Irish dates to the 430s. But although Palladius may have reached Ireland and ministered there before Patrick, Ireland's patron saint's fame overshadowed him. Whereas Palladius attended to an already converted congregation, Patrick targeted pagans in the north of Ireland for conversion. He went out on a limb in doing so. Patrick's conviction that he had been called by God to preach overseas to enemies of Britain may have been frowned upon. Christians in the late Roman period did not encourage missionary activity to the barbarians outside of their settled frontiers. Some may also have believed the future saint to have been unqualified for the task. Others may have questioned his motives, suspecting pecuniary interests. He nevertheless gained the support of the British Church, if not the Pope, and was ordained before he set out.

One of St Patrick's conversion failures was Niall of the Nine Hostages' son, Logaire, who died around the year 462. He was a man described as 'fierce and pagan ... the emperor of the barbarians' and the progenitor of a political kinship grouping whose territory at one time centred on Trim, co. Meath. Anecdotally, Logaire told his people that his father Niall would never have allowed him to convert, adding that he would rather be buried with his forebears at Tara than at any monastic Christian site. When captured by his enemies, Logaire promised never again to ravage the land. He swore an oath to keep his word to the sun and moon, earth and sea, day and night, and water and air. When he later broke it, the elements turned on him: wind left his lungs, the sun burned his skin and the earth engulfed him.

While Christianity became temporarily eclipsed in much of Britain when it was overrun by pagan war-bands, the religion remained potent in Ireland. Christianity survived the Dark Ages after the fall of Rome by clinging on in remote locales like Skellig Michael, a rocky outcrop eighteen miles from the Irish coast that rises 700 feet out of the sea. Writing in the nineteenth century, Cardinal Newman described the Dark Age Irish Church as the storehouse of the past and the birthplace of the future. Historians have also noted the remarkable resilience of the Irish Church in resisting the siren call of earlier gods. This period in Ireland has been called a golden age, one which stretched out to encompass the creation and safe-housing of magnificent religious works like the Books of Durrow, *c.* 650–700, and Kells, *c.* 800. Both are transcriptions of the Gospels; the former is famous for its symbolic representation of the four Evangelists in the form of Man, Eagle, Ox and Lion; the latter is a brilliantly illuminated copy of the

Gospels with full-page illustrations of Christ, the Virgin and the Evangelists.

Church leaders in Ireland ministered to the scattered, tribal Irish by founding monastic centres, many in wildly remote settings, such as the Aran Islands off the west coast, and in valleys deep within the mountains. Monks led a straitened existence, having to provide for their daily needs and maintain their buildings as well as cultivate learning and practise their devotions. They observed the most severe penances in an attempt to emulate Christ. St Kevin founded a great monastic site at Glendalough in the Wicklow Mountains, south of Dublin. It became the centre of the Celtic Church in Ireland and played a prominent part in the development of Christianity in western Europe. Followers of St Enda founded a monastic site in the Aran Islands even earlier than this. Missionaries from here went on to establish the more famous monastery at Iona, an island in the Inner Hebrides. They also founded a number of other satellite monasteries, including Clonmacnois on the Shannon, co. Offaly, founded by St Ciaran, and Killmacduagh, co. Galway. Other important early monasteries were founded at Kildare by St Brigid, Clonfert by St Brendan, and Lismore by St Carthach, to name but three.

It was missions from Iona that kick-started the conversion of the pagan peoples of northern Britain. Columba, a great-grandson of Neill of the Nine Hostages, arrived in Dalriada from Ireland to set up his church at Iona in the year 563. He was by then middle-aged, around forty, a man therefore quite old to make a new start in life. He may have been exiled from Ireland, or had left his homeland of his own volition, perhaps as penance for past misdeeds. An essential feature of Irish monasticism was the separation from home and kinfolk in emulation of Christ, a form of self-abnegation which Columba must have found appealing, and which has been imagined by the poet Thomas Moore.

> I long to tread that golden path of rays …
> [Where] sunbeams melt along the silent sea …
> And think t'would lead to some bright isle of rest.

That Columba had a fierce martial background is indicated by his later chasing raiders back to their boats by striding out knee-deep in water clad only in monkish attire. Records of his life indicate that his already established political and military prestige, as much as his spirituality, first commended him to the Dalriadan king, Conall mac Comgaill. Conall bequeathed the island of Iona to his fellow Irishman to bring order to the place, which up until then had been a haunt of pirates. The future saint – who may have already founded a number of monasteries in Ireland, including Durrow, co. Offaly, in 551 – arrived off the Scottish mainland determined to eschew worldly trappings and lead a monastic life. His fame may already have been such that his presence at Iona attracted pilgrims and aspiring monks. Remaining pirates were likely driven off as the monastic community grew. Satellite foundations followed, built to service the main monastic centre at Iona. It seems that Iona's primacy over dependent churches derived from a secular model of royal overlordship already familiar to Columba. Kinship, therefore, may have played an important role in determining who was who in the religious hierarchy in much the same way as in secular society.

Columba engaged in bouts of realpolitik on both sides of the Irish Sea, overseeing the regal ordination of the Dalriadan king Aedan Mac Gabhran and acting as peacemaker at talks to seal accords between rival kings. He had a vested interest in pouring oil on troubled waters: harmonious interchange allowed monasticism to prosper. Across the great spine of the Scottish Highlands he is said to have ministered to the wild tribes on Tayside. Bede asserted that it was Columba who first converted the Picts by using an interpreter to translate from Irish into the Pictish tongue. That Columba was allowed to minister to them reflects a degree of trust in him on the part of the local kings, which enabled him to come and go in their lands without hindrance. The same must have been true in Strathclyde, where he ministered to the northern Welsh. He died in the year 597, the same year Augustine arrived in Kent from Rome to preach 'the Word' to the pagan Saxons. Nevertheless, it was Columba's foundation at Iona which, more than any other, would bring to the Northumbrians traditions of scholarship, worship and artistic influence of Irish origin. Columba had wished for a simple funeral, without any large crowd gathering. His flock may have turned a deaf ear to his request but the elements did not. A great storm brew up on the eve of his burial, preventing anyone crossing by boat to Iona from the mainland. His simple grave was marked only by the stone on which he had laid his head for thirty years or more in his otherwise bare monastic cell.

Among those unimpressed by Columba's ministrations was the Anglian king Aethelfrith, mentioned previously in the context of halting Irish Dalriadan expansion southward. It was said that no Irish king dared make war on the English in his lifetime. Moreover, the prestige afforded by Aethelfrith's successes brought both Bernician Bamburgh and Deiran York within the king's remit. He became the kingdom of Northumbria's (Bernicia and Deira combined) first overlord. Aethelfrith used extreme methods to halt the spread of Christianity. On one occasion Bede recorded the massacre on the king's orders of 1,200 Irish monks at Chester. The excuse used by Aethelfrith was that the monks were actively praying for his defeat. Soon after this, in 617, Aethelfrith would himself be killed, slain by Anglo-Saxon rivals on the banks of the Idle River near Doncaster. The river is said to have run foul with pagan blood.

Aethelfrith's death left the door open for Christianity to spread. The victor of the battle, Raedwald, overlord of the southern English, installed Edwin of Deira (a future saint) as the first Christian king of Northumberland. But it was the arrival of an exiled Christian prince named Oswald, a young man who spoke fluent Irish and had been blooded as a warrior when fighting for his Dalriadan hosts in the north of Ireland, who would be destined to make the biggest impact on the region. Described as the first great crusading Christian prince, Oswald set out to reclaim Northumbria for Christianity after King Edwin's death at the Battle of Hatfield Chase, near Doncaster, fought on 12 October 633. At the head of an army of invaders from Dalriada, Oswald ordered a large wooden cross to be erected near Hadrian's Wall. It was a bold statement of intent, as well as a call on God's support. St Oswald's church at Heavenfield is said to mark the spot. Built on a highpoint overlooking a swathe of Northumberland's stunning landscape, like the Hill of Tara the site still retains a strong spiritual appeal. Near here Columba appeared to Oswald in a vision, a spiritual intercession on the future saint's part which would prove a timely moral boost. Oswald was faced on Northumbria's borders by King Cadwallon's rampaging Welshmen but was said to have been granted by the Lord 'a happy and easy victory'. Oswald would henceforth be known to the Irish by the sobriquet 'Lamnguin' – wielder of God's bright blade.

Oswald's military success, and the arrival at Bamburgh on the north-east coast of England two years later of a missionary abbot named Aidan, rejuvenated the flagging faith of the Northumbrians. Described by Bede as an Irishman of 'outstanding gentleness, devotion and moderation', Aidan had journeyed across the Irish Sea to minister to the Northumbrians at Oswald's request. Underpinning Oswald's pedigree as a compassionate Christian prince, a story is told by Bede of Aidan dining at Oswald's mead hall and of a silver dish of delicacies being distributed by the king to the poor begging outside. Impressed by the king's generosity, Aidan grasped Oswald's right hand and prophesised it would never grow old. We can easily imagine Aidan using parables and a judicious mix of reason and mysticism to win men and women over. He may also have worked to ensure the mighty did not get too grand – an important role in an age before electorates. From a later period, a badly damaged fresco at Knockmoy Abbey, co. Galway, shows three dead kings confronting three live kings: the motto reads 'We have been as you are, you shall be as we are'. Advisors in medieval times pressed kings to maintain an awareness of the march of time and the burden of possessions and false grandeur, saying, 'Of what value is the possession of undiminished wealth? Of what value knowledge, when none can know the whole truth?' Another anecdotal tale relates how a pagan priest on the cusp of Christianity likened life's passage to the swift flight of a sparrow entering a mead hall by one door and departing from another. The story served to make the point that there existed only a very brief period of awareness of light and laughter before the darkness and unknowability of death; 'this life of man appears but for a moment; what follows or indeed what went before we know not at all.'

Aidan chose the island of Lindisfarne, off the Northumbrian coast, as the centre of his diocese. The monastery there has been described as a daughter-house of Iona, an Irish foundation where many scores of Irish or Irish-trained monks gathered. Aidan travelled extensively on foot across the land, inviting those who had lapsed to re-embrace the Christian faith and encouraging those who still believed to further strengthen it. In the words of Bede, he and his followers stirred the population 'by words and actions to alms and good works'. So successful was he that a second wave of monastic foundations, based on the same Irish ecclesiastical and cultural model, soon spread across Northumbria. Aidan's successors were also Irishmen, sent south from Iona. This potent Irish–Northumbrian connection, started by three future saints, Columba, Oswald and Aidan, would endure in the decades to come, with Iona and the Holy Island of Lindisfarne becoming the fountainhead for the progression of Irish Christianity across Anglo-Saxon England and further afield in western Europe too.

Oswald was later killed by the pagan king Penda of Mercia, an Anglo-Saxon kingdom centred on the West Midlands in England. The fatal battle at Maserfelth, where this occurred, was fought a year or so before the Battle of Strathcarron, mentioned earlier. The two battles may have been linked; perhaps they were part of a concerted attack on Northumbria and Dalriada by Mercia and its allies. Legend has it that Oswald, by this time a king of enormous standing throughout Britain, died during the battle while praying for the souls of the fallen. He became the first English king to die a Christian martyr. His head, arms and hands were hacked from his body and impaled on stakes at Oswald's Tree – probably Oswestry in Shropshire, the site of a still impressive hill-fort. Oswald's brother, the thirty-year-old Oswy, recovered these items the following year. Oswald's head went to the monastic community at Lindisfarne, and the arms and hands went to Bamburgh. In fulfilment of Aidan's prophesy, the future saint's right hand is said to have remained incorrupt all the while on display. Other remains were buried in situ on the battlefield or gathered up and kept by the Mercians. Later in the century, Oswald's bones would be used by the late king's niece to endow a new monastery at Bardney in Lincolnshire. Bardney lay within the old kingdom of Lindsay, an area previously annexed by Oswald. According to legend the monks there at first refused to accept the dead king's remains because he was regarded as a foreign enemy, but when a bright light began to emanate from the remains they quickly changed their minds.

2

THE HORROR OF EVERY CLANG OF ARMS

By the late seventh century the era of Irish raiding on Britain's coasts had come to an end. Formidable English fleets now patrolled the sea-lanes. In 684 the area to the north of modern-day Dublin was devastated after an attack by an English flotilla. Internecine fighting in Ireland involved a bewildering number of rival dynasties focussed on long-running feuds and vendettas. Sometimes full-scale battles resulted, such as the one fought at Kells, south of Tara, in 718. The victor of the battle, Conall Grant, had little time to celebrate his success. He was killed shortly afterwards by the Irish high-king Fergal mac Maele Duin of the northern branch of Clan O'Neill. Fergal died in battle four years later near the Hill of Allen, a one-time fortress stronghold of Finn McCool where a chanting head belonging to a die-hard decapitated bard is said to have brought tears to the eyes of the victorious Leinstermen.

Ravaging territory to deny the population food and sustenance and to undermine the authority of a rival was commonplace in Ireland, as elsewhere in Europe. Kings and their retinues operated like itinerants, almost always on the move, living off the labour of their subjects. Disputes with neighbours meant they gave their own territories a reprieve while terrorising those adjacent. In 770 a warlord named Donnchad 'the wrathful and ruddy', from the southern branch of the O'Neill, plundered Leinster. Next year he struck north to ravage the lands of the rival northern O'Neill. He later harried Munster. His strategy was to overrun an area, steal or set crops and stores of food ablaze. By using these tactics and winning the Battle of Forchalad, defeating Congalach mac Conaing, king of Brega, Donnchad succeeded to the high-kingship in 778. The *Annals of Ulster* for that year bewailed that the battle was fought 'on a gloomy, sad Sunday [but] many a fond mother was sorrowful the Monday on the morrow'. Little other than bog prevented raiding from the Irish midlands eastward into Leinster's rich grasslands, whereas the broad Shannon deterred random excursions westward. Geography played a large part in determining friend from foe, but the nature of warfare in Ireland would change with the arrival of the Vikings from Scandinavia in the second half of the 790s.

The first batch of marauders beached their ships on the sands of Lambay Island, beside modern-day Dublin, and launched destructive raids on the mainland. Another group attacked Inis Murray Island, co. Sligo, then used the River Erne to attack inland. At the height of this early Viking raiding monks prayed for stormy weather. High winds that 'tossed the ocean's white hair' heralded days and nights free from Viking attack. Irish waterborne trade between Dalriada and Antrim was for a time curtailed. Whereas after the Battle of Magh Rath political ties had been cut with Ireland, the Dalriadans now suffered social and economic links severed with their homeland too. The route from Oslo fjörd to the Irish Sea became known as 'the sea road', and the islands and archipelagos of northern Britain became established settlement points and stopovers for seagoing communities. Sleek, seaworthy longships and the exceptional sailing prowess of the Vikings enabled them to bypass mountain, bog and forest and strike deep into the interior of Ireland through the country's many waterways. The Vikings were also adept at manhandling their boats across intervening bogs and drumlin-strewn moorland. They pillaged the monastic site at Iona and overran the Isle of Skye. Further Viking arrivals threatened the Hebridean islands.

Attacks mounted in 802 and 806 again laid Iona to waste; sixty-eight monks were butchered on the latter occasion. Surviving Ionan monks withdrew to Ireland, taking with them the Book of Kells, now on display in Dublin. Smaller monastic foundations were also ransacked. The Vikings completely destroyed one at Inis Murray in Donegal Bay in 807, first attacked in 795. Skellig Michael off the Kerry coast suffered assaults on a number of occasions, most notably in 824 when its abbot was seized as a hostage, later dying of mistreatment and hunger. Another fierce attack on the rebuilt Iona monastic site occurred in 825. Abbot Blathmac died when refusing to divulge the whereabouts of gold and silver associated with St Columba's relics. At Clonmacnois monastery, co. Offaly, a Viking king named Turgeis is said to have lifted his pagan wife onto the holy altar, at which point she began to talk in tongues in the manner of an oracle. Exactly what point this tale was supposed to make is unclear but perhaps it establishes a religious dimension to the attacks. Being heathens, the Vikings may have felt challenged by the Christian God. True or not, their continued depredations resulted in enormous losses to the Irish in destroyed manuscripts and precious religious objects. They sacked monasteries at Armagh (throughout the ninth century at least nine times), Clonmacnois (ten), Kells (five), Glendalough (four), Lismore (six) and Kildare (sixteen).The rich monastic foundation at Duleek, co. Meath, was plundered at least ten times between the years 830 and 1150.

By 845, the Vikings had established bases on a number of loughs and created in this way an inland continuation of 'the sea road'. The aforementioned Turgeis' fleet had entered Belfast Lough in 832 and had then concentrated on Lough Neagh before plundering the monastery at Armagh three times in a single month. Lough Ree to the north of Athlone is specifically mentioned as a Viking base in a prophecy of doom attributed to St Columba. Raiding parties operated along the Shannon and Erne with relative impunity, but when they ventured further north the fighting men of the northern O'Neill defeated them at the Battle of Magh Itha on the modern-day Fermanagh and Donegal border.

Historians have rightly applauded the northern O'Neill for repelling the Vikings, especially since the northern coast of Ireland lay in direct line of attack for Vikings settled in the Hebridean isles. It is thought that Viking settlements dating from this time were mainly sited on the east coast of Ireland. The Vikings also set up a semi-permanent base at the mouth of the Shannon, possibly the forerunner of Limerick Town. The first recorded mention of a Viking encampment in Ireland is for the year 836 at Arklow, co. Wicklow, possibly a temporary summer camp. A permanent, fortified Viking settlement near Dublin followed five years later in 841. Another was built further up the east coast at Linn Duachaill, co. Louth, where remains discovered near the village of Anagassan indicate a sizeable site. Trenches dug at this location have revealed a huge defensive wall protecting the site's landward flank. The *Annals of Ulster* entry for the year 841 reads, 'Pagans still on Lough Neagh'. They may have been over-wintering there for the first time.

As early as 811 the Irish had successfully pushed back against the encroaching tide of attacks. Reports reached the court of the Emperor Charlemagne that year of a great slaughter of the heathens in the north of Ireland, probably near the coast in modern-day County Down. Local Irish resistance everywhere stiffened and become better coordinated. When faced by resolute opposition the Vikings were beatable. At first they bettered the Irish in terms of torso and head protection but the defenders soon emulated them, acquiring, through trade or barter, leather jerkins, waxed linen shirts, swords and helmets. The notion that the Vikings were imbued with superlative bravery owes more to myth than reality: their early successes relied on surprise and unprepared defences. Later, they lost as many battles as they won. Being opportunists out to acquire loot, the early Viking raiders may have hoped to avoid confrontation with Irish armed forces, quickly taking to their boats when countered.

Irish chroniclers made a clear and early distinction between two types of Scandinavian: the Finngaill (white-haired foreigners, likely Norwegian) and the Dubhgaill (dark-haired foreigners, likely Danes). Ireland, with a population of perhaps half a million in the ninth century, for a time became their battleground, but it seems the Dubhgaill were largely vanquished by the midpoint of the 850s. Some returned to Scandinavia, others retreated across the Irish Sea to Anglesey. Temporary alliances of convenience brokered between erstwhile enemies were an ongoing dynamic throughout the first Viking Age in Ireland. Pacts between Irish and Norse were quickly forged but as quickly abandoned. As an example, the Irish high-king of Tara, Mael Sechnaill I, energetically opposed the Viking king Olaf 'the white' and his Irish ally Cerball mac Dunlaing, lord of Ossory, by securing the assistance of previously settled Norsemen. Olaf in turn allied himself with Aed Findliath mac Neill of the northern O'Neill and married Aed Findliath's daughter to seal their alliance.

Aed Findliath and Olaf's combined forces later ravaged the high-king's lands in Meath and by 862, the year of Mael Sechnaill I's death, had become sufficiently powerful for Aed Findliath himself to assume the high-kingship. Although much from this time is unclear, it seems Olaf either broke his alliance with Aed Findliath or was sidelined by the new high-king. The result was Olaf allying himself with Lorcán mac Cathal of the rival southern O'Neill. Open warfare then broke out between the opposing factions. Each side comprised a mix of Irish and Norse armies. Olaf sought to humiliate Aed Findliath by ravaging the area around Tara to the north of Dublin. He and his brother Ivar 'the boneless' famously broke into the ancient tombs of Newgrange, Knowth, Dowth and Drogheda in the Boyne Valley, looting them for precious metals. The backlash from Aed Findliath resulted in the pair being temporarily exiled from Ireland.

Viking warlord kings like Olaf 'the White' and his brother Ivar 'the boneless' were boundlessly ambitious men. While they were absent from Ireland, the city of York fell to Ivar's forces in the year 866. Ivar would go on to dismantle the Anglo-Saxon kingdoms of East Anglia and Mercia before rejoining Olaf in Strathclyde. The extent of Ivar's depredations and conquests almost defies belief. By 869, if not before, Olaf was back in Ireland, targeting the monastery at Armagh. Chroniclers mourned the loss there of 1,000 dead or captured by him. He then rallied his men and sailed to the west coast of Scotland, where he acquired a new base of operations at Dumbarton on the Clyde. In 871, he and Ivar are recorded as bringing back to Ireland in 200 longships 'a great prey of [captive] Angles and Britons and Picts' to be sold at Dublin's great slave mart. Gaining control of Dumbarton, Dublin and also York enabled the late-ninth-century Vikings to carve out a mercantile empire encompassing much of eastern Ireland, the Hebrides, western Scotland and northern Britain.

One Irishman who successfully challenged the Vikings and won them over was the southern O'Neill king Flann Sinna, known as Flann of the Shannon. Despite a rare defeat suffered at their hands on the River Liffey in 888, he managed to assert supreme authority in the east of the country. A decade later he had become strong enough to launch an offensive against Connaught, gaining the province's submission by the year 900. Perhaps Flann's greatest military success was his victory at Ballymoon, near Castledermot, co. Kildare, on 13 September 908, when he and his Norse allies crushed an invading army from Munster and killed their leader Cormac mac Cuilennain, the so-called bishop-king of Cashel, a man renowned for his piety and scholarship if not his martial prowess. Flann solemnly received his opponent's decapitated head, saying he would treasure it as a relic of the holy bishop. This and other confrontations in the first decade of the tenth century indicate that inter-provincial rivalries between Irish kings and their Viking allies had reached new heights, but this all changed in 914 when another large Viking fleet, in effect a second great wave of invaders, laid anchor in Waterford harbour. The newcomers built a large fortified settlement there. An Irish churchman from Munster would later recall 'immense floods and countless sea-vomiting of ships and fleets', adding that in all of southern Ireland there was not a harbour or a landing point without fleets of foreigners.

The newcomers struck northward three years later, their intention to capture Dublin, by this time in Irish hands. Desk-bound chroniclers complained of the weather. Snow, extreme cold and 'unnatural' ice is said to have prevailed unusually long into the year, rivers and lakes remained frozen over and there is said to have been a widespread loss of livestock. Clerics also discerned a worrying pattern in the night skies as comets set the firmament aglow and a mass of fire raged in the west; these are violent, imagined symbols, akin to stage effects to dramatise the political turmoil in Ireland.

A new Irish high-king named Niall Glundub mac Aodha confronted the invaders north of the Liffey at Magh Feimin on 22 August 917. The tide of battle that day turned when reinforcements led by Ragnall, a grandson of Ivar 'the Boneless', arrived and drove the Irish back to their camp. A twenty-day standoff on the plains of Cashel then saw Niall's army frustrated when the Vikings called his bluff and failed to disperse. Niall withdrew. According to the *Annals of Ireland,* another battle was fought, possibly linked to Magh Feimin, where 500 Irishmen including several notables fell in battle when attacked by Ragnall's brother, Sihtric Caech. After this fight Dublin fell to the Vikings.

The Irish attempted a dislodgment two years later. The Vikings defended a naturally moated stronghold at the junction of the Liffey and one of its tributaries at a place called Kilmohavoc. An earthen wall and ditch defence probably closed the V. It was a hallmark Viking encampment. Niall fell attempting to ford the river at modern-day Islandbridge. His army suffered the most serious defeat against the Vikings to date. Twelve Irish sub-kings are said to have died with him as well as many common soldiers. Chroniclers lamented the loss of so many leaders, saying, 'Where are all the princes of the western world ... where now the horror of every clang of arms?' The list of the dead has been likened to a roll-call of all the powerful families in the north of Ireland. The *Annals of Ulster* lauded Ragnall as the undisputed 'king of the Finngaill and the Dubhgaill', a terror to the Irish, and later to the English and Scots too.

Probably not until late in the tenth century did the Irish manage to make lasting inroads against the Dublin Vikings. Attempts on behalf of the Dublin kings to retain a foothold at York had been defeated by the English earlier than this. A grand coalition of Dublin Norse, Irish, Scots and Welsh led by Olaf Guthfrithsson had been defeated by King Athelstan at the Battle of Brunanburh in 937, and Erik Bloodaxe, one-time king of Northumbria, had been cut down in a 'gory fight' at Stainmoor in modern-day County Cumbria in 954. The campaign of Brunanburh is noteworthy for a number of reasons, not least because Olaf Guthfrithsson's ships from Ireland crossed Scotland's narrow waist from Clyde to Forth before entering the Humber and occupying York; the Viking ships would have had to be manhandled over dry land and hauled along the Carron and Kelvin rivers. Vikings based in Ireland are recorded as having dragged and pulled their ships from Lough Erne over Breifne to Lough Ree in midwinter the previous year, a distance of approximately 40 miles. Their command of inland waterways and their ability to move longships overland is therefore well attested.

Not until the year 980 would the Irish manage to gain comparable victories against the Dublin Vikings. Up until then the Irish had been held in what has been called a 'Babylonian oppression' by the Scandinavians. That year, the southern O'Neill king, Mael Sechnaill mac Domnall – sometimes referred to a Mael Sechnaill II but known henceforth in the narrative as Malachy – won a famous victory over them, one that ranks with Brunanburh and Stainmoor in importance, near the Hill of Tara; contemporaries called it a 'red slaughter'. Vikings from the Hebrides fell in heaps alongside their Dublin-based cousins. The relevant entry in the *Annals of Ulster* reads,

> The Battle of Tara was won by Mael Sechnaill son of Domnall against the foreigners of Dublin and the Isles, and very great slaughter was inflicted on the foreigners therein, and foreign power ejected from Ireland … there fell therein Ragnall son of Olaf, the son of the king of the foreigners … and many others.

Historians consider the Battle of Tara among the most decisive battles ever fought in Ireland. Many up until then enslaved Irishmen, women and children are said to have been freed from bondage. The defeated Norse king of Dublin, Olaf Cuaran, survived the carnage and lived out the rest of his days at Iona in religious retirement. The Vikings at Dublin recognised Malachy as their notional overlord, and until 1014 scant sources confirm an even spread of victories between Dublin Vikings and Irish. Although the former subsequently extended their settlements along the east coast to include Carlingford Lough and Strangford Lough, they became ever more engaged in day-to-day Irish politics. Many Vikings settled peacefully in Ireland and must have paired with local girls. Cohabitation and trade facilitated coexistence and cooperation. In time a mixed race grew up; Norse names like Lochlann and Gormlaith gained popularity and remained fashionable for newborn Irish boys and girls for generations to come. Early medieval Irish art and architecture is perhaps a fusion of Irish and Scandinavian styles. Rather than perceiving as an enemy, medieval chroniclers began to view the Norse as simply another element in Ireland's rich cultural mosaic.

The year 1014 is one indelibly marked in Irish history because of a great victory won by Ireland's most famous king, Brian Boru. His full name was Brian Boruma mac Cennetig. He hailed from an obscure Munster dynasty. Born at Kincora, near Killaloe, co. Clare, around the year 941, he would live a long life of approximately seventy-four years and would marry at least four times. All his wives were from outside his native Munster, Ireland's southernmost provincial kingdom. Rather than love matches, they were diplomatically arranged to underpin peace accords. Only from the age of thirty-five or so does Brian step into the light of history, upon emerging victorious from the Battle of Belach Lechta and gaining the kingship of Munster, based at Cashel.

In 982 Brian's Munstermen are recorded as raiding the lands abutting Leinster, a demonstration of force orchestrated by him to impress his northern neighbours but which drew an immediate armed response from Malachy of the southern O'Neill. A series of armed interventions resulted. Malachy led an army south into Clare and broke down the tree of Magh Adhair, the ancient meeting place and inauguration site of the kings of northern Munster. In a snub designed to invalidate Brian's claim to the kingship of Munster, Malachy's men tore the tree up by the roots, made it into logs and then carried it off to form the roofing of Malachy's new palace. Brian responded by bringing a fleet up the Shannon to attack Malachy's allies in Connaught. He also ravaged Ossory and Leinster, having first made terms with the Norse at Waterford and exchanged hostages with them, guaranteeing that each would not threaten the other.

After amassing a large fleet at Lough Ree, estimated as 300 riverine craft including a contingent from the Waterford Norse, Brian went on to successfully harry the Irish midlands. He came within a whisker of destroying Malachy's principal residence on the banks of Lough Ennell, co. Westmeath. He is said to have wasted and destroyed Malachy's lands, 'leaving neither man nor beast'. However, when he diverted twenty-five ships to ravage Connaught his forces were set upon and the crews massacred. Blood-red skies espied by frightened clerics heralded violence and betrayal to come. A series of reverses followed. Brian's army was brought to battle and defeated at Carn Fordroma, in Connaught, in 990. Six hundred Munstermen fell, including Brian's uncle Donal. Two years after this, when hosting in Meath, Brian is said to have taken 'neither man nor cow' and to have fled like a runaway. These instances sit ill with Brian's reputation for military prowess, but he recovered from these setbacks and after a period of fortress building once again raided into the midlands. Three hundred of Malachy's warriors were slaughtered. To settle affairs, Brian and Malachy for a time joined forces and looked to eliminate common rivals. They took hostages from the Vikings of Ireland and also later hosted together in Connaught. Far from being mortal enemies, the two men appear to have operated with cold expediency: sometimes they were allied, at other times they were at each other's throats.

By the year 996 or 997, Brian had become strong enough to demand hostages from Malachy. In doing so he was challenging the centuries-old O'Neill hold on the high-kingship. The two men met at Clonfert in 998. Brian was confirmed king of Munster and Leinster; Malachy lorded it elsewhere. In effect they divided

Ireland between them. Malachy ravaged Connaught; Brian did the same in Leinster. Together they worked to bring the kings of Connaught, Leinster and Dublin to heel – no easy task. One man in particular, Maelmordha mac Murrough, a claimant to the kingship of Leinster, would have no truck with submitting to an upstart king from Munster. He allied himself with his cousin Sihtric Silkbeard in Dublin. In midwinter of the portentous year 999, the eve of the millennium, the protagonists clashed at Glen Mama, near Lyons Hill, co. Kildare, a place of importance as a residential centre for the ancient kings of Leinster. The Leinstermen and Dubliners were eager for a fight but Brian's army prevailed. The battle has been variously described as 'a crushing defeat' for the Leinster–Dublin alliance and the 'quelling of a desperate revolt'. An ancient prophesy claimed that after a fight at Glen Mama 'Ath Cliath [Dublin] the fair would be burned, and the Leinster plain ravaged'. To make this forewarning good, Brian wasted Leinster and occupied Dublin.

The traditional date of Dublin's capture is New Year's Day 1000, a time associated with the coming of the antichrist, who for the Irish was expected to be serpent-like, a one-eyed scourge from hell. Though bearded and battle-scarred, Brian was easier on the eye but equally dangerous. He seized Maelmordha and held him hostage. He then ransomed him for a hefty sum. Sihtric Silkbeard had earlier fled north to Ulaid. Only when hostages had been provided did Brian allow Sihtric to return to Dublin and pay him homage. Sihtric and Maelmordha both now owed their allegiance to Brian.

Brian and Malachy inevitably clashed after the turn of the millennium. Much from this time remains obscure. Malachy continued to style himself king of Tara, although of the two Brian is considered to have been the stronger. Brian now turned on Malachy. Precise details are lacking, but it seems Brian broke the accord reached between the two men and made a bid for the high-kingship. Payback from a disgruntled Malachy came when Brian's scurriers were set upon north of Tara and overwhelmed, suffering heavy losses. Much of the raiding on both sides may have involved the plundering of opposing riverine fleets. In an attempt to prevent such incursions from Munster, Malachy built a great barrier across the Shannon at Athlone, but it proved a failure: Brian occupied Athlone, took hostages from the kings of Connaught and Meath and forced Malachy's submission. The monopoly of power enjoyed by the southern and northern branches of the O'Neill was in this way brought to an end. Malachy's capitulation dates to the year 1002, a decisive moment in Irish history. For the first time an overlord from Munster occupied the seat of Tara.

Brian did not have it all his own way. The north of Ireland continued to hold out against him. By repute, the northern O'Neill king, Aed O'Neill, was warned in a dream never to allow the Hill of Tara to come under Brian's sway. Aed's men blocked Brian's passage northward near Ballysadare, co. Sligo, in 1004, threatening battle. Brian fell back to rally more men.

To mark his achievements and thank God, Brian bestowed twenty-two ounces of gold on the monastery at Armagh. By the turn of the millennium the church there had gained religious primacy over all of Ireland with the possible exception of Dublin. Churchmen accepted Brian as their protector and benefactor and also accepted his right to be recognised as Emperor of the Irish, but continued stubbornness on the part of the northern O'Neills necessitated another great hosting by Brian in 1006. Brian's army boasted Munstermen, Leinstermen, the soldiers of Meath and Connaught, plus battalions of Dublin Norse. Keeping 'his left hand against the sea and his right against the mountains', the high-king marched through modern-day Sligo north to Donegal. From there he struck eastward into Antrim and then south through modern-day Down and Louth. The hosting disbanded upon returning to Meath in early August. Although an epic circuit, with much harrying and looting, no battles were fought. Only the kings of Ulaid, a region comprising much of eastern Ulster, provided Brian with hostages. It seemed to the chronicler of the *Annals of Ulster* that a *Pax Briannus* now prevailed: 'Sliab Cua has no troop; Vikings do not row around Eidnech; a lone woman crosses Luachair [unmolested]; cows without herdsmen low [safely] in the meadows.'

Brian's struggle for power was almost done but important pieces of Ireland's political jigsaw still remained missing. One fell into place in 1010, when during an exceptionally hot summer the Cenel nEogain branch of the northern O'Neills submitted to him near Newtonhamilton, co. Armagh, an area rich in legendary associations from the days of Cúchulainn and Finn McCool. The Cenel Conaill of Donegal, however, continued to resist. Brian's sons Murchad and Domnall ravaged Donegal the following year. Three hundred captives and numerous herds of cows were seized. Brian launched attacks by land and sea into Sligo Bay. He was rewarded when the Cenel Conaill chieftain, Mael Ruanaid, submitted to him on the plain of Ballymote, co. Sligo. Bards rightly lauded Brian's achievement; for a king of Munster to exert overlordship over the north of Ireland was up until then unprecedented.

However, this state of affairs was not destined to last. Three years later a major rebellion against Brian's rule broke out. The revolt started in the north and rapidly spread southward down Ireland's eastern seaboard. From Meath, Malachy sought to stem the tide of insurrection and fought an inconclusive battle against the Leinstermen and Dubliners at Drinan, near Ballymahon, co. Longford. His son Flann was among the 150 men who died fighting there. The Dublin Norse then sent a fleet down the coast to raid Munster, but were driven back after setting the town of Cork ablaze.

Romanticised versions of the causes of this new conflict blame a queen named Gormflaith as its instigator. One source is the twelfth-century *Cogadh Gaedel re Gallaibh*, which translated means *The War of the Irish against the Foreigners* – a propaganda tract. Gormflaith was the sister of Brian's enemy Maelmordha mac Murrough, the Leinster king who had been defeated at Glen Mama in 999. She had also once been the wife of both Brian Boru and Malachy and had indulged in carnal relations with Olaf Cuaran, the Viking king defeated by Malachy at Tara in 980. Gormflaith had sons by both Brian and Olaf: these were, respectively, Donnchad and the previously mentioned Sihtric Silkbeard. A sexual pawn in Ireland's interminable power games, it seems Gormflaith's brother

Maelmordha of Leinster had further promised her hand to Sigurd 'the Stout' of Orkney and also to king Brodar of Man in return for military support to confront Brian and Malachy.

Saga evidence reveals Gormflaith as beautiful but malign. The skalds claimed, with misogynistic undertones, that her best qualities were those over which she had no control, and that her character was evil insofar as she had control over it. Her alleged inciting of her brother Maelmordha to go to war with her two ex-husbands by slighting her brother's manliness may be far-fetched but helps to contextualise the relations between the rival factions. The Leinster royal dynasty could not stomach having to bow to a Munster overlord whom they viewed as an arriviste. Moreover, Irish and Norse noblemen were highly vulnerable to slights against their honour and easy to goad into avenging some suspicion of an insult. Maelmordha must have withdrawn his submission to Brian and lured Sihtric Silkbeard into his sister's web of intrigue. He sent the men of northern Leinster and his Norse allies into Malachy's territories in modern-day Westmeath, where they carried off 'a great prey of slaves'. Malachy appealed to Brian for military assistance, and Brian responded by leading a large army north. On the way he plundered Ossory. Brian's son Murchad meanwhile struck into Leinster as far as the monastery at Glendalough before advancing on Dublin. He re-joined his father near the modern-day city at Kilmainham.

The Munstermen laid siege to Dublin from early autumn to Christmas 1013. Convention demanded the besieged should offer battle or submit, but the defenders cast honour aside by refusing either to fight or yield. Shortages of provisions and inclement weather forced Brian's army to disperse. This allowed the Dubliners to strengthen their defences and await reinforcements from the Isle of Man and the Western Isles. Brian also used the time to good purpose. He assembled around him fighting men from Munster, Connaught and Meath, perhaps even from Scotland.

Fought within sight of the medieval town of Dublin on Good Friday 1014, the resulting Battle of Clontarf was probably the largest battle in Ireland during the Viking period. Opposing

Brian and Malachy were all the fighting men of Leinster and Dublin, plus other Vikings to the number of 1,000 breastplates, the latter described as 'all the foreigners of the western World'. Brian's and Malachy's forces were strengthened by a contingent from Connaught led by Taig O'Kelly. The only clues we have to unit sizes are from the Norse side. Brodar of Man is said to have arrived at Dublin with twenty longships, which might have yielded a landing force of upwards of 300 men. Sigurd of Orkney is thought probably to have brought fewer ships. Military historians assess Brian's enemies to have numbered around 2,500 men. Brian and Malachy's forces may have numbered somewhat more. It seems the two men may have ridden side by side to attend a council of war held somewhere north of the present city but that there was a last-minute rift between them, possibly a disagreement as to how the battle should be fought or if it should be fought at all. Malachy remained reluctant to fight until the eleventh hour. Without his support, Brian's strength would be greatly diminished. Brian had also detached his son Donnchad to lead a diversionary raid into Leinster. These men could not now be recalled in time.

Historians have since speculated as to why Brian, a king who up until then had shied away from committing himself to battle unless at an advantage, did not simply break contact with the enemy and march away. Several explanations present themselves: first, that Brian may not have been in a position to withdraw in the face of an enemy now determined to fight; second, that fragile alliances forged in Munster and Connaught would crumble should he be accused of 'turning tail'; third, that Brian, an old man, may have been forced to yield to pressure from his council of war, dominated by his hot-headed son Murchad.

Tensions grew in the king's camp the night before battle. Ill omens abounded. One involved a group of clerics arriving at the encampment demanding dues owed them by Brian. When told to come back after the battle, they prophesised it would by then be too late. Another involved Brian being confronted by a ghostly emissary who forewarned the king's fall on the morrow. Ominous occurrences also plagued the Manx and Orkney Vikings. Showers of boiling blood falling from midnight skies are said to have assailed their ships. Ravens with iron beaks clawed at terrified crews. A woman in Caithness was seen to weave on a loom where dead men's heads formed the weights, entrails served for warp and weft, a sword doubled for a shuttle and arrows acted as reels. As far away as Iceland priestly garments are said to have suddenly become drenched in blood. Continuing on this fanciful theme, the sagas would later place Sihtric Silkbeard, accompanied by a host of Valkyries, in the vanguard of Brian's enemies. More reliable sources claim he played no part, remaining behind at Dublin with a small reserve to watch the fighting unfold from the town ramparts.

The Orcadian and Manx Vikings probably led the host that exited from Dublin's northern gate, followed by the bulk of the Norse of Dublin, then by the main body of Leinstermen. They crossed the River Liffey and its tributary the Tolka and formed up facing north on flat land in the modern-day Dublin suburb of Clontarf, then just open land. Brian's army confronted them. In the distance the Munstermen and their allies would have had sight of the Liffey mouth where Viking fleets, row upon row of longships in the shape of sleek serpents, lay anchored or beached. On the battlefield the opposing troop formations were so compacted it was claimed a four-horsed chariot could be driven on the warriors' heads from one flank to the other. The constrained nature of the battlefield, packed with troops, militated against anything other than the launching or receiving of full-frontal assaults. Shields were held close, forming a defensive wall from behind which fighting men might jab at opponents with sword, spear and axe. Banners bravely fluttered in the morning breeze, drowning out the din of oaths and curses from men jostling into position. The Irish interspersed their colours between the various contingents, whereas the Norse held their standards aloft before their mid-battle in the centre of their line. Battle is said to have raged from one tide to the next, described by chroniclers as 'wounding, noisy, bloody, crimsoned, terrible, fierce and quarrelsome'.

One individual combat highlighted by the skalds tells of Brian's son Murchad, at the head of over a hundred sons of kings, felling thirty mail-clad Norse before being fatally stabbed. With exaggerated licence, owing more to modern dramas like *Game of Thrones* than actual combat, his swordplay was described as so fierce and heated that the gold inlay on the hilt of his sword melted away. Domnall of Alba, an ally of Brian's, is said to have famously clashed with the king of Norway's son. The latter had boasted the night before that no man in Ireland could withstand him. Domnall sent word back that he would prove to be the Norseman's equal in combat any day. When they met in battle both died at the other's hands. Maelmordha of Leinster also fell in battle, and by then Brian was probably dead too. In his seventies in 1014, too old to fight, Brian had remained well to the rear at prayer while the battle raged. It may have been when appealing to God for victory that a Manx axe belonging to King Brodar struck him down. Brodar shouted, 'Now man can tell man that Brodar felled Brian', but his glory proved short-lived. The Manx king was killed shortly afterwards and is alleged then to have had his stomach slit open, exposing his entrails, which, according to a whimsical Norse source, were drawn from him and wrapped tightly around a tree to prolong his torture.

Valhalla's halls also welcomed the Hebridean king Sigurd 'the Stout', run through by the Viking warlord Hrafn 'the Red', a man named either for his hair or for his bloody line of work. The list of those killed on either side included at least six sub-kings fighting for Brian, as well as a Scottish prince. Of the foreigners fighting with Maelmordha it was said that none of rank appeared in battle and left it alive. Adding credence to the claim that Malachy remained aloof from the fighting, nobody of note from Meath is named in the annals among the dead. Several accounts claim Malachy led his army away on the eve of battle, having refused to fight. Other accounts hold that it was Malachy's troops who drove the enemy back to their boats; that so packed together were the fleeing soldiery, many Vikings drowned attempting to reach safety. Hrafn 'the Red' was among those who survived the battle by swimming to safety, murmuring all the while that he would do penance at Rome for past misdeeds should he survive. An

Icelander named Thorsteinn also survived. Unable to regain his ship, he fell captive, allegedly while tying his bootlaces. Brian's grandson Toirdelbach drowned while pursuing the routed Vikings. A wave at the weir of Clontarf is said to have overwhelmed him. Sihtric Silkbeard avoided an otherwise inevitable death by staying in Dublin. He remained in control there and continued as Dublin's overlord until the year 1036.

Even in death Brian continued to affirm his personal pre-eminence. Clontarf became known as 'Brian's battle'. Prior to the fight he had made a will which expressed his wish to be buried at Armagh. A vigil extending over twelve nights preceded his interment. That he died in the hour of victory against a foreign foe turned him from just another warring high-king of Ireland into a national hero. The author of the *Cogadh* stated,

> Brian was not a stone in the place of an egg; and he was not a wisp in the place of a club; but he was a hero in place of a hero; and he was valour after valour.

Yet the strength of Munster sapped away upon his passing. Malachy would recover the high-kingship and live to the ripe old age of seventy-three. Histories which downplay his role at Clontarf may have been penned to conjure an almost miraculous victory won by the martyred Brian against all odds, but poets like Thomas Moore have not forgotten the other victor of the battle:

> Let Erin remember the days of old,
> Ere her faithless sons betrayed her;
> When Malachy wore the collar of gold,
> Which he won from her proud invader.

The Battle of Clontarf has often been portrayed as a straightforward encounter between Irish and Norse, a denouement of the struggle between the two. According to the late Reverend John Ryan, an authority on the battle, 'in the mellow haze of popular imagination' the battle became transformed from a complex internecine conflict into a 'clear-cut issue' between Irishman and Viking. It was, as we have seen, far more complicated and nuanced. Modern historians more readily stress the internecine aspects of the struggle, yet the chroniclers of the time were keen to emphasise the sizeable foreign elements unleashed, implying there to have been a threat from abroad to the established Gaelic order. The second decade of the eleventh century boasted dramatic Viking conquests elsewhere in Britain and on the continent of Europe. The narrative of the era is the fulfilment of Danish imperial pretensions. Cast as a victim, England is said to have 'lamented and shaken like a reed-bed struck by the quivering west wind' in the face of Viking aggression. The year 1016 witnessed a series of momentous battles in England, resulting in the Danish king Cnut placing a stranglehold on the country. Cnut's Viking empire came to comprise all of England, Denmark and a large slice of Norway. There is no reason to think his ambitions might not have extended across the Irish Sea to Dublin and its hinterland. Cnut may even have asserted rights of overlordship over Dublin and the Irish – details are lacking. Had not the Irish kings held back the Scandinavian tide at Clontarf, wider Danish ambitions might have been realised. For a time after Clontarf, anarchy prevailed in Ireland. High-kingship as a concept became almost meaningless.

3

NINETY HEROES CLAD
IN MAIL

Twelfth-century Ireland remained almost entirely forested, with extensive areas of bogland and swamp. Wild boar, pigs, deer and game birds abounded; so too did wolves and foxes. Famously, thanks to St Patrick, there were no snakes! Roads were mere trackways. Ownership of cattle and sheep continued to represent the main wealth of the landed classes. Dry, unforested land remained mainly rough pasture, but wheat, rye, barley and flax were being cultivated wherever possible. The chronicler Gerald of Wales claimed Ireland contained more grass than grain, indicating an economy based heavily on livestock. The main towns in Ireland were those founded by the Vikings, primarily the fortified encampments at Dublin, Limerick, Waterford, Cork and Wexford. Of these, Dublin remained the most important. Even after the death of Brian Boru, Dublin continued to be a target for warring Gaelic kings. Located on the coast, in close proximity across the Irish Sea to North Wales and the Isle of Man, with established trade links to northern and south-west England, it is not difficult to see why. The Viking base there rivalled another like it at Kiev, whence Russia was brought under the sway of the Scandinavians. Only in Ulster, thanks to the fighting prowess of the northern O'Neills, had the Norse failed to establish permanent coastal bases. Elsewhere, settlements sprung up where Irish kings built royal fortresses. Substantial bastions were erected by Brian Boru in 995 and 1012. The king of Connaught demolished one at Kincora that guarded Lough Derg. Stone and wood from the structure was thrown into the Shannon. Ireland's many monasteries also sheltered the native Irish. They too became proto-towns.

By the twelfth century Canterbury was asserting its primacy over the Irish Church and also acting as the main arbiter in ecclesiastical disputes. High on the agenda of English clerics was the reform of Ireland's slack marriage customs. At the Synod of Kells in 1152, Church leaders formally censured the Irish in this regard – possibly a pretext for broader reform. There was resistance from the Irish Church, especially at Armagh, which looked to Rome for guidance. Dublin, on the other hand, favoured closer ties with Canterbury. The synod may also have been called to address escalating violence in Ireland. A battle fought the year before the synod had pitted the forces of Munster against the combined might of Connaught and Leinster. One overawed chronicler described the slain in impressionistic fashion, claiming they were 'as many as the sands of the sea and the stars of the sky'. The battle resulted in the collapse of the O'Brian lordship in northern Munster, but Connaught was weakened as well, having suffered heavy losses.

In the year of the synod a great famine swept the country. Chroniclers wrote of a great dearth prevailing in Munster and of many perishing from hunger in the northern half of Ireland. Churchmen saw it as God's wrath on the sinful and warlike Irish. Matters came to a head when England's only pope, Adrian IV, decided to confer the overlordship of Ireland on his fellow countryman Henry II. Pope Adrian saw this as a way of introducing more drastic reform to Ireland. He granted Ireland to Henry to govern on the grounds that all the islands of Britain belonged to the Holy See at Rome. Contemporary chronicler Matthew Paris described Ireland as in 'a kind of [religious] limbo', imagining 'bestial men' being reluctantly brought to the faith.

A modern audience might regard his description as tantamount to encouraging colonisation by Church decree.

The idea of English dominion over Ireland may have pre-dated these events. Tenth-century King Edgar of England is reputed to have considered himself overlord of not only the English but also the Irish. He claimed jurisdiction over 'all the islands of the ocean with their most fierce kings as far as Norway ... and the greater part of Ireland with its most noble city of Dublin'. The source for this is the *Altitionantis Charter*, a probable twelfth-century forgery which attempted to justify the English Crown's claims to the lordship of Ireland. Cnut may also have asserted rights of lordship over the Irish. The Dane boasted a mighty fleet and forged alliances with the Dublin Norse. William the Conqueror may have included Ireland within his imperial remit. His son William Rufus, however, had better reason to seek to bring the Irish to heel: Irish support for Welsh and Anglo-Saxon rebels proved problematic during his reign. Dublin, Wexford and Waterford became particularly attractive stopovers for exiles who posed an ever-present threat to the newly established Norman state.

Standing on Pembrokeshire's rocky coastline, Rufus is said to have been able to discern Ireland in the far distance. Like Agricola, he bragged he would make himself master of the island, but never did. Rufus' successor, Henry I, proved more insular in outlook, content to allow the Scots their nationhood and to coexist with the Welsh. Ireland would never have been of interest to him, nor to the king that followed, Stephen, a Frenchman whose reign was punctuated by civil war. Not until the reign of Henry II did the conquest of Ireland first arise as a potential project.

Direct intervention in Irish affairs occurred in the end not at the Church's urging but in response to a call for military assistance from an exiled king of Leinster named Dermot mac Murrough, a man described as drawn 'in the darkest colours'. If not simply the victim of sustained hostile propaganda, it seems mac Murrough was a remarkably brutal king. In a long reign spanning over forty years his main achievement had been to extend his southern Leinster power base to include the whole province; he also controlled Dublin and its powerful fleet. Gaining the submission of the chief town of Ireland had been crucial to his success. He is said to have rounded up dissenters for elimination in the manner of a modern dictator, blinding, castrating or otherwise mutilating his victims. Seventeen of his chiefs are alleged to have been killed or blinded by him in a single year. His first recorded act of aggression, an attack on the important ecclesiastical centre at Kildare, dates to 1132. Kildare's abbess had been installed there by one of mac Murrough's rivals. The Leinsterman torched the place and ordered the abbess to be raped to invalidate her from holding a similar office in the future. Another of Dermot's exploits was to abduct the wife of Tiernan O'Rourke, the infamous one-eyed king of Breifne. The woman in question, Dervorgilla, had been young enough (probably aged around fourteen) to have been O'Rourke's daughter when first married in 1122. Her husband ruled over a region centred on modern-day Carrick-on-Shannon. Compared to Dervorgilla's homeland in Meath, the landscape around Carrick must have appeared bleak and inhospitable: reed-fringed lakes, impassable bogs and dark forests made for dispiriting first impressions. Her later abduction by Dermot mac Murrough may have been made at the instigation of Dervorgilla's brother, possibly to seal a land deal on the borders of Meath and create a buffer zone against O'Rourke's eastward incursions. Sexual or physical abuse of Dervorgilla by the much older O'Rourke may also have played a part in driving the young woman into mac Murrough's arms. Whatever the truth of the matter, in the light of the Church's condemnation of adulterous arrangements – the Synod of Kells having occurred the same year as the abduction – mac Murrough's seizure of Dervorgilla proved one embarrassment too many for the Irish high-king, who forced mac Murrough to pay O'Rourke one hundred ounces of gold by way of compensation. Within a year or so O'Rourke had his wife back. Resentment nevertheless remained. The fallout from these events was still very much a political issue on the eve of the Norman invasion of Ireland.

When the incumbent Irish high-king, Muirchetach mac Loughlin, died at the hands of an unknown assassin in 1166,

Tiernan O'Rourke's main ally, Rory O'Connor, and arch-enemy, Dermot mac Murrough, emerged as the main contenders for the high-kingship. With O'Rourke's help, O'Connor prevailed, gaining control at Dublin and winning a great victory over mac Murrough's Leinstermen at Ferns. With wife, daughter and bodyguard, mac Murrough fled to Bristol via South Wales. From there he travelled on to Aquitaine to seek the help of Henry II. Rory O'Connor meanwhile assumed the high-kingship of Ireland. The stage was set for a major foreign intervention in Ireland and a bitter struggle for power.

Since the great council meeting of 1155, any plans Henry might have harboured for invading Ireland had been put on hold. The time had not been right. England had just emerged from a long period of civil war. Henry's mother, the formidable Empress Matilda, insisted her son's first priority should be to reconcile himself with supporters of the former King Stephen, many of whom were still armed and dangerous. He should also, in her opinion, first consolidate his hold over his vast inherited Continental empire. These matters were still a priority when Dermot mac Murrough lobbied Henry in 1166. A year or two earlier, prior to his expulsion from Ireland, mac Murrough had arranged for the Dublin fleet to engage in six months of campaigning on Henry's behalf against the Cambro-Irish of Gwynedd. Having also backed the right side in the recent civil war between Stephen and Matilda, it seems the Leinsterman had forged close mercantile and military ties with Henry's England earlier than 1166. He was not just some random foreigner turning up out of the blue, as is sometimes assumed. In fact, Rory O'Connor's capture of Dublin and the chasing off of mac Murrough probably gave Henry deep cause for concern. Having a powerful and potentially unruly neighbour on his western doorstep was disquieting. Like Tuathal Techtmar in Roman times, mac Murrough had likely proved a useful client king to the English. Henry was nobody's fool, nor was he prone to making rash decisions. He always found time to weigh his options. On this occasion, although hard pressed by innumerable domestic issues, he acquiesced with his ally's request, agreeing for mac Murrough's return to Bristol to seek military assistance from among the knights of his realm. Whether he specifically targeted South Wales for the recruiting is not known, but he may have done. Close ties existed between South Wales and Leinster: a pool of under-employed knights in the future principality looked for leadership and reward. Many were landless men and likely therefore to be attracted to a lucrative foreign venture.

By the twelfth-century Bristol had emerged as England's second city and also an important trade hub with Dublin. Its flourishing slave market had once supplied Ireland's needs. The chronicler William of Malmesbury claimed the traders at Bristol bought up youngsters from all around England. After making the females pregnant they shipped them roped together to Ireland. William deeply sympathised with the victims, saying that 'it would make you groan to witness their misery'. By mac Murrough's time the practice had by and large been curtailed. The English Church had prohibited the trade, describing it as shameful.

Robert Fitz Harding acted for the king in his dealings with mac Murrough at Bristol. He introduced the Leinsterman to Richard Fitz Gilbert de Clare, Earl of Striguel. Better known by his nickname 'Strongbow', de Clare was approximately thirty-five years old in 1166. He was a man distrusted by Henry because of an earlier de Clare family affinity to his mother's great rival King Stephen. That Strongbow had fallen on hard times is indicated by Gerald of Wales, who claimed the earl had 'succeeded to a name rather than possessions' and was prey to creditors. When approached by mac Murrough to organise a mercenary band to help him in Ireland, Strongbow was therefore immediately receptive. Mac Murrough offered land, money, horses and equipment. Not only could Strongbow put the Irish Sea between himself and moneylenders, but he might also make his fortune.

The timeline between mac Murrough approaching Strongbow and the date of the first armed expedition to Ireland indicates that many obstacles had to be overcome before a deal could be struck. Initial conversations between the Leinsterman and the earl probably took place during the winter of 1166/7, but not until the spring of 1169 did a vanguard of warships and transports first beach at Bannow Bay, on the tip of Ireland's south-eastern coast. This invasion of Ireland by knights and soldiery from Wales can perhaps be seen as a logical transference of military ambitions from one warzone to another. A Welsh resurgence under Rhys Gruffydd had made Ireland an attractive alternative theatre of war for land-hungry adventurers. Strongbow did not number among these initial arrivals. Not fully trusting the earl, Henry II had put difficulties in Strongbow's way at every stage; at one point he had despatched him to Germany to accompany the dowager empress Matilda on a state visit. The English king toyed with Strongbow. Relations between the two men remained strained right up until the point of the earl's eventual departure for Ireland in the summer of 1170.

After safely disembarking on Ireland's south-east coast, the leader of the first Norman task force, Robert Fitz Stephen, prepared to mount a preliminary assault on the fortified Norse town of Wexford. Two further shiploads of men, led by a young adventurer named Maurice de Prendergast, arrived in time to reinforce him. Including mac Murrough's Irish contingent, the combined army numbered around 1,000 fighting men. Many of these early Norman adventurers were related, descendants of a famous Welsh princess called Nesta. The princess had borne illegitimate children by both Henry I and Stephen of Cardigan, as well as illegitimate offspring from her marriage to Gerald of Windsor. Their names, Fitzgerald, Fitz Stephen, Fitz Henry and Barry, would later resound in Irish history. They are said to have comprised just 'ninety heroes clad in mail'. The Irish initially set little store by them – but they should have done.

Irish soldiery was inferior to the Normans in almost every respect. Irish warriors relied on speed of movement rather than defensive armour. The overriding impression from contemporary commentators is of the Irish in the twelfth century fighting unprotected. Gerald of Wales claimed they went naked, meaning unarmoured, into battle. The famous line of verse, 'Fine linen shirts on the race of Conn, the Foreigners one mass of Iron', evocatively sets both sides in context militarily.

Spearheaded by mounted and heavily armoured warriors, the Normans were able to engage opponents and then retire in good order, quickly regrouping before returning to the attack. They could do this time and time again, wearing out an enemy. Trained from early youth in the art of war, the Norman knight was an elite equestrian warrior. Equipped at heavy cost, the largest part being the purchase and maintenance of one or more warhorses, a Norman's main offensive weapon was the lance. Earlier hurled overhand like a javelin, by the second half of the twelfth century the lance was more commonly couched underarm to deliver a devastating mounted charge. Other knightly weapons were a double-edged, straight sword and mace. The latter was a wooden club with a heavy iron head used when a knight's lance became splintered. Defensive armour comprised a kite-shaped shield that protected the complete left side of the rider, plus a conical helmet with nasal over a mail hood, as well as leg defences, hauberk and a long coat of chain mail or quilted armour. The escalating cost of equipping a knight encouraged an increase in the number of less well-equipped mounted cavalrymen, known as squires or sergeants. These were twice as numerous as knights in the forces that set out across the Irish Sea.

In support of these front-line fighting men were large numbers of Welsh archers; they were formidable bowmen, reputed by Gerald of Wales to be capable of discharging arrows that could penetrate an oaken gate four fingers thick and pin a knight's leg to his horse through two layers of mail. Made from the wood of the wild elm, when fired en masse bows could create an arrow storm capable of disrupting an enemy force over 200 yards distant. The Normans mounted their archers so that they could participate in rapid marches or pursuits. There were also auxiliary foot soldiers in the expedition, mainly Welsh and Flemings armed with spears, swords and pikes. Defensive armour for them consisted of a helmet made of leather strengthened with iron, and also a stout leather jacket.

The Irish relied on ambush and surprise rather than set-piece encounters. The Normans had in the past faced similar opposition in Wales. Irish terror tactics tested their nerve nonetheless – for instance, ritual dismemberment of a fallen enemy remained an unpleasant facet of Irish warfare. Hearts were removed from the dead, throats cut through, and heads carried off as trophies. The threat of being overwhelmed and mutilated in the dense, trackless outback of Ireland kept the invaders on their guard and sometimes unnerved them to the extent they might panic. During the reign of King Stephen, Ireland and other remote regions of the British Isles were described as the breeding places of 'men of an animal type, naturally swift-footed, accustomed to war, volatile always in breaking their word, as in changing their abode'. This is a quote from the life of King Stephen, the *Gesta Stephani*, written in the mid-twelfth century. An Irish warrior's ability to be in one place one moment and gone the next proved a trial for the Normans, just as it would for later opponents like Sir Walter Raleigh, who, in the sixteenth century, would recount how fighting the Irish was 'like beating at the air'.

The Normans would not only face the native Irish but also the urbanised Norse. In Ireland's bustling coastal towns the Norse remained a military force to be reckoned with. Described at Clontarf as wielding 'swords and Lochlann axes, spears and bows and arrows, with bodies encased from head to foot in mail', the Norse retained their fighting prowess well into the twelfth century. They were said by the main chronicler of the invasion, Gerald of Wales, to be 'born warriors in the Danish fashion, men with iron hearts as well as iron arms'. They remained hardy fighting men with armour and weapons little changed from the days of their Viking forefathers.

Alerted by news of the invasion, the Wexford Norse formed up on the opposite bank of a tidal inlet at Dun Cormick. Once it became clear they were not up against the usual array of lightly armed Irishmen but instead faced massed ranks of archers and infantry, supported by one or more squadrons of mounted knights, they hurriedly withdrew back down the coast road to man

Wexford's fortifications, pursued all the while by mac Murrough's spearmen. That some fighting occurred at Dun Cormick is attested by a memorial cross erected there to commemorate the Norman and Welsh losses incurred. Next day, the attackers massed outside Wexford preparatory to an all-out assault upon the walls. The Norse responded by casting down large stones and wooden beams on the attackers. A Cambro-Norman named Robert de Barri was among the first to scale the defences. Struck down in a melee on the ramparts, he fell headlong into the ditch below. He only survived because his comrades, at great risk to themselves, dragged him to safety. The Normans renewed the attack the following day, but by then the Norse had decided enough was enough. A herald rode out from the town under a flag of truce to seek terms of surrender.

Wexford's fall resulted in the first major land grants made to the Normans. As an example, mac Murrough gave Hervey de Montmorency, Strongbow's uncle, 200,000 acres of land between Wexford and Waterford – a staggering reward so early in the campaign. Described by Gerald of Wales as 'a fugitive from fortune, unarmed and destitute', the approximately fifty-year-old Montmorency had inherited nothing from his parents. Like his nephew, he had every reason to risk all in the Irish venture.

Having secured Wexford and taken hostages, the allies advanced northward via mac Murrough's capital at Ferns through an area today comprising Kilkenny and parts of Laois. The local king was a mortal enemy of mac Murrough's; he had previously blinded one of the Leinsterman's sons. Fighting became progressively harder. Skirmishing in thick, boggy woodland favoured the native Irish over the Normans. The defenders dug trenches in the bogs and 'plashed the woods' with wattled branches, making the trackways impassable to horsemen. The near-contemporary *Song of Dermot and the Earl* describes how

[the Ossorian king] bade his men throw up a trench, high and wide, steep and large, and to strengthen it at the back with stakes, and in front with hurdles, in order to dispute the passage of King Dermot the stout-hearted.

Not until they were driven onto higher, open ground vulnerable to cavalry attack could the opposing Irish be beaten. At the Battle of Clashacrow, 'the hollow of the slaughter', mac Murrough's allies finally lured their tormentors from dense, thicketed undergrowth, ambushed and destroyed them. Men cut down but still alive were despatched by the axe-wielding Irish. Decapitated heads were collected as future decorative items for their leader's citadel. From a mound of more than 200, one head is said to have immediately drawn mac Murrough's attention. Holding it up by the ears, the king is said to have bitten off the nose and lips.

Rory O'Connor was caught flatfooted by the developing crisis. The Ireland of which he was notionally overlord was personified in verse as an affrighted 'trembling sod'. Mac Murrough had already reoccupied his old capital at Ferns before the high-king's forces could be mobilised to confront him. Underlining the fact that rival Irish kings at times preferred to seek an accommodation rather than butt heads, mac Murrough's son Conor became the high-king's hostage. Mac Murrough gained additional territory in Leinster in exchange, but only on the condition he recognised O'Connor as his overlord and also expel his unwelcome Norman allies. But this would have been difficult: news of mac Murrough's generous land grants had by this time spread, attracting additional Norman knights to Ireland. Among them was Maurice Fitzgerald, a man said by Gerald of Wales to be 'intrepid in war [and] second to none in valour'. He arrived at Wexford with ten knights, thirty mounted archers and 100 foot archers. Approximately sixty years of age in 1169, he must have been among the oldest of the invaders.

Backed by these additional forces and the promise of more to come, mac Murrough determined to confront Rory O'Connor if necessary, refute the terms of the agreements made and seize the high-kingship for himself. Gerald of Wales depicts the Leinsterman as resolved not only to win back control of his own kingdom but also to bring Connaught under his remit. Mac Murrough wrote to Strongbow urging further reinforcements, adding that the knight should himself accompany them. As a lure he held out the promise of his daughter Eva's hand in marriage and the kingship of Leinster as an heirloom. Strongbow may have been introduced to mac Murrough's daughter in 1166–7. An informal engagement perhaps already existed. The fact that Eva accompanied her father into exile to meet with Henry II speaks volumes for the ambition the Irishman harboured for her. Given the inducements it seems clear that Strongbow would have travelled to Ireland to join his Cambro-Norman kinsmen much earlier than he did had it not been for Henry II's heavy hand holding him back. Mac Murrough and Henry II perceived traits in Strongbow to admire and fear. This led one to offer up a kingdom, and the other to shackle him. For the latter, having a foreigner bequeath substantial territory to one of his subjects risked the setting up of a hostile, quasi-independent state. In an attempt to prevent Strongbow's departure the English king threatened the sequestration of the earl's assets in Britain. Messengers from the king arrived just prior to Strongbow setting sail for Ireland, forbidding him to leave. Strongbow turned a deaf ear to the demands. He was determined now to make his fortune in what would become from then on until relatively recent times an enduring warzone.

In May 1170, Strongbow's advance party made landfall close to where Fitz Stephen's forces had disembarked the previous year. They were led by a knight named Raymond Fitz William Fitzgerald, known as Raymond 'le Gros' – later a name to become anglicised as Grace. To secure their bridgehead and await Strongbow's arrival with the main force, they constructed fortifications across the narrow, windswept neck of Baginbun Head. Even today these defensive earthworks are discernible. The bay's name is thought to be the conjunction of the names of two of the first boats to land: *Le Bag* and *Le Bun*. An earthen ditch and palisade protected the stronghold from an attack from landward and steep cliffs secured the invaders from attack from seaward. It was a classic Viking defence. Raymond's position nevertheless remained fragile. Nearby lay an army of hostile native Irish and Waterford Norse which had hurriedly assembled to confront them. Rather than await attack and risk being bottled up, the Normans sallied out from behind their defences to meet the enemy head-on. They drove ahead a screen of cattle to shield them. At the last moment they caused the cattle to stampede and disrupt their opponents. The leading elements of the Irish army were driven back upon their supports. The Normans then feigned flight back to their fortified camp, where the first wave of wildly pursuing Irish and Norse were cut down by missile fire from Welsh archers and Breton spearmen. Those not killed either fled or were captured. With more prisoners than he could guard, le Gros is said to have solved the problem by having the limbs of his Norse and Irish captives broken and then to have cast them into the sea. A female Welsh camp follower named Alice of Abergavenny apparently helped cut down the numbers by indulging in an orgy of blood-letting to avenge her dead partner. The chivalric code applicable in Britain and on the Continent was, it would seem, immediately set aside in Ireland. Wanton acts were carried out without fear of censure or reprisal. Bernard of Clairvaux, writing in 1149, had described the Gaels as mere 'beasts … shameless in their morals, unclean and stubborn … a Pagan race', words which would become a permit for unrestrained brutality.

The Battle of Baginbun and its bloody aftermath is now seen as a decisive moment in the attempted Norman Conquest of Ireland. Had Raymond le Gros's small force been wiped out, it is conceivable Strongbow might have lost heart in the enterprise. Fitz Stephen's and Fitzgerald's forces alone could never have achieved what Strongbow later did. Their men were more akin to freelance mercenaries. Some, like Maurice de Prendergast, had already defected to Rory O'Connor. The famous verse which states that 'at the creek of Baginbun, Ireland was lost and won' therefore has merit.

Strongbow's main invasion force arrived in Ireland from Milford Haven on 23 August 1170. His army linked up with Raymond le Gros's men outside the walls of Waterford. They had with them by this time 210 knights and over 1,000 other troops, mainly archers. Waterford was stormed, but only after two initial attacks had been repulsed. Having put up a fight, the inhabitants are said to have been slaughtered in heaps along the streets. Two days later, despite the carnage, Strongbow's marriage to Dermot mac Murrough's daughter Eva took place in the town. Strongbow required Henry's consent to marry outside England but went ahead without it. Henry's main issue with Strongbow's request to travel to Ireland may have been the prospect of this, a marriage which linked a premier English earl with the royal house of Leinster.

Mac Murrough and Strongbow next marched on Dublin. They left Robert Fitz Stephen behind at Wexford to secure the important bridgehead from there with Wales. The combined army was organised in three divisions. Milo de Cogan, described as a Norman knight of 'great worth and valour', commanded the vanguard, a mix of Anglo-Normans, Welsh, Norse and Irish. Raymond le Gros led the main body, men from Wales plus mac Murrough's Leinstermen. Strongbow led the rearguard, riding at the head of the troops he had brought over from Wales and a further unit of Irish. Rory O'Connor could muster much larger forces and could count on the support of the Dublin Norse.

Advancing over the high passes of the Wicklow Mountains, Irish scurriers led the army unobserved through mist-laden, forested foothills before emerging outside the walls of Dublin. The king of Dublin, a man named Asculf mac Torkil, sued for peace, but during the resulting truce elements of the Norman army broke into the city and slaughtered the garrison and many of its inhabitants. Mac Torkil and his family barely had time to reach the safety of their ships. Whether the Normans who broke the truce acted independently or on orders is unclear. Mac Murrough had very good reason to seek revenge on the Dubliners. His father had been killed by them and had then been buried in a grave beside a dead dog.

With Dublin occupied, mac Murrough and his aggressive new allies invaded O'Connor territory to the west, probably into modern-day counties Meath and Westmeath. They plundered throughout the region. In response, O'Connor put to death the hostages he had taken, including mac Murrough's son Conor. The high-king would have had little compunction in doing so: Rory's father, Turlough O'Connor, had been killed by mac Murrough sometime in the past. Like mac Murrough, Rory O'Connor had also ruthlessly clawed his way to power. What is more, mac Murrough's old rival, Tiernan O'Rourke, seemingly confronted O'Connor and made his continued submission conditional upon the hostages being executed. It may therefore have been at 'one-eyed' O'Rourke's bidding that Conor met his end. Despite such draconian actions, the high-king's position weakened further when the Normans successfully overran eastern Meath. The only brake on further inroads was mac Murrough's now failing health. Worn out and grieving for Conor, the Leinsterman is said to have retired to the monastery at his old capital at Ferns. He died there in May 1171. A fragment of a thin cross-shaft marking his grave can still be seen today in the churchyard. His death coincided with a compact, arrived at by O'Connor with a number of powerful Irish provincial lords, to confront the main body of Normans holed up at Dublin.

Dublin at this time comprised a small fortified settlement on the south bank of the River Liffey where high ground, later occupied by Dublin Castle, preserved the inhabitants from seasonal flooding. The siting of the original base was typically Viking, a habitable stockade protected on two flanks by the rivers Liffey and Poddle. Ready access inland and to the open sea was of paramount importance in the choice of the siting. The first attempt to dislodge the Normans was launched in late May by the returning Asculf mac Torkill's army, reinforced by a host of Hebridean warriors led by a fierce Viking berserker known as John 'the Wode'. Roughly translated, 'the Wode' meant 'the madman'. They launched their assault from below the city, from the Steine, an open space on the west bank of the Dodder Estuary that served as a temporary camp. As at Baginbun, it was as much through guile as fighting prowess that the outnumbered Normans overcame the forces hurled at them. While engaging the attackers outside the eastern gate, and probably getting the worst of the encounter, the garrison leader, Milo de Cogan, sent his brother Richard with a small mounted force of thirty knights out by the western gate to fall on the enemy rear. John 'the Wode' was trampled down and hacked to death while unsuccessfully attempting to re-deploy his shield-burh to face the surprise attack. Prior to that he had stood his ground and is credited with striking one knight such a terrible blow with his two-handed axe that it sliced off his victim's leg, despite it being encased in mail. John is also alleged to have felled a further nine or ten Norman knights before succumbing. Such amazing reports may have served as bragging rights for his eventual killer. Asculf mac Torkil earned less kudos by fleeing. He was captured before he could reach the safety of his ships and was later executed. The Normans first considered ransoming him but became so enraged by his haughty manner that in the end they beheaded him.

Had the returning Dublin Norse coordinated their assault better, by linking up first with Rory O'Connor's legions of Irishmen, Dublin may well have fallen to them. O'Connor and O'Rourke had several large contingents of men at their disposal. All were encamped nearby or en route to Dublin. O'Connor's army from Connaught lay at Castleknock, half a dozen miles or so to the north-east of Dublin. With him were O'Rourke's men from Meath and Breifne. A supporting force from the north of Ireland under the command of Rory mac Donlevy was positioned at Clontarf, north of the Liffey. A number of Leinster sub-kings and their Norse allies based themselves at Dalkey to the south. Domnall O'Brien, king of Thomond, a great-great-great-grandson of Brian Boru, lay encamped at Kilmainham. Completing the blockade, thirty longships under the command of Gottred, king of Man, waited in Dublin Bay. Though described as mostly unarmoured, Irish noblemen's bodyguards must have included a hard core of men who possessed iron helmets and mail shirts. They also boasted a mounted arm, but certainly not one to match the Normans in a cavalry charge. Irish noblemen are said to have ridden barefoot into battle. They may have avoided being chased from the battlefield by dismounting to fight.

Returning from Ferns after visiting his dying father-in-law, Strongbow assumed command at Dublin. These were desperate times for him. Much of his Irish support had abandoned him after Dermot's death. Only a victory over the forces now ranged against him would regain his lost status. While at Waterford the previous winter, he had received a summons from Henry II ordering him back to England. In the circumstances it might have proved prudent to have done so, but he chose instead to strengthen his position by making good his late father-in-law's promise of the kingship of Leinster. Strongbow rejected out of hand surrender terms offered by O'Connor that would have given him control of Dublin, Wexford and Waterford at the price of handing Leinster back to O'Connor.

The siege dragged on throughout the summer months. Soon the Normans were suffering severe privation from lack of provisions. Henry II's displeasure with Strongbow and the presence of Gottred's fleet militated against the besieged gaining supplies from Wales. In desperate straits, Milo de Cogan and Maurice FitzGerald led the call for a sortie to be launched against the main Irish camp. FitzGerald is credited by Gerald of Wales with making a rousing speech in support of the proposed foray, saying the besieged could not hope for help from the English, for, 'just as we are English as far as the Irish are concerned, likewise to the English we are Irish'. Raymond le Gros led the charge with twenty mounted knights shortly after midday. Milo and Strongbow followed at the head of successive waves of thirty and forty knights respectively. Mounted archers and foot soldiers supported the attack. A small force of loyal Irish also accompanied them. The whole attack probably numbered around 1,000 men. It fell like a thunder clap on the high-king's camp at Castleknock. Raymond le Gros is said to have simultaneously skewered two men on the end of his lance, testament to the knight's undoubtedly strong physique if not the chronicler's veracity. Taken by surprise, much of the Irish soldiery fled. Rory O'Connor went unrecognised in the confusion. Milo de Cogan attacked Tiernan O'Rourke's camp and killed the latter's son Aed. The slaughter is said to have extended well into the evening. The Irish were relentlessly hunted down 'across the green of Ath Cliath'. The Irish dubbed the fight 'the victory of the ashes'; but quite why is unclear. Some 1,500 Irishmen fell for the loss, allegedly, of a single Norman. Elsewhere, other Irish contingents quickly dispersed.

Upon news reaching England of the victory, an alarmed Henry II made remonstrations to Strongbow, now nearly a king in his own right, to submit to him. From Henry II's perspective Strongbow's involvement in Ireland had raised the concern that the earl might assert his independence from the crown. Henry feared Strongbow might use his Irish base to foment a revolt in Pembroke or seize it by force.

Was Strongbow actively seeking to set himself up in opposition to his liege lord and create a power base encompassing Dublin, Waterford, Wexford, Leinster and Pembrokeshire? Henry clearly appears to have considered it a possibility. The earl's earlier ignoring Henry's demands further argues the case. That Strongbow may have got cold feet is indicated, however, by his prompt despatch of Raymond le Gros to negotiate with the English king on his behalf. Le Gros was tasked by Strongbow with stressing that everything done in Ireland had been carried out in Henry's name. Henry nonetheless remained unsure of Strongbow's motives.

Meanwhile, Strongbow became aware of problems further south where Wexford had been placed under siege by the Irish, and where Robert Fitz Stephen had been taken prisoner. Milo de Cogan remained in Dublin when Strongbow marched out at the head of the relief army. Confronted en route by a hostile force, Strongbow led his mounted knights forward and scattered them, killing their leader, Dermot O'Ryan. Strongbow summoned Domnall O'Brien, king of Thomond, who, after the earl's marriage to mac Murrough's daughter Eva, was now the earl's brother-in-law. The two men overawed the coalition of forces opposing them. Strongbow also settled scores with men who had earlier betrayed his father-in-law, beheading at least one unfaithful sub-king.

Upon learning that Wexford had fallen and that Robert Fitz Stephen remained holding out in a hastily constructed fortress of turf and stakes at nearby Carrick, Strongbow headed south, making for Waterford. Hervey de Montmorency met him there and appraised him of the king's displeasure. He insisted the earl accompany him to England, and Strongbow at last demurred. With Montmorency in attendance, Henry and Strongbow confronted each other in Gloucestershire. The River Severn divided their forces; both were arraigned for war. Strongbow found the king preparing a strong fleet with which he planned to make a personal expedition to Ireland. After a recent shaming the king had suffered because of the martyrdom of Thomas Becket, he was in no mood to forgive or compromise. In the negotiations that followed it was only through the skilful mediation of Montmorency that Strongbow retained the lands inherited from his father-in-law, enfeoffed by the service of 100 knights. The coastal towns of Waterford, Wexford and Dublin and adjoining territories, as well as all other Norman bastions, had to be yielded to Henry. The Irish were not consulted at any stage. Henry's distrust of Strongbow remained acute. The juxtaposition of Leinster with Pembrokeshire, where Strongbow had close affinities, continued to create a danger for the king that from Ireland the earl might yet attempt to seize control of South Wales. Many of Strongbow's new tenants in Leinster were from Pembrokeshire. In good weather the Blackstairs Mountains in Ireland were clearly visible across St George's Channel from St David's Head.

Henry anchored his 200-ship fleet in Waterford Harbour on 17 October 1171. Although an unopposed crossing, navigating the Irish Sea was a nerve-racking experience. William Marshal, a later Lord of Leinster, would one day order the founding of the Cistercian monastery at Tintern in the Welsh Marches to give thanks to God for preserving him from drowning when his ship was struck by gales while making the crossing.

Upon Henry's safe landfall, Strongbow immediately surrendered the town to him. Having survived the long siege at Carrick, Robert Fitz Stephen appeared before Henry in chains. He was reprimanded for overstepping the mark by setting himself up as a virtual king in Wexford. Henry chastised Fitz Stephen for being the first of his subjects to enter Ireland without his consent, and for presenting others with the opportunity for wrongdoing. Imprisoned in Desmond's Tower at Waterford, the knight also had the lands allotted him by mac Murrough seized by the king. Henry appointed his own man, William Fitz Aldelin, governor at

Wexford. Another of the king's men, Robert Fitz Bernard, gained the custodianship of Waterford. Hugh de Lacy became governor of Dublin. These old Viking towns now became the westernmost outposts of the vast Angevin empire. The chastised Strongbow retired to his base at Kildare.

More of an opportunistic adventurer than an out-and-out soldier, Strongbow has since been described as something of 'a limp spear'. According to Gerald of Wales, the earl was smooth-shaven, softly spoken, fair-featured and of a sanguine temperament. Gerald considered him almost feminine. Belying this, other descriptions of Strongbow claim him to have been tall, well formed and warlike; all agree, however, that his temper was 'composed and uniform'. In the end he proved no match for Henry. The king allowed the earl to stew in Leinster while he himself spent time at Dublin, drawing up the city's first charter. Over the coming years Irish society in the areas controlled by the English was reorganised along feudal lines, Church reform was progressed, silver coinage introduced and trademark Norman motte-and-bailey castles established around the country like grim sentinels, vying with Ireland's iconic round towers from the Viking age for dominance on the skyline.

4

WOLVES UPON LAMBS

Rory O'Connor may or may not have submitted to Henry II while the latter lorded it in Dublin. Gerald of Wales says he did but his account is at odds with others. Henry remained too distracted by his own problems at home to have had time to exert himself militarily in Ireland. Unforced, it seems unlikely O'Connor would have made submissive overtures. Better attested is that Tiernan O'Rourke and a number of other sub-kings kneeled before Henry at Christmastime, but even they perhaps did so with fingers crossed.

Henry had been under tremendous pressure prior to his departure for Ireland. He remained a troubled man. The murder of Thomas Becket had outraged Christendom. The Pope for a time boycotted all meetings with Englishmen and later proclaimed an interdict (an ecclesiastical censure) on the country. He may even have threatened to imperil Henry with excommunication; had he done so the king would have become vulnerable to deposition. Even without such immediate concerns, Ireland and its politics would always be something of a sideshow for Henry II. Being king of England, duke of Normandy and count of Anjou, with a vast Angevin empire which extended from the Solway Firth to the Pyrenees, he had more pressing concerns. Ireland was poor, backward and underpopulated. As long as no single fellow countryman became overly powerful across the

Irish Sea at Dublin, as Strongbow had threatened to do, Henry probably remained content to let affairs run their course. Most of Ireland in any case remained outside of Norman control. A vast, unconquered land of daunting mountain tracts and great bogs abutted the Norman enclaves on the east coast. Henry's successors would discover that too small a military force would be unable to make decisive inroads into Ireland, while too large a force would starve.

Contemporary descriptions of England's first Angevin king portray him as a complex, restless man of medium height, with reddish hair and piercing blue-grey eyes. Peter of Blois claimed Henry's eyes appeared 'dove-like' when calm but gleamed 'like fire when aroused'. The image on his tomb at Fontevrault, near Chinon in Anjou, depicts a clean-shaven man of regular features. Subordinates were wary of crossing him. This may help explain why Strongbow was quick to make over to Henry all the territory he had won in Ireland. Even a casual turn of phrase could arouse the king's temper.

Prior to leaving for Ireland, Henry had taken the precaution of closing the channel ports to prevent papal legates entering the country to foment trouble behind his back. Only on his return seven months later, having dealt with Strongbow, did he prostrate himself and submit to Pope Alexander III's demands. He did so after crossing from the south coast to meet with papal emissaries at Avranches in Normandy. He refused to acknowledge that he had ever wished for Becket's death but accepted guilt in prompting it. Henry promised he would remain obedient to the Pope as long as the latter treated him as a Christian king. Pope Alexander praised Henry for stamping out vice among what he termed to be 'the barbarous and uncivilised Irish'. Henry was therefore making his plea from a position of renewed strength.

If he had ever planned to lead an expedition against Rory O'Connor in Connaught, this pressing need to make his peace with the Pope – as well as to curtail a brewing rebellion from within the royal family – prevented it.

His absence from Ireland may, however, have been taken as a sign of weakness by the native Irish. Rory O'Connor forged alliances with erstwhile enemies and called in the support of friends. He led a major offensive into Meath, destroying Norman fortresses at Trim and Duleek, raiding as far as the outskirts of Dublin. Strongbow suffered defeat in battle at Thurles to his brother-in-law Domnall O'Brien in 1174. Four knights and 700 common soldiers were killed by the Irish, proof that the Normans were not always the remorselessly efficient war machine sometimes claimed; also that family ties counted for little in the bear pit of twelfth-century Irish politics.

When news of Strongbow's reverse reached Waterford, the locals rose up and slaughtered the town garrison. Strongbow was for a time blockaded at Wexford. Raymond le Gros rushed to his aid from South Wales, bringing over a newly recruited force of Norman knights and Welsh archers. The Normans, though badly shaken, quickly rallied and were soon busy rebuilding destroyed castles and raiding as far west as the Shannon. Among those who ventured furthest west was the adventurous Robert Fitz Stephen, who ranged into modern-day Cork and Kerry. The following year, Domnall Cavanagh mac Murrough, another of Strongbow's brothers-in-law, asserted his rights to Leinster, but was almost immediately slain in battle at Naas, south of Dublin. Irish chroniclers claimed Domnall to have been killed treacherously, saying that two hired assassins in Strongbow's pay felled him from behind.

Soon after this, Strongbow was again recalled to England. In his absence, Raymond le Gros led a Norman force to capture the Norse town of Limerick. The expedition had been sanctioned by Strongbow before his departure but was seen by Henry as overstepping his authority. Strongbow's uncle Hervey de Montmorency cautioned Henry's council that le Gros sought not only to exert control over Limerick but the whole of Ireland. Henry ordered le Gros's withdrawal. In the meantime, Domnall O'Brien again rose up in revolt. Raymond le Gros's recall was put on hold and Strongbow returned to Ireland. Further Irish risings were now stretching the available Norman resources to the limit. At Slane Castle, co. Meath, the forces of Melaghlin mac Loughlin attacked Richard Fleming's garrison. Fleming and around 500 of his men were killed. Panic set in across the region, leading to the abandonment of garrisons nearby, including those at Kells and Derrypatrick. The sole Norman success at this time was le Gros's triumphal march on Limerick, where on 6 April 1176 the Irish cordon around the city collapsed. Strongbow, however, never heard the welcome news. He had died of an infected toe the day before.

Despite his naysayers, of all the inroads made by the Normans, Strongbow's achievement in Ireland ranks among the most astonishing. It is true that Raymond le Gros, Milo de Cogan and Robert Fitz Stephen were his enablers, and that much attributed to Strongbow was carried out by others, yet the fear the earl engendered in Henry II of a Leinster–Pembrokeshire axis developing paved the way for the later English occupation.

At the treaty of Windsor, almost a year before Strongbow's death, Henry II had formally appropriated for himself the kingdoms of Leinster and Meath, including all the land immediately abutting Dublin. Redistribution of property was carried out on a lavish scale. Native owners were regarded as without rights. Even when the Irish received royal grants, these were generally interpreted to cover only the life of the grantee. In contrast, 100 Norman knights gained land for military service in Leinster, plus sixty in Limerick, sixty in Cork and fifty in Meath. Henry also established the rule that all colonists in Ireland remained subject to English law. Centuries later much of the territory under Henry's control would become known as the Dublin Pale, an area where English law and language prevailed. Also known as 'the land of peace', the Dublin Pale at its maximum extent stretched from Drogheda in the north to the mountains of Wicklow in the south, but was never much more than 20 miles or so in width. Beyond this was by definition 'the land of war', an area outside direct English governmental control. The notional boundary of what became the Pale cut across lands previously controlled by clans like the

O'Briens and the mac Carthaigs. These warring clans remained a menace to English colonising attempts. Domnall mac Carthaig is alleged to have fought twenty-one battles in Munster during the early phase of the English occupation. Even if an exaggeration, the claim serves to establish his warlike credentials. The Irish high-king Rory O'Connor retained a tenuous overlordship elsewhere; this juxtaposition Henry was happy to preserve.

Internecine warfare, the curse of medieval Ireland, continued apace. O'Connor was never able to reconcile all the Irish sub-kingdoms to his rule any more than Henry was able to restrain his unruly Normans. In 1177 Henry had little option but to grant lands in Cork to Robert Fitz Stephen and Milo de Cogan after they had occupied the town of Cork and the surrounding countryside in the manner of a *fait accompli*. The same year, O'Connor blinded one of his sons when rebellion threatened from within the royal family of Connaught. The reasons for this act are obscure; maybe his son wished to take the fight to the Normans without his father's support, or perhaps he sought to usurp the high-kingship.

In repelling the more boisterous of the Normans, Rory O'Connor in the end proved himself up to the task. This occurred when the warlike Hugh de Lacy, foremost among the 'gentlemen buccaneers' who accompanied Henry II to Ireland, probed westward in an attempt to expand his remit across the Shannon. De Lacy's forces were beaten off with heavy loss by Rory O'Connor to the west of Clonmacnois, co. Offaly. The monastery there had been plundered by de Lacy's men much in the manner of the Vikings, which of course the Normans had once been themselves. To strengthen his position in Meath, de Lacy would later marry one of Rory O'Connor's daughters. This was done without Henry II's sanction and therefore inevitably incurred the king's wrath.

Another Norman adventurer's achievements, those of John de Courcy, have been described as among the most amazing in the history of the occupation of Ireland. Described by Gerald of Wales as 'fair-haired and tall, with bony sinews and limbs ... brave and impetuous', de Courcy hailed from Cumbria. Many of the men he would later endow with land were from the north-west of England. Given a grant by Henry II to occupy lands in eastern Ulster, he determined to assert himself at the important ecclesiastical centre of Downpatrick as Lord of Ulaid (*Princeps Ulidiae*), to mint coins in his own name and construct a number of formidable castles. Downpatrick, near the south-western arm of Strangford Lough, was in 1177 an open town, famous as the last resting place of a number of saints: the saying went that 'in Down three saints one grave do fill, Brigit, Patrick and Columcille'. De Courcy's invading army marched northward from Drogheda in the depths of winter to lay claim to the region. By skirting the Mourne Mountains, they appeared on Downpatrick's southern outskirts unannounced.

De Courcy rode upon a white horse that day, bearing a shield with birds painted upon it; an attempt, it was said, on the part of the Norman to fulfil an ancient prophecy that such a rider would one day enter Ulster and conquer it by force of arms. De Courcy's army comprised just twenty-two knights, 300 mounted archers and a number of Irish auxiliaries. He attacked the fortress at Downpatrick and the monastic site at the Mound of Down (*Rath Celtair*), driving out the Irish in a series of skirmishes, carrying off much booty. His men arrived half-starved and spoiling for a fight. They 'ate, drank, plundered, killed and destroyed' at Downpatrick until the town was in ruins. The Pope's legate, Cardinal Vivianus, witnessed their arrival and endeavoured to intercede to conclude a truce, but de Courcy would not allow it.

After their initial repulse the Irish soon regrouped. Led by a local king named Rory mac Donleavy, famous for being 'the last Irish king of Ulaid', they greatly outnumbered the Normans. Like Raymond le Gros at Baginbun, de Courcy was forced to dig in to prevent being overrun. Chroniclers remarked on the astonishing bravery shown by the Irish when launching their attacks. Fierce forays made by them resulted in a number of de Courcy's men being killed and others captured. The fighting became a virtual repeat of the earlier Baginbun battle. The position taken up by the Normans was once again on a peninsula, this time between Dundrum Bay and Strangford Lough. Accounts speak of de Courcy building a defensive line from sea to sea. Ingress could only come from the west, between the Annacloy and Blackstaff rivers. Even then, a marsh, ditch and hedge provided almost insurmountable frontal obstacles to an attacker.

Having been reinforced in the meantime, de Courcy had with him around 1,000 men, including 140 heavy cavalry. He disposed his army in three bodies, led respectively by de Courcy's brother Amory with around seventy supporting archers on firm ground to the south; de Courcy with the main body including most of the archers in the centre; and Sir Roger Power with a smaller contingent of foot soldiers to the north on marshy ground beside the Annacloy River. Mac Donleavy's horsemen first attacked Amory's men, but were disordered by the perimeter ditch and hedge and from missile fire from bowmen drawn up in advance of the Norman position. The arrow storm is said to have 'so galled them that they began to shrink back'. Amory then launched a counter-charge which broke them. Unhorsed several times, on the last occasion he might have been slain had not three of his men alighted beside him grabbed spears from the clutches of men already dead or dying and held out until relieved. The Irish attackers proved no match for de Courcy's main body when it arrived. De Courcy and his knights fell upon their victims 'like wolves upon lambs'. On the other flank attempts by mac Donleavy's men to infiltrate the marsh beside the Annacloy River were repulsed by Sir John Power's archers. To Power's front after the battle there were said to have been heaps of 'dead corpses, harnesses, legs and heads'. Combined missile and shock action had won the day, but advantageous deployment on behalf of the Normans was also a key factor.

The struggle for control in north-east Ireland was clearly a long-drawn-out affair, sometimes favouring the invader, at other times the natives, but despite the fierce tenor of the times warring in the region was never continuous. De Courcy relied on Irish allies as well as his elite Norman forces, but he failed to consolidate power over the neighbouring region to the west of the rivers Bann and Blackwater. Like the Shannon, these defended river systems proved too strong an obstacle to overcome.

Gerald of Wales considered de Courcy one of the four great men of the early conquest period. His life is instructive of the forces at work in Ireland in the late twelfth century. Norman lords were prepared to defy the English king and even ally themselves with enemies of the Crown. In de Courcy's case these were the Manx Vikings and the fierce northern O'Neills. De Courcy also fostered the cult of St Patrick, so by any measure he should be considered an honorary Irishman. He linked his conquest at Downpatrick to the saint and re-established a major ecclesiastical centre there. In addition to the Benedictine abbey, three monasteries close to the town were founded by him. One of the first castles in Ireland was also erected nearby. Under de Courcy's rule, English and French speech largely replaced Gaelic in the region.

This same pattern of entrenchment and uneasy coexistence between Irish and Normans would be emulated by Normans elsewhere in Ireland as far south and west as Cork, delineating the limit of initial Norman cultural penetration, even if not the full extent of raiding, harrying and rapine. By marrying into the indigent ruling class, incomers to Ireland could gain security of tenure and the Irish retain or regain otherwise lost lands, albeit often down the female line. Strongbow started the trend and John de Courcy emulated him by marrying King Godred of Man's daughter, gaining both a wife and a powerful fleet. As mentioned earlier, Hugh de Lacy followed suit around the year 1180 by wedding Rory O'Connor's daughter. Like Strongbow's marriage to Dermot mac Murrough's daughter Eva, these unions were entered into without first seeking Henry II's permission. In the case of de Lacy, now the Irish high-king's son-in-law, Henry worried the knight might be aiming too high and that he might perhaps one day seek to claim the high-kingship of Ireland.

A veteran of Henry II's wars in North Wales and later Normandy, Hugh de Lacy had earlier been granted the governorship of Dublin and then also the province of Meath; his fief was an area of land described as a 'palatinate, containing half a million acres of the rich midland plain'. These rights were obtained on the promise to the king of fifty knights in time of war. De Lacy was a hard-nosed and ambitious man, evidenced by his murder of Tiernan O'Rourke while engaged in talks with him. O'Rourke had ancient claims to Meath, so the Irishman's removal well suited de Lacy's interests. The murder took place on the Hill of Ward, co. Meath. O'Rourke's spiked, eyeless head later adorned one of Dublin's gates. His trunk was hung from a gibbet to the north of the town.

That de Lacy had quickly become an enormously powerful lord in Ireland is borne out not only by his ruthlessness but also by the scale of his construction works. His fortress at Trim on the south bank of the Boyne occupied 30,000 square metres and remains the largest castle ever built in Ireland. The original construction comprised a huge ringwork defended by a double palisade and an external ditch, sited on a hilltop. Rory O'Connor once attacked it and burnt it, but de Lacy had it rebuilt. De Lacy's son Walter continued to improve the castle. The final completion is dated to the 1220s.

De Lacy had an uneasy relationship with Henry II, twice being recalled to England to account for his actions. In a replay of fears occasioned by Strongbow's rise, Henry became worried by the power amassed by his governor at Dublin. As a counterweight he knighted his youngest son, John, and named him Lord of Ireland (*Dominus Hiberniae*). Henry might have styled John full king in Ireland had not Pope Alexander III, for reasons that are unclear, withheld permission. Being Henry's youngest and favoured son, the rueful nickname 'Lackland' bestowed on John by his father reflected a desire on the king's part to see him established with territories he could call his own.

Aged just eighteen or nineteen, John arrived at Waterford Harbour on the midday tide on 25 April 1185. He came with a substantial army: 300 knights and supporting pages and foot soldiers. To the annoyance of the native Irish and many established Normans, he arbitrarily granted the men in his retinue extensive lands and titles. All but the youngest members of John's entourage were awarded land. Philip of Worcester and William de Burgh were among the major recipients: the former gained lands in southern Tipperary, the latter in Connaught. Other beneficiaries were Ranulf de Glanville and Theobald Walter, who both gained land in County Limerick; these grants would need to be wrested from the Irish at the point of the sword. It cannot just be that John was ill advised; immaturity and arrogance must also have played a part.

The earliest description of John is a character study written by Gerald of Wales in the late 1180s. It confirms the young lord's flippancy and youthful folly, and also his high-handedness and unearned confidence in his own abilities. Perhaps the latter betrayed an insecurity in John, the result of being the male runt of a large Angevin litter. Other writers have written of John's paranoia.

Described as 'great quaffers, lourdens, proud, belly swains, fed with extortion and bribery', John's newly arrived knights heaped scorn on the Irish nobility who attended upon them by insulting their deportment, domestic habits and unfashionable beards. Head hair and facial hair were considered manly adornments by the Irish, so poking fun at them cannot have endeared the newcomers to their hosts. The *Historie of William the Marshal* tells of John and his cronies 'sniggering' all the while attending on the Irish. It is little wonder therefore that the kings of Thomond, Desmond and Connaught rose up against the new arrivals, possibly encouraged to do so by Hugh de Lacy, who cannot have been enamoured at the prospect of having a teenage royal bully and a pack of chancers lording it over him. Even previously feuding clans like the O'Briens, mac Carthaigs and O'Connors united in a bond of amity to confront John. As a result, John suffered a number of sharp military defeats. Being ganged up on in this way did not help, but neither did John help himself: he failed to deploy sufficient numbers of archers and relied too heavily on armoured cavalrymen in wild, wooded countryside where light cavalry would have been a more sensible option. What is more, he withheld pay from his troops. Many of his soldiers quit his service and indentured with the locals to avoid starving. John should have overwintered at Dublin to gain a better knowledge of the administration and the men in Ireland who mattered, but instead he sailed back to England at the earliest opportunity. His brother Richard had made his name at the same age by crushing the proud barons of southern France, so it cannot be said that John's youth was a barrier to endeavour. On his return he blamed Hugh de Lacy for his failures. He also accused the baron of pocketing tribute due to Henry II from Rory O'Connor in Connaught, a defamation he knew would resonate with his cash-strapped father.

In the end it was not an Englishman who would put paid to the quasi-renegade Hugh de Lacy. On 26 July 1186, a shadowy assassin named Gilla-Gan-Mathiar O'Maidhaigh, a man known as 'the youth without bowels' due to his wraith-like thinness, struck him down. The news of de Lacy's demise cannot have cost Henry II much sleep. He promoted de Courcy to the viceroyship of Ireland and started planning another Irish expedition for John, but problems elsewhere put an end to this. On the other hand, Henry did manage to overturn the papal objections to John being made Ireland's king. Lackland was soon disporting a crown of peacock feathers and gold, even though a formal coronation never, it seems, took place.

In such dangerous times, Ireland's high-king Rory O'Connor was perhaps unusual to have lived long enough to consider retirement. In 1183, thirteen years after the Battle of Dublin, he handed over to his son Conchobhar the kingship of Connaught and also his claim to the high-kingship of Ireland. Two years later he had second thoughts. Perhaps he had been coerced to take a back seat and resented the fact. He forged an alliance with Domnall O'Brien of Thomond and called in support from mercenary Normans. A brief war erupted. This resulted in the partitioning of Connaught with Conchobhar. The split proved temporary, as Conchobhar again ousted his father. His raiding from Connaught resulted in the burning and demolition of Kildare Castle, with the entire garrison burned alive within. This was a crime that could not go unpunished, and so John de Courcy and two of Rory O'Connor's younger sons invaded Connaught, They brought Conchobhar to battle, but were roundly defeated by him on some forgotten battlefield.

Militarily, Conchobhar was a match for anybody. His successes might have secured for him the lordship of Connaught had he not been assassinated a year later, probably by men close to him in the pay of one of his brothers. In his seventies, too old to make another comeback, Rory O'Connor could not then prevent his half-brother Cathal O'Connor from seizing power. Rory lived on for a further ten years or so, dying at Cong near Galway in 1198. With echoes of the sleeping Finn McCool, poets lauded him as 'the last of the Gaelic monarchs of the Gael [now] slumbering by the vast eternal voices of the western vale'.

Thirty-seven years old when he gained the kingship of Connaught, Cathal O'Connor maintained an anti-Norman policy by reasserting the dynasty's claim to the high-kingship. He once described himself as 'a beautiful salmon with red rounded fins' who would one day oust the Normans, whom he likened to 'blue shoals of coarse fish, with ugly shapes'. He made the statement after almost drowning in Lough Ree, so had a sense of the ridiculous. A violent storm had sunk his ship and scattered his fleet, and thirty-six of his men had died. Cathal was a cultured man who played chess and discoursed with bards. He was not, however, too effete to fight. When in 1195 John high-handedly bequeathed Connaught to William de Burgh without recourse to Cathal, the Irishman rallied the men of the west to his banner and promoted himself as a national saviour. Exploiting divisions between the Norman lords, Cathal attracted a strong mercenary following. He launched destructive raids across the Shannon, burned de Burgh settlements in Tipperary and drove off his rival's cattle. At some point, though, he overextended himself. A series of military setbacks followed. Cathal kept control over Connaught, but a third part of the province became held in fee to the English crown as a barony and the remainder was taxed by them. More focused on negotiable wealth than physically occupying the badlands west of the Shannon, John (by then king of England) recognised Cathal's claims. The papacy did so too. John admired Cathal and presented him with a fine warhorse. Cathal thanked him, removed the heavy, ornate saddle and rode bareback at the king's side in the Irish manner, to the astonishment of all.

*

It was Richard I's untimely death in 1199 that catapulted John to the throne of England. Henry II had died ten years earlier. The change ushered in a more aggressive phase in Anglo-Irish relations. John made it English policy to encourage new English settlers, and this proved destabilising for the Anglo-Normans already settled, as well as for the native Irish. Royal agents, ignorant of the ways of the Irish, asserted control over swathes of the more fertile countryside. Strongbow, Hugh de Lacy, Robert Fitz Stephen, Maurice Fitzgerald, Miles de Cogan and Raymond le Gros had all died within twenty years of the first landings in Ireland. They left minors to inherit their lands, so, despite the widespread anger generated by the royal grants, there could be little armed opposition from the Norman families already established in Ireland. Several Irish lords from the time of the Norman invasion were also dead, Domnall O'Brien in 1195 and Rory O'Connor in 1198 being two examples. Feuding between their successors hindered the formation of a common front against the Anglo-Normans.

Prominent among the newcomers to Ireland were the previously mentioned Theobald Walter (King John's butler) and Hubert de Burgh. That Theobald Walter was a ruthless man was made clear when he and a Norman party from Cork assassinated Diarmait mac Carthaig of Desmond and his entourage. Men like Walter had little difficulty bringing swathes of land in modern-day Limerick and Tipperary under their control through mounting terror raids. The concentration of their fortresses bordering Crown lands underpinned their status as fierce Marcher lords. In the case of Hubert de Burgh, castles built by him at Tibberaghny, Kilsheelan, and Kilfeacle (all in modern-day Waterford) shielded a shallow, recently pacified hinterland. Further west, castles at Carrigogunnell and Castleconnell on the banks of the Shannon guarded Limerick Town.

*

The arrival of the premier knight of his day, William Marshal (Strongbow's son-in-law), to Ireland in 1207 marked a new chapter in the struggle for control of the country. Marshal was at odds with the English king, and his arrival in Leinster upset the balance of power in the region. In particular, John's viceroy, Meiler Fitz Henry, became rattled. He sacked Marshal's urban foundation at New Ross, co. Wexford, killing twenty of Marshal's men, and then confronted Marshal's forces and those of Hugh de Lacy the younger, fighting a winter war against them in 1207/8. John de Gray, Bishop of Norwich, then superseded the exhausted Meiler Fitz Henry in 1208. A turbulent period in Irish history followed when William Marshal wilfully disregarded de Gray's orders by providing succour to a prominent Norman landowner in Ireland named William de Briouze, a nobleman who had been outlawed from England by King John.

Described as 'a hard man of the Angevin regime', de Briouze had once been close to both Richard I and John. His dramatic fall from grace would prove consequential to Irish history. The cause of the rift between John and de Briouze was a failure by the latter to pay off ruinous debts. The amount owed the Crown by de Briouze has been assessed in excess of £3,000. Owing money rarely caused the king to remorselessly hound a subject, so more than this may have been at stake, and it is hard not to conclude that the pressures put on the de Briouzes for repayment of debts owed more to belligerency on the king's part than an anxious treasury. King John's version of events was that de Briouze had reacted with unwarranted violence when royal debt collectors sought to recover lands and possessions in Wales as part payment. Specifically, these were the Marcher castles at Hay-on-Wye, Brecon and Radnor. In open revolt, de Briouze and his sons torched the nearby town of Leominster and attacked their lost castles, killing a number of John's soldiers. When arraigned as a rebel, he and his family fled to Ireland.

Another version of events claims that John's ire against the de Briouzes became stoked when word reached him that Matilda de Briouze had bad-mouthed him when requested to provide her son as a hostage. The de Briouzes had not been specifically targeted in this regard: the request for hostages was made during a fit of royal paranoia and was part of a much wider sweep of the king's baronage, which included William Marshal. A papal interdict on John, the reasons for which are outside of the scope of this book, had led the king to fear his barons would be absolved by the papacy of their allegiance to him. The taking of hostages was a way John saw of forestalling this.

When the de Briouzes fled from Wales to Ireland, John amassed a large army, which he transported in an invasion fleet of 700 ships. Some 800 knights with attendant pages and warhorses packed the transports. There were also ancillary operatives: sappers, masons, carpenters and the like; men needed for the erection of fortifications and laying siege to castles. John's aim was not only to bring de Briouze to heel but also to force the submission of other noblemen he distrusted in Ireland. He also sought to enforce taxation in Ireland for a renewal of his Continental wars.

Although much from this time is unclear, a more widespread conspiracy may have been afoot against John. De Briouze, de Lacy and others may have been in league with the Scots and French. Indicative of this, John confronted the Scottish king and forced his submission before setting out for Ireland. Before John's embarkation, William Marshal travelled to South Wales to meet with the king in person. It was a typically precautionary move on the part of Marshal. To make amends for supposed misdeeds he promised substantial reinforcements for the royal army upon arrival at Waterford. By skilfully knowing when to back down, Marshal survived the later purges of John's barons in Ireland.

John's massive armada landed at Crook near Waterford on 20 June 1210. A number of Irish sub-kings and their retinues flocked to John's banner as he marched north through Leinster to Dublin. As a punishment for Marshal's earlier warring on Fitz Henry, the king quartered his army on the earl's lands, centred on Kilkenny. John maintained a strong bodyguard, never less than ten strong. Earlier mishaps in Ireland were not repeated. John's youthful arrogance and ineptitude had moderated with age. In less than two months his army defeated the de Lacy forces. The king followed up by dispossessing Walter de Lacy of his landholdings in Meath. With the support of de Courcy, who was once more in favour, John then drove Walter's brother, Hugh de Lacy, from Ulster. The latter might have mounted ambushes during John's risky passage north, but the king's commanders struck east to the coast and seized Carlingford Castle; they built a bridge of boats across Carlingford Lough before sending the army over unopposed. When marching north, the columns of men avoided the dangerous Mourne Mountain passes by hugging the coast. John took ship to Ardglass, south-east of Downpatrick. From there his forces captured Dundrum Castle.

In the face of John's advance, William de Briouze's wife Matilda and her elder son and the de Lacys fled by boat to Scotland, but were shipwrecked and seized by Lord Duncan of Carrick. Matilda promised John payment of the money the family owed, but no thirteenth-century baroness could have made good on such large debts. When Matilda finally admitted that she and her husband could not pay, John had de Briouze outlawed and had Matilda and her son William seized. De Briouze managed to escape to the Continent dressed as a beggar, avoiding the fate awaiting his wife. While in captivity at Windsor Castle Matilda was starved to death, probably on John's direct orders. Matilda is said to have succumbed after eleven days under lock and key. She was found dead at the feet of her son. De Briouze died in exile in Paris a year later and was buried in the abbey of St Victor within the city.

In Dublin more than twenty Irish chieftains submitted to John, but a number of others remained hostile. One in particular, Aiden O'Neill, refused point-blank to provide John with hostages, while others simply stayed away. John had a bad reputation with respect to hostages dating back to the suspected murder of his nephew

Prince Arthur at the commencement of his reign, exacerbated now by the treatment of Matilda. Meanwhile, de Gray added to his master's successes by raiding westward and destroying a number of castles still holding out against John, including the Old English castle at Clones, co. Monaghan. De Gray then suffered setbacks in modern-day County Offaly when set upon by the forces of Cormac O'Melachlin. Thousands of settlers in Offaly were alleged to have been killed, and de Gray's base at Ballyboy Castle, key to controlling the ancient route linking the wild Slieve Bloom Mountains to the Bog of Allen, co. Kildare, was set ablaze after John returned to England.

One reason for John's hurried departure from Ireland was the stirrings of revolt in Wales. Henry II's fear that his barons might establish a Cambro-Gaelic power base in the twelfth century remained salient for the more paranoid John in the thirteenth. The once powerful de Lacys had held lands in Herefordshire, and William Marshal controlled much of the de Clare landholdings in Pembrokeshire and castles as far east as Cardiff. William Marshal's lands have been described as the equivalent of a 'great feudal state', a potential counterweight to royal ambitions. John strove to bring Wales under the same level of control as Ireland. This meant mounting expeditions into the wild, mountainous north, where his Welsh rebels retained numerous inaccessible boltholes.

No matter how cruel, despotic or unscrupulous, it seems John managed to retain the loyalty of his Irish barons. Later, with a French invasion of England imminent – a little-known period of our history which lies outside the scope of this narrative – 500 Irish knights under the leadership of William Marshal would travel from south-east Ireland to back the English king, mustering on Barham Down, near Canterbury.

John was very much a hands-on king in Ireland. Through conquests in Meath, Limerick and Ulster new Crown land was amassed and the process of anglicisation sped on. Several new towns in Ireland were founded during John's reign and a common coinage introduced. The period also witnessed an increasing pace of feudalisation along English lines. John gained the backing of a large number of Gaelic and Anglo-Irish lords, but he remains to the English 'bad King John', the monarch who lost a vast Continental empire and who, on his death, left London under French occupation and Dover under siege. Alone of English kings, John's tomb effigy has him depicted with sword drawn, a pointed reference to the lasting shambles of his reign. Chronicler Matthew Paris spoke for all the late king's critics when observing that 'foul as it is, Hell itself is made fouler by the presence of John'.

5

BRAVE HEARTS

John's successor, the boy king Henry III, rarely travelled abroad during his long reign and never went to Ireland. He matured fast; he had to. By the age of nine he spoke with unusual gravitas and dignity. He embraced the spirit of Magna Carta – the charter by which the English barons had sought to constrain John – and urged his barons to do so too. In 1255 he ordered the terms of the charter to be read out in the county courts of England, perhaps also at Dublin. The same year John died, Magna Carta had arrived in Dublin. From then on Ireland routinely received new legislation passed in England. Henry also oversaw important improvements to Ireland's fortifications. The defence of the lordship required ongoing management of Dublin's frontiers and the maintaining of an armed presence in the interior. Summonses for military service (scutage) were served in Connaught, Ulster and Munster, implying that firm inroads had been made by the English westward and northward by the time of the young king's succession. Alongside quotas for knightly service, all adult males were expected to serve in defence of their tenancies. Even men of limited worth had to own a horse – a necessity when campaigning over difficult country.

By 1240, the stage was set for a royal visit by Henry III to Ireland. Factional fighting there, unchecked by the restraining hand of the king, had inevitably weakened the English position and fostered alliances of convenience with the native Irish. Officials at Dublin spoke of a degeneracy setting in among the Anglo-Irish lords due to the brutalising effect of frontier life; also perhaps because of royal neglect after the death of King John. Problems for Henry closer to home in the end took priority. He cancelled his visit and instead demanded armed support from Ireland to campaign in Wales. Some 3,000 kern (Irish foot soldiers; in Gaelic the *ceithern*) were called for by the English king to support his quest to bring the Welsh rebel Dafydd Llewellyn to heel. Contrary winds prevented their timely departure from Dublin. The Irishmen arrived at Holyhead too late to participate in a campaign that had by then run its course. Unemployed, they ran riot and devastated the Isle of Anglesey, much to Henry III's anger. Although getting off to a bad start, the wild Irish fighting abroad would become commonplace in the coming centuries.

Irish forces under the command of Aed Muimnech, brother of the king of Connaught, had previously violated the sanctuary of Tibohine, co. Roscommon, and plundered it. Many other churches and sacred places were also targeted by them. Churchmen referred to the defilers as a 'shower from Hell; sons of malediction, beyond salvation.' The Irish soldiery, the 'shag-haired crafty kern', certainly looked the part; they are said to have worn devilish tokens on their heads and to have jubilantly caroused while picking over the possessions of dead men, raping their female captives. Shakespeare makes several references to this ubiquitous soldiery. In *Macbeth*, the bard mentions 'the merciless MacDonald' being supplied by swarms of kerns and Gallowglass from the Western Isles:

> ... Mark, king of Scotland, mark;
> No sooner justice had with valour armed,
> Compelled these skipping kerns to trust their heels,
> But the Norwegian lord surveying vantage,
> With furbished arms and new supplies of men
> Began a fresh assault.

Richard II, *Henry V* and *Henry VI* also mention the English being affrighted by the Irish. In *Henry VI*, 'the uncivil kernes of Ireland are [up] in arms, and temper clay with [the] blood of Englishmen'. To one of Shakespeare's contemporaries, Barnaby Rich, the kern were 'the very dross and scum of the country ... hags of Hell, fit for nothing but the gallows'. Rich saw them as symptomatic of an arcane and backward land, where 'if the father hath been a kern, the son will be a kern'. Long, plaited locks of back-combed hair and half-shaven skulls were styled in the manner of Norse berserkers of old. During the Elizabethan wars in Ireland a contemporary described them as

> ... a kind of footman, lightly armed with a sword, a target [round shield] of wood, or a bow and sheaf of arrows with barbed heads, or else three darts, which they cast with a wonderful facility and nearness, a weapon more noisome to the enemy, especially horsemen, than it is deadly.

By the mid-point of the thirteenth century, Henry III was backing further advances into Gaelic-controlled areas in both the north and west of the country. An increasingly insecure Connaught had become victim to the sort of damaging raids mentioned above. The Shannon barrier had been breached. The death of Cathal O'Connor in 1224, a year of terrible disease and foul weather, had sparked a period of protracted violence in the west. In 1246, a large army led by Richard de Burgh, Maurice Fitzgerald and John Cogan crossed the Shannon at Athlone and razed the surrounding countryside. The English in Ireland (descendants of the first Cambro- and Anglo-Normans) had by this time 'dressed down' for war. They preferred to ride light, unprotected horses and armed themselves with bow, spear and sword, in the manner of the Irish. Roscommon was attacked and the monastery at Boyle plundered. The invaders also raided O'Connor strongholds in Clew Bay, near Westport, co. Mayo, and an island in Loch Ce, co. Roscommon, the home of the chiefs of Clan mac Dermot, vassals of the O'Connors.

The raiders were harried throughout by small bands of Irish horsemen who set ambushes and launched attacks at night, torched tents and speared anyone they encountered. The battered English army was forced back across the Shannon. Even so, the damage done by them had been enormous: Connaught was said by a chronicler to have been left 'bare of food, raiment and cattle ... depriving the inhabitants of peace and happiness ... [leaving them] ... nothing but discord and slaughter' – a vignette of the fate native Ireland faced over centuries of foreign domination. The same kind of thing happened in central Ulster when the River Bann was crossed. Unrestrained land-grabs inspired widespread antagonism, triggering dramatic battles for control.

A new candidate for the high-kingship arose in the form of Brian O'Neill, king of Tyrone, a distant descendant of Niall of the Nine Hostages. He sought to style himself high-king at Tara and thus invoke time-honoured legitimacy. He gained the support of other disgruntled Gaelic leaders from as far afield as Connaught and Thomond, and in 1258 was accepted in the north as Ireland's high-king. Two years later, styling himself King of Tara, he marched on Downpatrick at the head of a large army.

Rather than being opposed by English magnates, the Irish were faced by a hastily assembled force under the command of ignoble commanders with names like Roger Taylor, backed by loyal Irish tenants. The clash led to a resounding O'Neill defeat. The self-styled high-king fell in battle, side by side with twenty-three sub-kings and other notables. It was later told how 'Brian O'Neill, king of Cenel nEogan, to whom the Gaels gave hostages, and who paid neither tax nor tribute to the king of England', was slain by the Gaels themselves and by 'some of the foreigners at Dun da Lethgas'. A Lament for O'Neill written to mark the event speaks also of one of Brian O'Neill's young captains:

Alas deep grief overspread the country,
To anticipate the death of O'Devlin.
Gofraidh, our grief unto the Judgement Day
Generous of his banquet was the youth.

After decapitation, Brian's salted head was taken across the Irish Sea to London to be gloated over at Henry III's leisure. Being a religious and perhaps squeamish man, the king may have foregone this pleasure, ordering instead that the grim relic should cheer the day for his subjects when crossing London Bridge. The colonising English had little need to honour age-old traditions on the windswept hilltop at Tara. Military control of key towns like Dublin, Drogheda and Downpatrick had by then proved enough of a bridgehead to contain, if not fully subjugate, the Irish.

As a reward for their resilience against the insurgents, the citizens of Down were excused taxes by Henry III's government up to a value of £100. The defeat struck Gaelic aspirations in the north a severe blow. No more could a king of the O'Neill claim overlordship over 'all other kings of Ireland'. The long line of contenders for the Irish high-kingship that perhaps began with Cormac mac Airt and his henchman, the still comatose Finn McCool, ended with Brian O'Neill. Brooding over the defeat, the bard Gilbride mac Namee chastised Munster, Leinster and Connaught for welcoming the English in the first place. He claimed that only the men of Ulster had remained resolved to raise arms against them. He applauded the 'brave hearts of Ulster's sons', described by him as 'a patriot band', saying they alone had always stood firm against the invaders.

By the early part of the thirteenth century, Dublin had emerged as both a cosmopolitan trading centre and the seat of English royal authority in Ireland. Norse-Irish, known as Ostmen, rubbed shoulders with New English, Old English, Welsh, Flemings and a motley assortment of traders, including merchants from London, York, Bristol and further afield. All bustled to and fro between the town's many markets. Dublin also boasted one of the earliest Norman castles, added to and extended during the reign of King John. Further to the north in Down, Carrickfergus Castle may have been the first stone castle to have been built by the Normans. Many stone castles replaced earlier motte-and-bailey structures. They followed in the wake of a long line of similar castles built in Normandy, England and Wales. In Ireland, the mounds of former mottes exist today at Ardscull, co. Kildare, Callan and Knockgraffon, co. Tipperary, Clonard, co. Meath, and Granard, co. Longford. Stone defences at Carrickfergus were in place as early as 1178 and rectangular towers and an inner bailey four or five years later. A middle ward to strengthen the castle's seaward defences was added at the end of the first decade of the thirteenth century. A final phase, probably sponsored by Hugh de Lacy, provided promontory defences and a formidable gatehouse to protect the landward approach. The most remote of the Norman castles in western Europe was at Greencastle, co. Donegal, built in 1305, with the impressive name of Northburg.

Urban centres known as boroughs (from the word 'burg') also sprung up. Examples are Carrickfergus, Clonmel, Downpatrick, Drogheda, Dundalk, Kildare, Kilkenny, Naas and New Ross. The latter was a port founded by William Marshal that competed for trade with the royal port at Wexford; this was presumably a cause of friction between Marshal and King John. By 1250 it was one of the wealthiest ports in Ireland, with as many as 400 ships berthed at any particular time. The older Norse towns at Cork, Limerick and Wexford also prospered, but none could rival Dublin. By the year 1300 there were around fifty towns extant in Ireland compared to around seventy-five in Wales. Ireland was also dotted with newly founded monastic houses. Many were established in urban centres. Eighty foundations are known to have existed by 1230. Most Irish settlements, however, remained rudimentary. A pilgrim from the Pyrenees named Raymond of Perelhos, when visiting St Patrick's purgatory chapel in Donegal, recorded the Irish he came into contact with as being little better than indigent herdsmen, without shoes or breeches. Whether he would have noted the same characteristics of the indigent populations of rural Wales, England or Scotland is open to question; discriminatory descriptions of the Irish, whether in Ireland or in the Highlands of Scotland, often feature in medieval travelogues.

Reform of the Irish monastic system had been initiated by the churchman Malachy. On a visit to Rome in 1142, almost thirty years before the Norman invasion, he had visited the great

Cistercian founder Bernard of Clairvaux. A number of monks had travelled back with him to found the first monastery of the same order in Ireland, at Mellifont, co. Louth. This called time on Ireland's by then lax and disorganised monastic system. The arrival of the Cistercians brought uniformity. Rigid daily programmes for monks became the order of the day. The new monasteries, of which there were thirty-eight by 1272, were designed with a fixed layout in mind: an open quadrangle, with the church built at the northern end; the sacristy and chapter at the eastern side; refectories and kitchens to the south; and store rooms to the west. Monks' dormitories made up a second story on two sides of the quadrangle. The simple, well-ordered life of a Cistercian appealed to the Irish. It seems many monks left the old monasteries and flocked to the new ones. Other orders were introduced into Ireland at much the same time: Augustinians, Franciscans and Dominicans. Cathedral building also increased: soon there were two in Dublin, plus others at Kilkenny, Kildare, Cashel, Killaloe, Limerick and Clonfert.

English military penetration of Ireland reached its zenith in the Middle Ages after the midpoint of the thirteenth century, with armies pushing west into modern-day Kerry, Clare and Galway. But expansion was halted when the invaders suffered a resounding defeat in August 1261 at a place called Callann, near Kenmare, co. Kerry. The annals speak of a great hosting made by the English there against the mac Carthaigs. The main protagonists were the Munster Geraldines, led by John Fitz Thomas and the Irishman Finn mac Carthaig, king of Desmond. The Irish had an intimate knowledge of the mountainous and forested terrain and this negated any advantage the Geraldines had in cavalry, boosting the effectiveness of the fleet-footed Irish, armed with spears, knives, bows and slings. Mac Carthaig was also able to choose where and when to fight. The site of the ambush he sprung was a place where two cascading rivers joined beside the castle of Ardtully, near Kilgarvan, built on the site of an earlier monastery. The invaders suffered a heavy death toll. John Fitz Thomas and one of his sons fell in battle, along with fifteen knights, eight barons and several other young noblemen, plus innumerable common soldiers. A plaque on the battlefield describes the victors as liberating the kingdom of South Munster from English domination.

Mac Carthaig's success was to be short-lived. After raiding enemy territory and burning down a number of English strongholds at places like Macroom, Dunloe and Killorglin, he eventually over-reached himself. At Kinsale in midwinter 1261/2 he confronted Miles de Cogan, the grandson of Milo de Cogan and John de Courcy. Having rejected Miles' peace overtures, mac Carthaig was brought to battle in a set-piece fight and defeated. He and a number of his noble retainers were killed. This ended the war, but the prestige up until then afforded the invaders suffered a major knock because of the earlier defeat.

One man who somehow managed to escape the slaughter at Callann was Walter de Burgh, the son of Richard de Burgh. Walter had succeeded his father as lord of Connaught in 1243. He had subsequently been elevated to the earldom of Ulster by Henry III. More than any other foreigner, he won the hearts of the Irish, being, it was said, 'the best of all the English in Ireland'. By his late twenties or early thirties he had become the holder of the biggest area of unbroken lordship in the British Isles, including all the rich agricultural land of county Galway between the Corrib and the Shannon, an area later known as Clanrickard Burke.

On one notable occasion in 1262, Walter de Burgh shared a room and a bed with a Clan O'Connor chieftain named Fedlimid; it was the outcome of necessity rather than passion, on a drunken night in midwinter. The O'Connors of Connaught were among the first of the Irish to realise the military potential of stone-built castles. This made them formidable opponents. On the basis of their submission to de Burgh, Henry III confirmed Fedlimid's right to lands held in Connaught in much the same manner as he might have done for any expatriate Englishman. This, however, brought the O'Connors into conflict with other powerful neighbours, leading to innumerable fights.

That frontier warfare in Ireland remained uncompromisingly brutal is attested by the so-called 'Carnage of Clare' around 1278.

According to the annals, the MacNamaras and O'Briens seized all 'the men, fair-haired women, little boys, servants, kern, horseboys and herdsmen' of their neighbouring enemies and made of them 'one universal litter of slaughter'. The fact that dark-haired women appear to have been spared would suggest an ethnic basis for the killings. Yet the wars were not simply a process of genocidal encroachment and bitter counter-moves: two years after sharing O'Connor's bed, de Burgh turned on his own countrymen, specifically the Fitzgeralds, and drove them from Connaught, capturing a number of their castles. A characteristic of thirteenth-century Irish warfare, as in the Viking age, was the speed by which alliances and accommodations might be overturned without any underlying ethnic basis. Another was the introduction of foreign fighters (*gall Oglach*) from the Hebrides and Western Isles, men known now in the anglicized form as Gallowglass. The first of them originated from Norse-Scottish families like the MacDonalds, MacSweenys, MacCabes and MacDowells. Men like John 'the Wode', who fought at Dublin in 1171, were their forerunners.

Described as the lustiest fighters of the Irish and a warlord's 'castle of bones', a Gallowglass' axe resembled a double-bladed hatchet, affixed to a shaft much longer than usual. Each warrior was attended by two horseboys who carried armour and provisions. In battle, the boys (young men really, akin to kern) bore three light javelins, which they hurled before coming into hand-to-hand combat with the enemy. Although only of nuisance value against heavily armoured opponents, these missiles were capable of killing or injuring horses and unarmoured troops. The fierce MacSweenys and their like were all initially freelancers. They proudly claimed they owed no one allegiance. They chose who they fought for – presumably the highest bidder. As time went on, however, the various families of Gallowglass became attached to specific lordships. The MacSweenys rose to the chieftaincies of three septs of the O'Donnells in Tyrconnell. By the fifteenth century there were even Gallowglass contingents defending the Dublin environs, contractually bound to the Fitzgerald earls of Kildare. The O'Connor royal bodyguard boasted a contingent of

Gallowglass. Eight-score of them were provided by Dougal mac Sorley of the Western Isles in 1259. Such soldiers made a strong impression on contemporaries. During the Hundred Years War between England and France, they were described as 'long-haired, moustachioed, saffron cloaked, barefooted, axe and claymore wielding mercenaries', who rode back from battle with severed heads dangling from their stirrups.

In the summer of 1270, Walter de Burgh and Ireland's deputy justiciar, Richard of Exeter, launched an invasion of O'Connor lands in Breifne. It was in the nature of a pre-emptive strike: the O'Connors and O'Briens had massed their forces, concerned that the erection of a strong de Burgh castle at Roscommon would lead to the English reneging on previous agreements made regarding territorial rights. The *Annals of Loch Ce* retain the English schedule for the coming days: day one, from Roscommon to Elphin, via Tulsk, the route of the modern N61 (approx. 15 miles); day two, Elphin north-eastwards for a further 9 miles toward modern-day Carrick-on-Shannon. The English army, which lay between Carrick and Jamestown, is said to have included 'all the foreigners of Erin', implying a much larger than usual raiding army. Fedlimid O'Connor's unpredictable son, Aed O'Connor, described as 'an able and dynamic man with a ruthless streak', and his ally Turlough O'Brien had placed their forces on the east bank of the Shannon, whereas the English were marching on the west bank. De Burgh may have been loath to commit his whole force on the east bank, fearing his line of retreat might be compromised should he suffer a reverse. When de Burgh's army crossed the river the next day, Exeter's force remained on the west bank.

De Burgh set up camp in a largely unpopulated, wooded region of lakes and round hills, skirting the modern-day border country between counties Roscommon and Leitrim. Aed O'Connor indicated his willingness to submit to de Burgh by following the protocol of the day, presenting himself at his opponent's camp. Hostages were taken by the Irish to ensure their leader's safe conduct. When the talks broke down, two of the hostages were killed out of hand by the Irish. A third hostage, Walter de Burgh's brother William, was held captive. Fearing for his brother's safety, de Burgh attempted a withdrawal in the face of the enemy, a tricky military manoeuvre at any period of history. O'Connor seized his opportunity and ordered an immediate pursuit.

The Irish are said to have raged around their prey for two full days and nights, in the manner of 'furious, tearing lions', denying their enemy food or rest. Tired and discouraged, the English found themselves cut off from the nearest bridging point by Turlough O'Brien's forces at the as-yet-undiscovered ford of Athankip, probably named for a distinctive tree or group of trees. Forced to fight, de Burgh is reputed to have killed O'Brien in single combat, but the delay this occasioned enabled Aed O'Connor's main body to fall on the earl's rearguard and destroy it. When this final attack came, the outcome was a fearful slaughter of the English. The account of the battle in the *Annals of Ulster* speaks of how the Irish 'committed slaughter innumerable on the foreigners'. Not only was the English rearguard routed, the vanguard also broke. Nine knights were killed on the moor and a hundred barded horses abandoned. De Burgh managed to escape by crossing the river to safety. How many of his men reached the relative security of Athlone is not known. On the east bank, O'Connor, knee deep in corpses, took his revenge for the killing of Turlough O'Brien by executing de Burgh's brother William. The Earl of Exeter's contribution to the debacle, if any, has gone unrecorded.

Athankip was perhaps the most comprehensive defeat inflicted on the English forces up until this time. Coming just nine years after Callann, the disaster represented an unequivocal check on English colonial ambitions. Their attempted penetration of western and south-western Ireland has been described as 'more like a spear-head than a broad shield'. The English could never for long occupy ground gained, being always at the mercy of the native Irish.

Aed O'Connor followed up the victory at Athankip by raiding colonists' settlements and destroying a number of English castles. Two years later he captured the strategic stronghold of Athlone and pulled down the bridge across the Shannon. Upon his death in 1274 chroniclers lauded his greatness by proclaiming him 'the most dreaded and triumphant of all the kings of Ireland in his day', saying how for nine years he resolutely defended 'the Family of Tara'. Walter de Burgh predeceased him, passing away at Galway after a short illness. He is said to have died a broken man, still mourning his brother. The Gaelic resurgence had swept him and his kind from the wild west of Ireland and now threatened 'the land of peace' in the east. An Irish poet had once written to ask the spirits of the heroes of old not to 'reproach our defeats with thy victories'. The likes of Finn McCool could for a time now rest easy; the oppressed Gaels at last had good reason for restored pride. But could it last?

6

VANQUISHED SO SUDDENLY

By the year 1301 the Scottish War of Independence was at its height. The English army had been wasted by endless campaigning in a hostile land against a Scottish enemy loath to confront the English in open battle. In 1303, the largest army yet from Ireland sallied forth in support of the English but saw little fighting. The Scots maintained hit-and-run tactics until finally submitting to Edward I. The wars for Scottish independence lie outside the scope of this narrative, but it is important briefly to touch on the epochal battle of the period, Bannockburn, fought in June 1314, where, prior to defeating the English, Robert Bruce uttered words redolent of Calgacus in the first century AD. Paraphrased here, he declared, 'If they [the English] find us fainthearted and beat us openly they will have no mercy on us … it would suit our skill to set bravely against cruelty, and make our fighting stand in that way.' After the battle, Robert Bruce harried the English as they fell back from Scotland. His brother Edward Bruce in the meantime made plans to lead a full-scale army into Ulster. Born around the year 1280, by the age of twenty-seven Edward was Robert Bruce's sole surviving male sibling; the others had been tracked down and hanged as rebels by the Bruces' rivals. For the best part of a decade, Edward Bruce was just one slip away from the hangman's noose.

The chronicler John Barbour (famous for his pronouncement that 'freedom is a noble thing'), in the 1370s claimed Edward to be 'lacking in measure'. The poet may have sought to glorify Robert Bruce at his brother's expense. In the same work he claimed Robert to be another Caesar or Charlemagne, which, his victory at Bannockburn notwithstanding, he was not. That Edward, like Robert, was a warrior of some talent is attested by his intelligent campaigning in the summer of 1308, when he won two important victories over Anglo-Scottish forces in Galloway. He was rewarded by his brother with the lordship there. Edward also distinguished himself at Bannockburn. On the eve of battle, Robert placed his brother in charge of one of the three divisions of spearmen in the army. Each numbered around 2,000 men. Edward's division bore the brunt of the English attack on the first day of battle but held steady. The next day, on a constricted battlefield which favoured the Scots, Bruce's army boldly advanced upon the English and, after a hard fight, broke them. Edward was in the forefront of the fighting: in one episode from the battle, related in the *Vita Edward II*, the formidable Earl of Gloucester met his death when clashing with Edward Bruce: 'Suddenly the Scots make a rush, the earl's horse is killed and the earl [of Gloucester] falls to the ground ... burdened by the excessive weight of his body [armour] he could not easily get up.' Even so, Robert was wary of heaping too much of an accolade on his younger brother. Although Edward later gained the earldom of Carrick, he was overlooked when the more prestigious titles of Lieutenant-General of Scotland and Earl of Moray were handed out.

Robert Bruce also had to reward Irishmen and the men of the Western Isles, the MacDonalds and their ilk, who had supported him over the previous decade, and many of whom had fought in the vanguard at Bannockburn. He may have looked to lands in the north and west of Ireland to set such men up as his surrogates; in this way, they could anchor the Bruces' power on either side of the North Channel – a new Dalriada. This was the probable reason for Edward Bruce's subsequent travail into Ulster. Robert Bruce saw several years of raiding into English-occupied Ireland as a way of usefully diverting the English king's attentions from Scotland, while at the same time utilizing Edward's warlike talents. By spreading terror through raiding and harrying, Edward might undermine the authority of English rule and expose Edward II's weaknesses. As significant would be the damage inflicted on crops and infrastructure, especially in a time of famine, which applied across much of Western Europe at the time. Due to climatic conditions and blight, the second decade of the fourteenth century witnessed starvation on a biblical scale. The coming invasion would seriously worsen an already desperate situation in Ireland, but would otherwise help to relieve the burden of large standing armies in Scotland living off the land – in effect, exporting famine.

Edward Bruce's army in Ulster started out as just two battalions but quickly gained the support of a number of Irish chieftains, most notably Domnall O'Neill, king of Tyrone. O'Neill met up with Edward Bruce at Carrickfergus and swore fealty to him. The Irishman had for some time been troubled by English incursions into his lands. He opposed the pace of their land grabs with both pen and sword. When Peter Bermingham of Tethmoy slaughtered over thirty chiefs of Clan O'Connor at a banquet in 1305, the atrocity was later used by Domnall O'Neill to highlight English intransigence when composing a remonstrance against the invader's 'sharp-toothed and viperous calumny' to Pope John XXII. The remonstrance was a powerful and compelling statement of national identity and independence. In it he cited 'wrongs wrought inhumanely on us' by the English, and urged the Pope to smite and correct the guilty party 'like a naked blade'. He added that it was no wonder the Irish were now fighting for their very lives, for they had been denied the right of being freemen; instead they had been reduced to slavery. The missive harked back to the origins of the country's woes, relating how Pope Adrian had 'by a certain form of words' conferred Ireland upon Henry II, and had thus condemned the Irish to be 'mangled by the cruel teeth of all the beasts'.

Peter Bermingham of Tethmoy was a particularly cruel and treacherous beast, who is alleged to have hunted Irishmen 'as a hunter doth the hare'. Domnall O'Neill must have had him in mind when he composed the phrase 'evil English barons', who plunged the Irish 'into an abyss of sorrowful slavery'. Taking its cue from the remonstrance, another contemporary chronicle, the *Triumphs of Turlough*, described the English in Ireland as 'an abominable perverse gang ... cruel and insatiable, overbearing, surly, sullen, full of spiteful malevolence and ill-design'. All this was true of the villainous Bermingham. After killing his dinner guests in 1305, the lord sold his victim's heads on to their enemies at a hefty premium.

Peter Bermingham was not alone in terrorising the Irish. Another oppressor, Sir Thomas de Clare, the brother of the Earl of Gloucester, had an Irish house guest dragged along the ground while tied to the tail of a horse, then decapitated. The headless corpse was afterwards raised up and hung by the legs from a beam. Other miscreants were also cited in the remonstrance. One in particular, John Fitz Thomas, Earl of Kildare, was accused of selling an Irish nobleman's head and having the son of the victim thrust into a filthy prison, to be later quietly done away with. Domnall O'Neill also complained to the papal authorities that at the English king's court at Dublin any person who was not Irish could accuse any Irishman without restriction, whereas all Irishmen, save only prelates, were refused recourse to law. Unequal practices regarding the dower rights of Irishwomen married to Englishmen were also highlighted. Little wonder the patriotic Irishman was easily seduced into supporting Edward Bruce's claim to the high-kingship of Ireland.

The Bruces could assert an illustrious ancestry that included direct links to Brian Boru, Strongbow, Dermot MacMurrough and the Hiberno-Norse king Olaf Cuaran. What is more, they were descended from the lords of Galloway, a branch of the kings of Man. Their Norman pedigree might have been more prominent than their Gaelic, but in the hurdy-gurdy politics of fourteenth-century Ireland such distinctions would have counted for little. In his remonstrance to the Pope, Domnall O'Neill referred to Edward Bruce as having 'sprung from our noblest ancestors'. Robert Bruce had earlier addressed the Irish, stating:

Whereas we and you and our people and your people, free since ancient times, share the same national ancestry and are urged to come together more eagerly and joyfully in friendship by a common language and common custom, we have sent over to you our beloved kinsmen, the bearer of this letter, to negotiate with you in our name about permanently strengthening and maintaining inviolate the special friendship between us and you, so that with God's will our nation may be able to recover her ancient liberty.

He invoked the same sense of nationhood when he wrote of the Scottish:

For as long as a hundred of us remain alive, we will never on any conditions be subjected to the lordship of the English. For we fight not for glory nor riches nor honours, but freedom alone, which no good person gives up but with life itself.

In the hope of raising a pan-Gaelic front against the English, Edward Bruce used similar language as his brother and Domnall O' Neill when describing the Welsh and the Irish as the Scots' natural allies. He claimed all were from one root of origin and kinship, adding, 'both bear hardly the yoke of slavery and curse the lordship of the English'. Irish sympathy for the Welsh during Edward I's wars had been widespread. Such a claim had merit. Words attributed by historian Geoffrey of Monmouth to the magician Merlin, that 'the Celts shall load with chains the necks of the roaring ones [the Saxons] ... and the rivers will run with blood', might, it seemed, come to pass.

Edward Bruce took hostages from the Irish lords of Ulster. All the Gaels of Ireland agreed to grant him the lordship and called him King of Ireland. He was crowned as such on Knocknemelan Hill, near Dundalk. Domnall O'Neill's remonstrance to Pope John was in part made to seek papal approval for Bruce's crowning. O'Neill confirmed that the Irish lords had unanimously selected Edward to be their king, describing him in glowing terms and probably stretching the truth when using adjectives like 'pious, prudent, humble, chaste [and] exceedingly temperate'. Domnall considered the Scotsman militarily capable of 'snatching' the Irish 'from the 'house of bondage'. Nevertheless, fearing a dangerous upsurge in nationalistic fervour, the Pope remained unenthusiastic and never formally recognised Bruce's claim.

Moving southward through the Moyry Pass to Dundalk, the Scots burned and pillaged English settlements along their route. The Moyry Pass was the traditional channel from Ulster into the Irish midlands and the east coast. Because of its narrowness, it was also frequently the scene of ambushes. On 29 June 1315, the Scots and their Irish allies attacked Dundalk, destroying buildings and massacring the population, English and Irish alike. They then headed back into Ulster. Walter de Burgh's son Richard, known as 'the red earl', raised an army in Roscommon. Some indeterminate skirmishing followed between opposing armies at Inishkeen, co. Monaghan. Bruce and his Irish allies then fell back into Ulster. The area around Coleraine was sacked by them and the bridge over the River Bann destroyed to prevent pursuit. On 10 September 1315, at the religious site of Connor, co. Antrim, de Burgh's well-equipped force became heavily outnumbered. Edward Bruce crossed the Bann in boats and attacked and defeated them east of the river. The Scotsman was able to re-supply his army before the onset of winter from stores previously amassed there by de Burgh. The bulk of de Burgh's army escaped and managed to fall back on Carrickfergus, which was then placed under close siege by the Scots. The castle finally fell to them in August 1316. De Burgh withdrew westward into Connaught, where several of his castles were threatened by other enemies, the O'Connors. A near contemporary description of him as becoming a 'wanderer up and down Ireland all this year, with no power or lordship', captures his plight.

It was only after further military successes for the Scots and their Irish allies against an English lord named Roger Mortimer, at battles at Kells, co. Meath, and Athy, co. Kildare, that Robert Bruce, King of Scotland, arrived in Ulster to reinforce Edward.

Robert came to Ireland at the head of a sizeable force in January 1317, in time for a planned march with his brother on Dublin. He sought to further worsen Ireland's plight and alleviate Scotland's own supply problems by moving his army to Ireland and living off the land. In the end, Dublin's defences proved too strong for the Scots to breach. Moreover, the invaders found they lacked sufficient supplies to risk a protracted siege. They struck westward toward Limerick and Tipperary. Robert Bruce returned to Scotland, but not Edward. Settlements along the way again suffered devastation. The ruthlessness with which the Scots ravaged the land has been likened to William Wallace's brutal harrying of northern England prior to the Battle of Falkirk, and to William the Conqueror's earlier devastation of the north of England after the Battle of Hastings. Western Europe had been afflicted by torrential rainfall and flooding the year before; two successive years of crop failure had led to acute shortages of food and rising prices. Nowhere was this more seriously felt than in Ireland, where disease among cattle and sheep and the presence of a voracious foreign army exacerbated an already acute situation. Pollen samples indicate a collapse occurring in arable farming and a move back toward pastoralism in areas previously under the plough. They also bear witness to a retrenchment eastward for English settlers, attempting to avoid the twin horrors of famine and war.

Having spent an extensive period of time in England, the previously defeated Roger Mortimer returned to Ireland at the head of a large army in the spring of 1317. He probably arrived too late to intervene in the Bruces' foray across the country. Appointed by Edward II as viceroy of Ireland, his objective was to defeat Edward Bruce and quell discontent among the native Irish. He arrived at Youghal on the south coast after having made the crossing from Haverfordwest. Almost immediately he was busy campaigning in the Wicklow Mountains, an area that had previously been under government control but had since been destabilised by the Bruce onslaught. Despite English inroads, the high passes of the Wicklow Mountains remained under the control of the O'Byrnes. In this sense, Dublin, being within a night's march of the mountains, remained very much a frontier city. Crucial to English success remained re-establishing control of communications within the lordship of Dublin. This meant clearing the route known as the king's highway, which extended down the valley of the River Barrow and connected much of modern-day counties Dublin, Kildare, Louth, Meath, and parts of Westmeath. Both Kildare and Meath had been formally shired in the same manner as English counties. Communications further to the south, toward English-controlled Wexford and Waterford, were probably secured by sea.

How successful Mortimer was in securing the king's highway is unclear. More certain is that he failed to bring Edward Bruce to battle. By the time of Mortimer's recall to Westminster, the Scotsman remained firmly entrenched in Ulster, albeit largely bereft of Irish allies. The native Irish had in the main become disillusioned with him and now doubted his ability to make a difference in their struggle with the English. Moreover, the latter had regained control of the Irish Sea, making it difficult for Robert Bruce to reinforce his brother from Argyll. In Mortimer's absence, Sir John Bermingham, the son of the murderous Peter Bermingham of Tethmoy, seized the baton in confronting Edward Bruce. He surprised him near Dundalk on 13 October 1318. Bermingham's army comprised approximately 1,500 men, including archers and horsemen, the latter being described as bedecked in coats of mail from head to foot. Bruce's army was a polyglot force of Scots, lightly armed Irish and renegade Old English. They outnumbered Bermingham, but not by much.

Bruce occupied a position three miles north of Dundalk on Faughart Hill. When battle opened next day, Bruce kept his more lightly armed Irish allies in reserve behind his right flank and relied on the long spears of his Scottish troops to repel Bermingham's heavy cavalry. The commanders of the small Irish contingent had pressed Bruce to await reinforcements before offering battle, but this advice Bruce rejected. Bermingham ordered his archers to target the Irish spearmen to prevent them from assisting Bruce's main body. If driven back they would expose the enemy right wing and threaten Bruce's line of retreat northwards through the Moyry Pass. Even so, the attackers were at a disadvantage; Bermingham's men had to strike uphill if they were to dislodge the defenders. His cavalry were driven back by Bruce's schiltron of long spears time and again. One counter-attack launched by Bruce sent a number of the assailants fleeing as far as Dundalk, a mile and a quarter to the rear.

In desperation, Bermingham is said to have employed the ruse of sending an assassin dressed as a jester, 'a man in a fool's coat', into the Scottish camp. Once close enough to Edward Bruce, the rag-tag clown, if it can be believed, clubbed his victim to death with a leaden ball attached to a chain. He was then himself struck down by the men of Bruce's bodyguard. Barbour claimed that after Bruce's unexpected demise the Scottish forces 'were vanquished so suddenly, few in that place were slain'; in other words they fled unpursued. Although the manner of Bruce's death has all the hallmarks of a fireside tale, something untoward must have occurred to bring about the Scotsman's sudden demise. The descendants of the likely assassin, a butcher named John Maupas from Drogheda, received a pension from the Crown right down to the seventeenth century. The *Lanercost Chronicle*, the chief English source for the battle, however makes no mention of the assassin; instead, it describes the Scots as forming up in three columns, at such a distance each from the other that 'the first was done with [by the English] before the second could came up, then the second [done with] before the third could render any aid'. The third column was then routed just as the two preceding ones had been. Edward was said to have fallen in the fighting, beheaded after death. Men who died with him included an unidentified MacDonald lord and a McCrorie chieftain.

If the manner of Edward Bruce's death is a puzzle, not so the outcome of his dismemberment. His body was divided into four quarters, which were sent to the four chief quarters of Ireland. A grateful Edward II received Bruce's salted head in a wooden pail and elevated the despatcher to an earldom. Edward Bruce's foray in Ireland had destabilised the country and drawn English forces away from the Scottish borders. Even more than the English, the Irish must have been relieved to see Edward Bruce eliminated. Because of his depredations and baleful presence in Ireland, his murder at the hands of either the assassin or an unnamed English soldier was seen as the best deed performed 'for the men of Erin ... since the beginning of the world'.

The victor of Faughart, Sir John Bermingham, became a prominent victim of a later mass killing. He and members of his family, as well as 200 of his soldiers, were killed near Ardee, co. Louth, on 10 June 1329, becoming casualties of what became known as 'the Braganstown Massacre', committed by local men, many of them Bermingham's tenants. The affair was unusual in that the knight's demise was at the hands of fellow Englishmen. Bermingham hailed from 'the wild Leinster marches' and had brought with him from there a private army of 200 kern. The knight also had a penchant for Irish ways and rough living. His lording it over the English settlers of Louth in the manner of a Gaelic chieftain was widely resented. The English of Louth saw the arrival of Bermingham's large Irish retinue as a vanguard of native intruders. Tension boiled over when Bermingham's soldiers killed a local man during a quarrel. The townsfolk of Ardee hunted down and killed two of the assailants. Others from Bermingham's entourage sought sanctuary in a local Carmelite chapel, but were dragged from its confines and put to death. The hue and cry became more widespread: a posse of men from Louth turned out, armed as if for war. They met up on the Braganstown causeway and marched on Balibragan, Bermingham's estate, demanding that other kern incriminated be handed over to them. When this was refused, they slaughtered all they could find, including the unarmed Sir John Bermingham, two of his brothers and 'a further nine of his name'. His countess was assaulted and a squire accompanying her and her children was cut down when waving a white wand of peace. The *Book of Howth* claimed the killings served to hinder the pacification of the region, described as 'the only key and wall thereof' against the encroaching wilderness. The feuding that continued in the fallout of the massacre deterred incoming colonisers and perhaps halved the local population for a time.

Four years later, at Carrickfergus Ford, another brutal murder occurred. The victim was twenty-year-old William de Burgh, known as 'the brown earl', a man said to have brought 'an unusual ruthlessness to Irish baronial politics'. Not only were men like Bermingham and perhaps de Burgh, with their swagger and Irish ways, resented by hard-working colonists, the arrival of a new wave of English nobles was also begrudged, especially since so little help had been forthcoming from England during the period of the Bruce ransacking. The Scottish invasion had exposed the English as unable or unwilling to protect their acquisitions across the Irish Sea. Work done to develop a settled state of affairs begun by King John, which had extended for a further hundred years after his death, had in the space of a few short years been undone. As in the Far East after the Second World War, the military debunking of a colonial power fatally weakened the English administration at Dublin; what has been described as a 'process of disintegration' set in, whereby the country was reduced to chaos.

The Irish and in some cases the Old English were emboldened to strike at their oppressors. The *Book of Howth* claimed, 'Ireland could never [at this time] be brought to conformity, for God never did permit any to reign that sought earnestly the commodity thereof'. Previously dispossessed Gaelic chieftains recovered ground and numerous small battles and skirmishes were fought. The Irish emulated their recent oppressors in arms and tactics. Castles built by the Normans fell to the Irish and became the strongholds of Gaelic warlords.

The high point of what has since been seen as the 'Gaelic resurgence' occurred on 10 March 1318 at the Battle of Dysert O'Dea, just a few months prior to Edward Bruce's death. It saw the Clare O'Briens and their allies confront an English force led by Richard de Clare, an ancestor of the great earl Strongbow. The trigger for the fight was de Clare's attempt to put an end to incessant Irish harrying of his lands. The *Triumphs of Turlough* describes how these raids were carried out, mentioning specifically 'flocks of sheep, herds of cattle, horses in frightened droves, plough teams, wolfhounds in packs, agricultural implements, clothing and weaponry' being seized. Of these, the Irish are said to have 'left not a jot, but speedily and completely swept clean and forcibly brought away'.

Shortly after one such raid, Richard de Clare, described as 'a knavish man of an overbearing temper', marched out from Bunratty Castle at the head of an army assessed at around 1,000 strong. His force comprised mounted knights and archers, light horsemen and a mixed force of Old English and native Irish infantry. The latter probably comprised spearmen and slingers. Indicating de Clare's strength to be typical for such a foray, Irish chroniclers described it as 'a general hosting'. Before the final leg of the chevauchée, the commander slept at his fortress at Quin, near Ennis, co. Clare. The English may have hoped to meet the Irish in open battle or take them by surprise, but they would be disappointed. Upon learning of de Clare's intentions, their quarry fell back into a region known as 'the ruined entrenchments', possibly the rocky terrain of the Burren, where better knowledge of the ground would allow them to launch ambuscades and hit-and-run attacks. The Irish also called in non-combatant members of their clans. The order given was to 'bustle up in silence … for to attack you comes a battle-flagged array of enemies'. The leading Irish warriors donned shirts or hauberks of mail over padded coats and conical iron helmets, equipment that may have been bartered from the Scots or stripped from the Scottish dead.

In the make-believe world of storytellers, on setting out from Ennis de Clare and his commanders soon became disconcerted by the unnatural stillness and emptiness of the landscape, and were soon startled by the appearance of a banshee, a ghostly manifestation of the Irish war-maiden Morrighan, an entity associated with the Irish pagan Goddess Dana. Described as 'a hideous hag, with elf-locks rough as heather, long as sea-wrack, and with bleary, dripping, red-rimmed eyes', when asked her name, she replied, 'a war-maiden of the Danu, the dismal of Burren, come to warn of impending doom'. Affrighted by this unexpected manifestation, de Clare's soldiers drew their weapons. Soon assailed by javelins from de Clare's bodyguard, the banshee immediately transformed into a bird in flight, and, availing herself of a sudden rushing wind, rose above her attackers and was gone. Eerie intercessions like this punctuate the military history of Ireland: another tale imagines Morrighan beside a riverbank washing a heap of bloodstained armour and helmets; this despite the very same, untarnished armour being worn by the frightened onlookers, readying themselves for battle. It is not difficult to see where Shakespeare found his inspiration for his play *Macbeth*, populated by portents, ghostly apparitions and calliagh hags.

When approaching the monastery at Dysert, with its round tower jutting skyward and its nineteen ghastly heads adorning the Romanesque doorway, seeming silently to look on, de Clare's scouts spied in the distance cattle being driven off by the Irish across a ford. This most likely occurred near the modern-day Macken Bridge, which crosses the Ballycullinan Stream, north-west of the small hamlet of Kilkee. The enemy intention seemed clear: to put the river between themselves and the English. Mailed knights rushed forward and cut down stragglers, but were then set upon by Irish reinforcements approaching unseen from the west, having skirted the southern shore of Lough Ballycullinan. One group was led by the famed Gaelic hero Felim O'Conor 'of the Red Sword'. A well-orchestrated trap had been sprung. Another Irish contingent approached from the north. Ahead of them they spied the red-sworded O'Conor and his men immersed in their bloody work. Abandoning their horses, mantles and missile weapons – and without, it was said, 'consideration or respect by loon for lord' – they too fell upon the already hard-pressed English, hacking and hewing their way through the mass of disordered soldiery.

Richard de Clare and his eldest son were among those slaughtered. Few Englishmen survived the rout that followed. Upon hearing the news of the defeat, de Clare's wife set fire to Bunratty Castle and fled by boat down the Shannon. English power in the region never recovered from the disaster. Gaelic warriors willing to accept casualties and fight it out was, for the invaders, a decisive change, something altogether new. No more could the descendants of the victors of Baginbun and Dublin count on defeating the Irish in open battle. The Gaelic resurgence and the distinct lack of interest in Ireland shown by successive kings of England had resulted in a weakening of the English position, throwing the colonists very much on the defensive. Lack of effective leadership undermined recovery. The effect was to encourage periodic Gaelic uprisings and a steady encroachment by the Irish into previously English-occupied territory. More aggressive clans like the O'Briens, O'Tuathals and the MacMurroughs on occasion even threatened Dublin directly. They were described by one worried observer as 'an advancing tide'.

*

This was also the era of the Black Death. Richard Fitz Ralph, Archbishop of Armagh, estimated the pandemic killed two-thirds of the English nation in Ireland. Eight Dominicans of the Blackfriars monastery in Kilkenny are known to have died in a single day. Because of the devastation wrought, English revenue from Ireland dropped drastically to an amount that barely covered the fixed costs of governance. For a time in the fourteenth century, owing to both the plague and the Gaelic resurgence, Ireland became unviable as a colonising project. Not until the beginning of the fifteenth century did the country regain sufficient strength in manpower to generate renewed economic growth and increased tax yields. England's new king, Edward III, may have claimed lordship over the whole island, but in a practical sense the English controlled only the immediate hinterland of major coastal towns like Dublin and Waterford. Gaelic and Old English lords retained virtual independence elsewhere. From a New English perspective, lands beyond the Rivers Bann and Shannon were analogous to bandit country. Territory under royal authority was only secure if adjacent to an acquiescent local nobility. Beyond Ireland's great riverine divide to the west, probably only Galway met this criteria.

The powerful earldoms of the Butlers of Ormond (the descendants of Theobald Walter, King John's butler) and the Fitzgeralds of Kildare were key to underpinning English rule in the narrow corridor focussed on Dublin, Drogheda and Kilkenny. Both families were, however, critical of the neglect shown to Ireland by the English Crown. In an attempt to remedy the situation, Edward III made his son Lionel, Duke of Clarence, his royal lieutenant there.

Married in 1352 to an Irish heiress, the immensely tall Clarence was already in possession of a vast Irish inheritance. He travelled to Dublin in the summer of 1361 accompanied by fifty knights, 300 men-at-arms and 540 bowmen. Forays made by him into the Wicklow Mountains upon arrival served to announce his intent of securing the lordship by demonstrating military might. Dublin Castle was strengthened and he set up his campaign headquarters there. Some part of the civil administration was removed to Carlow to make room for his considerable entourage. Clarence proved to be an energetic governor. He refortified Drogheda and then set off to campaign in Meath, where the capture of Dermot mac Murrough's ancestor, Art Caomhánach mac Murrough, and the Irishman's subsequent death in custody removed one of the most dangerous rebel Gaelic leaders at large. Two years later, Clarence made a triumphal progress through the Irish midlands from Cork to Drogheda, via Trim Castle, which for a time became his base. More significantly, new law statutes were passed by his administration at Kilkenny. The main outcome was to forbid all subjects of Edward III from using the Gaelic language, marrying Irish wives, fostering Irish children or observing Brehon law. Descendants of colonists who did not know how to speak English were required to learn the language on pain of losing their land and belongings. Sports like hockey were to be dropped and martial pursuits like archery and lancing adopted. As well as to discourage Irish pastimes, this was to build a force of citizen militia which could be called upon to defend English property. At last, the English were being seen to push back against the resurgent Gaelic tide. Another statute followed up on the first tranche, requiring all Englishmen in Ireland to maintain a martial stance, ordering landowners to defend their estates to the utmost, and to hold their ground. These were all measures designed to slow a process of so-called cultural degeneracy among the English born in Ireland. In particular, the statutes referenced the inability of the English colony to withstand Edward Bruce's depredations, the parlous state of the earldom of Ulster ever since, and the need to counter the claims of Domnall O'Neill's remonstrance. As we have seen, O'Neill had not minced his words. He had summed up his petition by declaring the English in Ireland to be 'of utmost perfidy … crafty foxes and greedy wolves … the very worst of them'.

Clarence's Kilkenny statutes have since been assessed as sweeping in scope and aim; their codification became the definitive way the English in Ireland were expected to deport themselves right down to the seventeenth century, and have been described as the first sustained attempt to force absentee landlords to take responsibility for the defence of their lands. Yet the English never really had sufficient resources to implement and police them effectively. The wording of the statutes also proved unacceptable to many already gaelicized English, and may have served to alienate others. Clarence departed for England almost immediately after their publication, *c.* 1367, vowing never to return to Ireland. The nature of the country and the difficulty of navigating a path between the rival groups in Ireland in the end proved too much for him. He was not a politician; moreover, he may have been suffering from impaired health, something doubtless brought on by the rigours of campaigning in the damp, fever inducing outback of Ireland. He died a year later, aged just thirty.

Clarence's replacement was Sir William Windsor, a man who already by the time of his appointment had acquired estates in Cork and Waterford. Windsor was an ideal candidate for the post; a veteran of the king's French campaign of 1359/60, with previous experience of confronting opposition in Ireland when earlier serving under Lionel of Clarence. As a further incentive to take up the position, he was allocated 1,000 marks by way of a bounty. Inducements like these had to be made because the governance of Ireland was seen by many as a poisoned chalice.

Windsor was made the king's lieutenant in Ireland in the spring of 1369. He agreed to serve there for three years, with a budget of £20,000, and the revenues of Ireland to fund military operations. These proved insufficient, forcing him to resort to more draconian measures to increase revenues, including an increase in general taxation.

A year after this, an insurrectionary force led by Brian O'Brien crossed the Shannon and defeated the Earl of Desmond, before marching on Limerick. O'Brien and his Munster allies were for a time feared to be attempting a complete reconquest of Ireland. Windsor's demand for money from Dublin became all the more urgent. In the summer of 1371, complaints about his exactions reached the ears of Edward III. The result was an order to forestall the most severe of his demands. Money dried up. Unpaid soldiers deserted in droves. Windsor was briefly recalled to court to face charges of mismanagement, but was exonerated by Edward, who valued his subject's martial qualities, if not his diplomacy or fiscal acumen. A second tour in Ireland became a virtual repeat of the first. Once again, subsidies for troops were denied him at Dublin. Officials there defied the Crown by stating that money must be found from England if Windsor was to re-arm. Uprisings were allowed to run their course for want of soldiers to confront them. Windsor was again recalled to court, this time to answer charges of extortion and oppression. He survived his trial and would later trade hunting down Irish insurgents for English ones during the Peasant's Revolt of 1381–2. He died, probably in his mid to late fifties, in 1384.

Perhaps best likened to a merry-go-round which could not be slowed, this cycle of recall and return in the face of a mounting threat proved disastrous for the good governance of the Irish colony. Had Edward III not been embroiled in a long-running war with France, he or his son, the Black Prince, might have made a better fist of things. Edward III has sometimes been described as a profligate king who denuded the crown's coffers by waging irresponsible wars on the Continent. Edward's government was always desperately short of money, especially so for Ireland.

A parliament called in the spring of 1376, which might have voted funds for Ireland, could not be attended by the king because of illness. Worse, his son, the Black Prince, died while the parliament was in session. Edward died shortly afterwards, on 21 June 1377, to be succeeded by his ten-year-old grandson, Richard, the son of the Black Prince and Joan 'the fair maid of Kent'. Ireland was once again about to enjoy the attentions of a hands-on king.

7

BLOOD OF THE CONQUEST

Richard II would be the only English monarch to visit Ireland between the years 1210 and 1689. Had he not done so, Ireland would have faced almost half a millennium of royal neglect (at least in person). Unlike Henry III, who became king when aged just nine and relied on William Marshal to rule as regent, Richard's reign progressed without a formal regency being established. A number of former retainers of the Black Prince controlled the privy administration. They dealt with petitions and acted as the boy-king's council. This was opposed by a number of leading members of the House of Commons, who worried that a clique had taken control of the government and was acting extravagantly. What is more, the cost required to maintain garrisons at Calais, Dublin and on the Scottish borders resulted in increased levels of taxation, and became the trigger for riots in Essex and Kent in 1381 – this was known as the Peasant's Revolt, mentioned earlier.

A number of chamber knights came to dominate the king's inner council. Among them was Robert de Vere, Earl of Oxford, made Marquis of Dublin. Marquis was up until then a title unknown in England, and outranked a mere earl. De Vere later became the king's deputy in Ireland and gained what has been termed 'quasi-regal' authority there. That he was a favourite of the king's was borne out in the autumn of 1386, when he was raised to the title Duke of Ireland, ranking alongside Richard's three uncles, Lancaster, York and Gloucester, probably much to their displeasure. The de Veres had once owned land in Ireland, but it had since been sold off. Personal ambition and what we would today call 'presentism', the need to be constantly at court, predicated against de Vere spending time at Dublin, despite his prestigious title. Rather than leave Richard's side, he appointed another man to deputise for him at Dublin. Envious contemporaries saw de Vere as an upstart who had gained everything through royal patronage and nothing by his own efforts. He became widely hated for feathering his own nest. Richard was said to be so blinded by the twenty-four year old, 'if [de Vere] said black was white, the king would not have gainsaid him'. It was even rumoured that Edward might make his favourite full king of Ireland. If not a homosexual relationship, Richard and de Vere appeared to contemporaries closer than was considered seemly. Historians have suggested their relationship might have been a compact of brotherhood: a chivalrous pairing, not necessarily a sexual one. Whatever the truth of the matter, after a brief period of open warfare waged by Richard's barons against de Vere, the marquis was forced to flee to the Continent, never to return. He lived for just a further five years, 'in poverty and distress', falling victim to a wild boar's charge in the forests of Louvain, in November 1392.

Perhaps to distance himself from his troublesome barons, Richard II arrived in Waterford Harbour in the autumn of 1394, two years after de Vere's death. He departed from Haverfordwest in Pembrokeshire at the head of a 5,000-strong ship-borne army, transported in 500 vessels. An Irish chronicler remarked that 'such a fleet did not come to Ireland since the Norse fleets came'. Unsurprisingly, given that Richard was the first English monarch to take the trouble to make such a journey in living memory, his visit was a success, both militarily and diplomatically, yielding the recovery of much land lost to the resurgent Irish. English bowmen are said to have quickly put any opposing Irish forces to flight. The main rebel grouping was led by a wily insurgent named Art mac Murrough, the self-proclaimed king of Leinster, son of the same mac Murrough who had died in English captivity in 1361. Art enjoyed some success in making penetrating raids into modern-day counties Carlow, Kerry and Kildare, but upon Richard's arrival found himself blockaded and had his cattle seized and homesteads and crops burned. In the end, he was forced to make a humiliating submission.

By the turn of the year, Richard was receiving other regular submissions from cowed Irish lords. Some sent their sons to him to be knighted and instructed in chivalrous pursuits. On 18 February 1395, Donnchad O'Byrne prostrated himself before Richard and swore to serve and obey him with 'every kind of submission, service, obedience and fealty ... to keep [the king's] laws, commands and precepts, and to continually obey them without complaint'. Such assent may seem remarkable. An aspect of absolutism is discernible. Richard II assumed the ancient 'high-kingship' of Ireland of Tara for himself; he made no distinction between his English and Irish subjects, but also brooked no dissent. Richard saw all of Ireland as his lordship and treated all Irishmen willing to pledge their loyalty as his true liege subjects. No ethnic edge or racial distinction was discernible – perhaps an unusually non-prejudicial stance for its time. Richard enjoyed the rich, outward displays of authority – the pageantry and affected manners, having Irish lords prostrate themselves, the act of knighting them and granting each 'the kiss of peace'.

Heading Richard II's campaign in Ireland was James Butler, 3rd Earl of Ormond, a nobleman who three years earlier had made inroads of his own into quelling the worst excesses of the resurgent Irish. On 4 September 1391 he had captured the key Ossorian stronghold of Kilkenny Castle and had expelled its governor. Although done without the express consent of Richard, the English king could hardly afford to alienate so powerful a lord, so he belatedly recognised his subject's right to have done so. Richard II is said to have conceded, 'I am unwilling that the said Earl or his heirs should by reason of [his actions at Kilkenny] be in future times ever vexed or molested by us or by our heirs.' Having taken advice from old-timers in Ireland, it seems Richard recognised Butler as Ireland's premier earl. He also took to him personally, and doubtless rewarded him for his loyal service. Irish annalists would later laud Butler as 'the head of the chivalry of Ireland'. In July 1392, the earl was appointed Lord Chief Justice of Ireland. After Richard's fall he kept the post, and later gained the governorship of Kilkenny and Tipperary. He died in September 1405.

Richard was clearly pleased with the progress he had made in Ireland; justifiably so, since he had quickly stamped his mark. Plans were made while at Dublin for the complete pacification of the country. Provisions included a general pardon for all rebel English who had in the past allied themselves with the Gaels and the creation of a more extensive English controlled area, stretching from Dundalk to the Boyne, then down the River Barrow to Waterford. Also a priority was the expulsion of all the remaining rebel Irish chieftains, the main one being the previously mentioned Aed mac Murrough, a lock-horned stag of a man, whose black warhorse was valued at 400 cows, and whose dress comprised a many-coloured cloak, a high, conical cap covering the nape of his neck, a long coat and under-coat, all bright yellow. Mac Murrough had himself claimed to be the 'rightful king of Ireland' and for the English 'to be unjust' in seeking to deny him his birthright. When brought to bay, Mac Murrough's land holdings were divided up among more pliant Irish chiefs, who swore their allegiance to Richard and his deputies. Richard also toyed with the prospect of embracing a number of Gaelic lords and bestowing on them status rights as Englishmen.

While Richard revelled in his success, his uncle, Thomas, Duke of Gloucester, took a more jaundiced view. He accompanied Richard to Ireland but did not remain long. He viewed the situation there with dismay. In the north-east, the O'Neills of Clandeboye ruled unimpeded from the Glens of Antrim to the northern parts of modern-day County Down. The Dublin government controlled little more than Leinster and the coastal towns – by the end of the century much of the east coast from Bray to Arklow would be in the hands of the rebel O'Byrnes and O'Tooles, lords of Wicklow and its mountain fastnesses. Gloucester considered the common

Irish people 'poor and wretched'. He later asserted the place to be 'a land neither of conquest nor of profit', adding 'that what might be gained one year would likely be lost the next'. These were sobering words, which would ring true down to the age of the Tudors. Richard II's self-glorified success in Ireland would prove, like much of his life's efforts, wishful and transient.

While in Ireland, riding high on the heady scent of power and pumped up by hubris, an increasingly upbeat but inwardly paranoid Richard plotted the downfall of those who had either previously opposed him in England or who now represented a threat to his regime. On his return to England, arrests followed thick and fast. Chroniclers claim the king sought to assuage all former humiliations suffered at the hands of his barons. French onlookers, with the benefit of impartiality, saw his actions as a necessary cull of the lords who had earlier sought his downfall. Historians still argue over the rights and wrongs of these times. On balance, however, Richard gets a negative press. On his watch, England appears to have become little better than a police state. Some of the terms of Magna Carta were set aside. Treason laws were used as a means of political oppression. Real power was invested in a number of Richard's newly made men, who arrested supposed traitors and punished them in kangaroo courts rather than allow them to be tried by their equals, as required by statute. A clause in Magna Carta guaranteed that an offender would be dealt with 'according to the lawful judgement of his equals and the law of the land', not arbitrarily by men of much higher status. Gloucester fell victim to the reign of terror unleashed. Ill and bed-ridden, he was murdered on Richard's orders.

Another who for a time fell from grace was Roger Mortimer, 4th Earl of March and 6th Earl of Ulster. Mortimer had a considerable stake in securing Ireland and regaining family land holdings in Meath, Ulster and Connaught, earlier lost to the Gaelic resurgence. Richard appointed him lieutenant of Ulster on 28 April 1395, before leaving to return to England, but it seems the king was later angered when reports reached him that Mortimer had acted half-heartedly when chasing down a family member who had rebelled. That the young Mortimer was immensely popular in England may also have been a factor in arousing the king's jealousy. In the autumn of 1397, Mortimer returned from Ireland to attend a parliament at Shrewsbury. The reception he received in Shropshire was said by the chronicler Adam Usk to have been 'rapturous'. Vast crowds, all of them dressed in the Mortimer colours of red and green, turned out to welcome him. To make a show of his loyalty to Richard, the returning earl swore on the Canterbury Cross to observe all ordinances agreed. The earl was brought back into Richard's fold. Some consider he might have been named as the childless king's successor. It is an interesting what-if to consider what might have resulted had the earl not been killed on his return to Ireland at the Battle of Kellistown, in co. Carlow. Mortimer was not only a scion of one of England's most powerful royal families, he was also a direct descendant of Dermot mac Murrough, Strongbow's father-in-law and therefore distantly related to the rebellious Art mac Murrough, whose forces he faced that day. At Kellistown, Mortimer bedecked himself in Irish garb against forces controlled by the irrepressible Art – mainly the fighting men of Clans O'Toole and O'Byrne, mac Murrough's surrogates. Mortimer wore just a plain linen tunic rather than mail armour and quilted aketon, and is said in the *Wigmore Chronicle* to have unwisely ridden well ahead of the main army. Dressed like this, his badly mutilated corpse at first went unrecognised among the slain.

News of the disaster at Kellistown is said to have filled Richard with fury, provoking in him a desire to revenge himself on the rebel Irish. The king's fantasy of unfettered high-kingship over Ireland was dashed by his cousin's death and the intransigence of Art mac Murrough. Richard sailed to Ireland, but first prepared himself spiritually. He is said to have left for Ireland wracked by doubts, aware of his own mortality and the risks he faced, reflecting gloomily on the dangers navigating the Irish Sea, uneasy about the state of England he left behind. Before departure he made his will, in which he detailed his funeral arrangements, asking to be laid to rest with his sceptre and ring. He imagined that 'our body [might]...be snatched from the sight of men by hurricanes or tempests of the sea', or 'we should pay the debt of nature in distant lands'.

A French squire, named Jean Creton, witnessed the king's arrival at Waterford on Sunday 1 June 1399, and noted the unkempt and ill-dressed Irish porters who waded waist-deep into the channel to unload the king's ships. Richard made Kilkenny his headquarters. A number of Irish chiefs appeared and made their obeisance, but not the unruly mac Murrough. Richard's entourage has been described as not large – approximately 500 men-at-arms and 2,100 archers, led by men of great rank, like the dukes of Surrey, Albemarle and Exeter, plus the earls of Gloucester, Salisbury and Worcester – but it was almost certainly strong enough to deal with mac Murrough had the Irish chieftain ever been tracked down. His forces burned Glendalough in the Wicklow Mountains, but were soon bottled up at Arklow on the coast by the insurgents.

Richard was still busy in Ireland when his great English rebel, Henry Bolingbroke, landed in Yorkshire from Burgundy with a small force of men on 1 July 1399. The details of Bolingbroke's grudges against Richard lie outside the scope of this book. Suffice to say, Richard's concern for the security of his Irish lordship and his desire to avenge the death of Mortimer proved to be his undoing. Bolingbroke's invasion of England could not be countered in his absence. Locking horns with mac Murrough had to be postponed. Even so, the need to prepare for an orderly departure as well as contrary winds prevented the king from embarking from Waterford until the latter part of July. By the time he reached the Welsh coast most of his supporters had deserted him. His end was a dismal one. Tricked into a meeting with Henry Bolingbroke, Richard was seized and incarcerated. His deposition and murder soon followed. Bolingbroke then had himself crowned Henry IV.

For all his faults, no other medieval English king, save John, had so determinedly looked westward toward Ireland to stamp his authority as did Richard. Had the king been less autocratic and vengeful, and had he lived longer, he might have made a significant, positive impact on Anglo-Irish relations and forged stronger links between London and Dublin. There is some evidence that Richard, from quite early on in his reign, saw Ireland as a potential bolt-hole, with Dublin as a possible replacement capital whence he might direct affairs of state. Had that unlikely event come to pass, and had Richard successfully united his two kingdoms, Irish history might have taken an altogether different tack, Finn McCool's long sleep might have been secured, and the wars in England between the Houses of Lancaster and York avoided.

*

The fifteenth century in Ireland witnessed an upsurge in ecclesiastical building and rebuilding. Many of Ireland's greatest monasteries date from this time. Notable examples are Muckross, co. Kerry, Timoleague, co. Cork, Ennis, co. Clare, and Claregalway, co. Galway; all are foundations which flourished up until the year 1535, when Henry VIII's dissolution plans placed them on the endangered list. There was also a revival in castle and fortification building, a reflection of a growing awareness of the threat posed to the so-called 'land of peace' by the still rumbling Gaelic revival. Many extant town walls at places like Youghal, co. Cork, Fethard, co. Tipperary, and possibly Athenry, co. Galway, date from the first half of the fifteenth century. The Crown specifically sponsored this castle building, defining the immediate limits of English ambitions by doing so. The young Henry VI, grandson of Henry IV, offered a £10 incentive for anybody who built a fortress to his specifications. These proved to be smaller than the earlier Norman ones: just a simple tower with walled and turreted enclosures. Such structures eventually became status symbols for Old English and Gaelic lords alike. Anyone who wanted to be taken seriously on the frontier had to have one. They still exist in Ireland in great numbers, although sometimes only the towers now remain. Monsieur de la Boullaye le Gouz, writing around 1664, stated that the castles and great houses in Ireland normally consisted of just four walls, but were extremely high, the roof thatched with straw; and just a square tower without windows, or, if with windows, they had such small apertures as to give very little light within, hardly more than a prison. They also had scant furniture; floors were covered in rushes, beds were made of straw. A good example of a walled castle of this type is at Aughnanure, near Lough Corrib, co. Galway, a six-storey tower built by the O'Flahertys around 1500. The O'Flaherty motto was 'fortune favours the strong'. Within the castle walls, other than the well-preserved tower house, are the remains of a banqueting hall, a watch tower, bastions and a dry harbour.

Henry IV may of necessity have maintained a somewhat closed, myopic world view, while later kings like Henry V and Henry VI looked westward to France: one for war, the other for peace. None appear to have troubled themselves overly much with Irish affairs. Meanwhile, Art mac Murrough continued to pose a threat to English rule in Ireland though his lands remained confiscated. In 1400 he recovered them, but continued on an unruly course. The following year, Art's allies the O'Byrnes suffered a resounding defeat at Bray, on the coast near Dublin. At the Battle of Bloody Bank, 403 of them lost their lives when the Mayor of Dublin ambushed them. In 1415, the year of Agincourt, Art mac Murrough and his son Donnchad openly warred with the English at Wexford. Perhaps Art recognised Henry V's absence in France meant there could be no likelihood of immediate retribution. Being an astute politician as well as a belligerent warlord, he later made sure to re-acknowledge his fealty to the Crown as soon as news reached him of the English king's unexpected success. In an age when, if not wary, a nobleman's head and limbs might end up at opposite ends of the country, mac Murrough managed to die shriven of his sins in his own fortress at Ferns, probably with his boots off. His death occurred, according to the *Annals of Loch Ce*, 'after the triumph of unction and penitence'.

Because of the actions of men like Art and his son Donnchad, by the midpoint of the fifteenth century direct English influence in Ireland was restricted to less than half the landmass. These were, though, the richer and more populous parts of Leinster and Munster – choice territories that had been carved out by the Norman conquistadores in the twelfth and thirteenth centuries. During the reign of Edward I, colonising English knights exercised control out of all proportion to their numbers. A century later they had become as unruly as the Gaelic lords they sparred with. The inability of the Dublin government to adequately protect settlers in border areas resulted in an exodus back within the lordship of Dublin or to their country of origin. The Irish council spoke of 'the English blood of the conquest [being] ... in a manner worn out of this land'.

Such, perhaps, was the state of play in Ireland when the thirty-eight-year-old Richard Plantagenet, Duke of York, arrived at Waterford in the late 1440s. He came as senior member of the Lancastrian establishment. His appointment as Henry VI's lieutenant, dated to 1447, was (it seems) a reflection of the English king's desire to sideline his cousin. York had a double claim to the throne of England and posed a dynastic threat to the ailing Lancastrian regime. York had done his best when fighting the French during the latter stages of the Hundred Years War, but had become troubled by the direction the prosecution of the war had taken. He had good reason to be concerned. Within a few weeks of arriving at Dublin, three French armies had invaded Normandy, rapidly overrunning the province. Historians have since pictured York waiting in the wings in Ireland, readying himself to take the stage and seize control from a floundering government in England. If so, during his fourteen months spent in Ireland, he still managed to engage fully in Irish affairs. Before returning to England in the autumn of 1450, he made important inroads against the rebel groups holding out in the Wicklow Mountains – still, as late as the mid-fifteenth century, a smouldering war zone on the lordship's doorstep. York's rule at Dublin has since been described as 'firm and even-handed', and was at the time considered by the Anglo-Irish as something of a 'golden age' of stability and positive reform. York also gained the submission of rebellious Gaelic chieftains, among them the leaders of the MacMahons, O'Reillys and MacQuillans, whose forces are said to have amounted to

3,000 armed men. By the time of York's departure, even the leaders of Clan O'Neill had ratified indentures with York to provide him with 500 men-at-arms and 500 foot soldiers in time of war. This agreement was made at Drogheda on 27 August 1449. They looked to York to protect them from any future commandeering momentum of colonialists, possibly even to support them in their desire to see an equivalent of Home Rule introduced. Later, in 1460, legislative independence would be asserted at the Drogheda Parliament, when it was stated:

> The land of Ireland is, and at all time has been, corporate of itself by the ancient laws and customs used in the same, freed of the burden of any special law of the realm of England, save only such laws as by the lords spiritual and temporal and the commons of the said land had been in great council or Parliament there held admitted, accepted, affirmed and acclaimed.

Richard Plantagenet never got the opportunity to make a difference in addressing the longstanding problems in Ireland, or the demand for self-rule. In the autumn of 1450 he travelled back to England with a sizeable force, ostensibly to confront the Lancastrian administration over its failures in France. This was as a consequence of an earlier revolt of Kentishmen under the command of a man named Jack Cade, also thought to have come from Ireland, who had called for York to intervene and topple the government. York arrived back at London with much brazenness. His return was unheralded: Henry VI had not ordered it. The duke is said to have appeared at the head of 'a great multitude ... harnessed and arrayed in the manner of war', some part of which may have comprised Irishmen loyal to him. York portrayed himself as a reformer, but Henry VI's queen, the formidable Margaret of Anjou, saw him for what he was, a prince of the blood who craved power. York blamed his return in part on the fact he had not been paid the salary he was owed while in Ireland. It was a failure he declared would threaten the lordship's collapse.

He said he would not abide it being put about that Ireland was lost through his negligence.

For a while York kept his distance, but, in February 1452, in what became known as 'the Dartford incident', he allowed his frustrations to boil over. At the head of an army drawn up in a strong defensive posture behind the River Darent in Kent, with 'much great stuff and ordnance', the duke publicly accused his enemies in England of seeking to undermine him through envy, malice and untruth. This was the first occasion York directly threatened the use of force to get his own way. The threat failed. Henry VI called his bluff AND encamped an army on Blackheath, a few miles to the west. York capitulated, and might have faced trial and death had not Henry sought to build bridges. The king should have trusted the counsel of others and done away with his rebellious subject. York was able to fall back on Dublin for refuge and attend the parliament convened at Drogheda, where the proclamation of independence, mentioned earlier, was presented to him.

York was later killed at the Battle of Wakefield in January 1461, leaving his eldest son Edward, Earl of March, determined to avenge his death and seize the baton of Yorkist ambition. But first Edward had to face a Lancastrian army led by, among others, James Butler of Ormond, first earl of Wiltshire and fifth earl of Ormond. Like the Ormond earls before him, James maintained a strong allegiance to the Lancastrian regime. Born in Ireland in 1420, he was dubbed a knight when aged just six. In the late 1440s he was seen by York's enemies as a possible counter-weight to the duke in Ireland. As late as the autumn of 1450 he remained uncommitted one way or the other between the rival camps in England. Only in 1452 did he make up his mind to back Henry VI. For his reward he gained the lieutenancy of Ireland, over York's head. By the end of 1454 he had become a key player in the Lancastrian war effort. He fought on the king's side at the first Battle of St Albans the following year – a Yorkist victory – then again at the Battle of Mortimer's Cross, Herefordshire, in February 1461. Here, several thousand Irishmen under his command combined with a Welsh and a Breton contingent to confront Edward, Earl of March's forces. The Irishmen are said to have assailed Edward's battle line with javelins and daggers, amazing the fierce men of the Welsh Marches by their impetuous, unrewarded bravery; they fell in heaps when the massed ranks of English bowmen loosed their arrows upon them. For a time gaps in their ranks were made good by men in support, but at some point a complete collapse in morale occurred and a rout ensued. This was followed by an inevitable slaughter, during which up to 3,000 may have perished. James Butler was later captured by the Yorkists and executed.

Edward also relied on Irish allies. Some may have fought at his side at Towton, the decisive battle of 1461, which secured Edward's first period of kingship. In 1474, sometime after having been crowned king for a second time, Edward presented Henry O'Neill, lord of Tír Eoghain, with a livery of scarlet and a golden chain, styling him 'the king's friend'. The O'Neills may have made good their promise to York to provide fighting men when called upon. Henry O'Neill led expeditions into eastern Ulster in 1469, 1470 and 1476, acting on behalf of Edward. (Edward IV was not only King of England, but also held the title Earl of Ulster.) In 1470, Henry captured Ringhaddy Castle, located just above the shoreline at the northern end of Strangford Lough. From there he marched on Omagh, co. Tyrone, capturing the town after a six-month siege. Thirteen years later, Henry handed the lordship over to his son Conn Mor, the brother-in-law of Gerald Fitzgerald, 8th Earl of Kildare. He died on 15 June 1489. Commentators at the time saw these acts of repossession carried out by the Tír Eoghain branch of Clan O'Neill, mainly against the rival Clandeboye O'Neill, to be 'the utter decay of Ulster' and against English interests.

The fighting during the War of the Roses for a time spilled over into Ireland. Another Butler was its instigator. After Towton, the late James of Ormond's brother, John Butler, a Lancastrian fugitive, managed to avoid capture. After laying low in Cumbria or Strathclyde, he arrived back in Ireland and drummed up strong support in Kilkenny and Tipperary. Thomas FitzGerald, Earl of Desmond, a man with Yorkist leanings and also an eye to claiming the now attainted Butler landholdings, confronted him. Open warfare broke out in the spring of 1462. With 1,000 helmeted horsemen and an unknown number of foot soldiers, John Butler's forces retook their lands and plundered Westmeath. They also captured and occupied Waterford. But when brought to battle at Piltown, near Rogerstown Castle, they fell prey to Geraldine crossbowmen on the banks of the River Pill. Many of Butler's men drowned trying to make it to the far bank – picked off while floundering in the mud. Survivors retreated north-east to Kilkenny, pursued by Fitzgerald's horsemen. The *Annals of Ireland* estimated 400 captured and interred, besides 'all that were eaten by dogs and by the fowl of the air'. John Butler made his escape from the debacle and fled to Portugal.

The Battle of Piltown effectively ended Lancastrian hopes of raising forces in Ireland. Providing an insight into Edward IV's grandiose and inclusive nature, when later reconciled to the Yorkists after the murder of Henry VI, in 1471, attainders against John Butler were rescinded. Edward even took the Irishman to France when campaigning there in 1475. Indicative of the respect in which he held his new ally, Edward described him as 'the goodliest knight he ever beheld and the finest gentleman in Christendom'. Living up to his reputation, Butler died in 1476 while on crusade in the Holy Land.

Too tied up with consolidating the Yorkist monarchy in England, the first years of Edward IV's reign saw a marked resurgence of Gaelic self-interest in Ireland. Edward IV's reign was among the most bloody in our history. Like his grandson, Henry VIII, he had a fiery temper and on occasion an eye for the axe. When one of his subjects ignored his commands to attend on him, the king is said to have vowed, 'If you come not at the third command you will die.' Again like Henry, Edward could be 'over-bearing and insensitive', yet on other occasions appears to have recognised unease among those presented to him. On one occasion, when patting an overawed subject's shoulder, he whispered 'ye sit still and be quiet'. The order might also have been made to the troubled Irish, who, in large measure, retained a fondness for the Yorks and may have patiently awaited further devolution and perhaps self-rule. That Edward could not attend to Irish affairs in person meant that the feudal lords of Ireland ruled without undue English interference. They became men of the ilk of the Earl of Warwick in England, 'the so-called Kingmaker', 'over-mighty subjects' who, in some cases, may have used revenues collected to feather their own nests. It was an age of such men, among them later the king's own brothers, George of Clarence and Richard of Gloucester.

Edward appointed Thomas Fitzgerald of Desmond as steward of Connaught and constable of Limerick Castle in the summer of 1462. A further promotion to the deputy lieutenancy of Ireland followed soon after. This was presumably in recognition of the earl's victory over John Butler at Piltown. Edward was taking something of a risk putting his trust in Desmond. The earl was closely linked with the Gaelic lords of Munster and was distrusted at Dublin; moreover, his power base lay far 'beyond the Pale', in the south-west of the country. His main ally was a kinsman, another Thomas Fitzgerald, the 7th Earl of Kildare. (These two men with the same name are referred to henceforth in the narrative as Desmond and Kildare respectively.) Another of Desmond's close associates was Roland Fitz Eustace, Ireland's Lord Treasurer. Edward ordered Desmond to govern with Fitz Eustace's advice, and for him to have 'special respect to the observance of our laws and statutes there', in particular to stamp down on what he called 'that damnable and unlawful extortion and oppression used upon [the Irish] called Coign and Livery'. This was a system whereby Gaelic warlords nurtured private armies at the expense of lesser chiefs. It represented a tax on clan members, over and above other taxes collected by the English, and was outlawed by the Dublin administration. The term appears to have originated from a system whereby unpaid, uniformed soldiers were enabled to extort goods in kind from the countryside – a licence for ravaging and rapine.

Returning to the topic of 'over-mighty' subjects arising during Edward's reign, the sixteenth-century chronicler Holinshed wrote how the Desmond clan were virtual princes in south-western

Ireland; that they 'did [illegally] put upon the king's subjects ... the Irish impositions of Coign and Livery, cartings, carriages, lodgings, cosherings, bonnaught and such like, which customs are the very breeders, maintainers and upholders of all Irish enormities'.

It soon transpired, however, that Desmond, for whatever reason, was not up to the job of king's deputy in Ireland. Taken prisoner while campaigning in modern-day county Offaly, forces from Dublin had to be diverted to rescue him. By 1467 the situation had become sufficiently serious to warrant the despatch of Edward's legal hitman, John Tiptoft, Earl of Worcester, known as 'the Butcher' for his brutal treatment of diehard Lancastrians. Tiptoft brought with him 700 mounted archers to restore order. When parliament was reconvened at Drogheda in February 1468, he passed a bill of attainder on both Desmond and Kildare. Rather than being simply guilty of failing militarily, the charge against them was written up as 'horrible treasons and felonies ... as well [as their being] in alliance ... with the Irish enemies of the king ... giving them horses and harness and arms, and supporting them against the king's faithful subjects'. Two of Desmond's sons were seized and tortured before being executed. To the shock and puzzlement of contemporaries, Desmond himself was then executed, on 15 February 1468. Kildare got off more lightly by procuring a pardon. Fitz Eustace was also implicated. The Lord Treasurer had to face charges of inciting Desmond to declare himself 'king of Ireland'. He too might have been executed, but, by vigorously defending himself, he had the charges dropped. Later, he would become a founding member of the Brotherhood of St George, a military order charged with the defence of the Pale.

News of Desmond's execution sparked a minor rebellion. Desmond's armed affinity in Munster ravaged Meath and Kildare, adding to the woes of the government at Dublin. The *Annals of Ulster* lauded the late earl, saying, 'Ireland never had a foreign youth that was better than he,' adding that he was killed treacherously. Others claim the earl's demise to have had more to do with his adoption of 'Coign and Livery', in pursuance of his own private ends. Less plausibly, anti-Woodville traditions implicate Edward's queen, Elizabeth, in plotting Desmond's demise – a conspiracy-laden allusion to the earl's earlier disparaging her marriage to the king. Being older than Edward, a commoner previously married and with two strapping sons, many frowned upon Edward's choice of consort. Desmond appears to have been among them.

To prevent further turmoil in Ireland, Edward had the heavy-handed Tiptoft recalled to England. Richard III, Edward's younger brother, later confirmed the displeasure felt by Edward when news reached him of Desmond's death, saying it had been an act committed against 'all manhood, reason and good conscience'. Tiptoft got his just deserts. Under a briefly restored Henrician administration, he was executed on Tower Hill. Allegedly the executioner, at Tiptoft's bidding, struck at the earl's neck three times, in honour of the Holy Trinity.

8

THE GREAT EARL

When Richard III fell in battle at Bosworth on 22 August 1485, the victor, Henry VII, built bridges with erstwhile enemies in England by marrying Richard's niece, the late Edward IV's daughter, Elizabeth of York. In doing so he sought to symbolically unite the red rose with the white. His action ushered in a new age and the passing of medieval England. Seeking to broaden his appeal, Henry pardoned Yorkists willing to accept his right to rule, including the secretly hostile John de la Pole, Earl of Lincoln, the late Richard III's nephew and lieutenant-general of Ireland. After Richard's death, Lincoln became the eldest surviving male representative of the House of York. He may have been Richard III's proposed heir, but, rather than make a direct bid for the crown himself, he sought to promote the cause of an even stronger candidate. This was his cousin, Edward Plantagenet, Earl of Warwick, the son and heir of the late George, Duke of Clarence – Edward IV's and Richard III's brother, alleged to have been executed by immersion headfirst into a butt of Malmsey wine. Lincoln set in motion the final great military campaign of the Wars of the Roses, raising the spectre of impostors to the throne emerging from Ireland to threaten the fledgling Tudor state.

In 1485, Warwick was a somewhat withdrawn ten-year-old boy. Richard III, mindful of the boy's pedigree, had incarcerated him with others of the Yorkist bloodline at Sheriff Hutton Castle, in the North Riding of Yorkshire, a place likened by historian P. M. Kendall to 'a stone chalice, holding the remaining blood of the House of York'. After Bosworth, Henry VII had the earl removed to the Tower of London, the fortress prison where Warwick's cousins, the Princes in the Tower, had sometime earlier disappeared, and where Warwick's father Clarence had been put to death.

The genesis of Lincoln's conspiracy to impersonate the imprisoned Earl of Warwick and destabilise Henry's regime remains shrouded in mystery. Rumours were circulating that Warwick had escaped from the Tower and was rallying support in pro-Yorkist Ireland. An impostor named Lambert Simnel, groomed to impersonate Warwick, had been sent from England to Dublin. News broke of the supposed Warwick's arrival in Ireland early in 1487. Henry arranged for the real Warwick to be taken from the Tower and to be paraded through the streets of London in an attempt to quash the claim, but many preferred to believe the lie that the genuine earl had escaped to Ireland, and that the youth on display was the impostor. The Tudor king had been aware of the existence of a number of plots against him for some time. A series of revolts had broken out against Tudor rule in 1486. Commissioners had been appointed to investigate, among them the Earl of Lincoln. If a covert supporter of the risings, Lincoln carried off his subterfuge very successfully. Only when Lambert Simnel was safely ensconced in Dublin did he reveal his hand by fleeing the kingdom to Burgundy, where he enjoyed the support of his aunt, Margaret Plantagenet, Duchess of Burgundy – a regent described by the Tudor essayist Francis Bacon as possessing 'all the spirit of a man and the malice of a woman'. Being the sister of the late kings Edward IV and Richard III, she remained an enthusiastic backer of anyone who would challenge Tudor rule.

With rebellion in the offing, she hired 2,000 German mercenaries, under the command of Martin Swartz, to bolster Lincoln's endeavours. These reinforcements arrived in Ireland on 24 May 1487. Soon afterwards, Lambert Simnel was crowned with a golden circlet taken from a statue of the Virgin Mary as King Edward VI, at Christchurch Cathedral in Dublin. It was a grand occasion, with file upon file of gloriously adorned prelates and clergymen, richly attired nobles and knights in attendance on the precocious ten year old, including the Archbishop of Dublin and four other bishops. From a dark, dank recess in the nave, an effigy of Earl Strongbow, the cathedral's founder, gazed sightlessly on the proceedings. If a number of supposed relics of Christ, also housed within the cathedral confines, were called upon to intercede while the bishop of Meath delivered the sermon, nothing is recorded. What was clearly elaborated was the boy's claim to the throne of England as the son of George of Clarence, the brother of Edward IV and Richard III, who, it was alleged, had sought to send his son overseas to Ireland for safekeeping on the eve of his death; this was all on the assumption that the princes in the Tower, Edward V and Richard, Duke of York, were actually dead by this time – something that even today attracts skeptics.

Was Ireland's strongman, Gerald Fitzgerald, 8th Earl of Kildare, taken in by Lincoln's subterfuge? It seems unlikely, yet most Irishmen failed to suspect the young 'king' of merely being a stalking horse for Lincoln's own dynastic ambitions. On the contrary, most would have seen Lincoln's endorsement as carrying great weight. Not all accepted the charade, however. Lincoln had to be physically restrained from assaulting the archbishop of Armagh, one of several men who refused to take part in the ceremony. Fitzgerald must have hoped to gain personally by promoting a Yorkist comeback. Ireland lay outside Henry VII's direct control. Fitzgerald was not going to rush to embrace the new regime whilst the possibility of a Yorkist comeback was on the cards – especially since his main rival, the Earl of Ormond, enjoyed the favour of the Tudors. If a sacrilegious ceremony played out at Christchurch would help cement his position, then so be it.

Despite calls for the Yorkist army to remain in Ireland, placing the onus on Henry VII to make the first move, Swartz's men, reinforced by a force of English archers and men-at-arms and a sizeable contingent of Irish infantry, soon felt strong enough to launch an invasion of England. The official Tudor estimate of rebel strength was 8,000 men, a sizeable army for the time – as strong in numbers as Henry VII had brought to the battlefield at Bosworth. Half, however, comprised 'beggarly, naked, and almost unarmed' native Irish, led by Thomas Fitzgerald, the brother of the Earl of Kildare. Bolstering the kern were more heavily armoured, axe-wielding Gallowglass, who remained the dominant professional soldier caste of Ireland; they were probably the equal of an English man-at-arms in a hand-to-hand fight. The other half of Lincoln's army comprised Anglo-Irish volunteers, plus Swartz's mercenary force, armed with pikes, halberds (bladed pole weapons), two-handed swords, well-drilled handgunners and crossbowmen. It was a sizeable and balanced force, but relied for reinforcements on the north of England rising in support of the imposter. Given the high mercenary contingent, it was important to get buy-ins from Englishmen with a firm stake in the future. Machiavelli points this out in *The Prince*:

> Mercenary and auxiliary troops are both useless and dangerous … they are disunited, ambitious and without discipline – faithless and braggarts among friends, but amongst enemies cowards … ready to serve in peacetime, but when war comes, they will either run away or march off.

The invaders landed in Cumbria on 4 June. Numbers increased along the way, but not by much. Lincoln hoped the gates of York would open to him, that old loyalties would be re-awoken, but the gates of the city remained firmly shut. The rebel earl led his forces southward, gambling that support for the Tudor king would prove as brittle as it had for his dead uncle. By 14 June Lincoln's army was in the vicinity of Southwell, just north of the Trent and the strategically important town of Newark. Having averaged twenty miles a day, his exhausted troops rested before crossing the river.

Henry VII's army lay at Nottingham, just a few miles away to the south-west. Not only was Henry's army larger, it was also stronger in heavy cavalry and guns than Lincoln's. What is more, it boasted many more archers, each backed by a billman – an infantryman armed with a scythe-like pole weapon.

During the long summer evening of 15 June, the Yorkists crossed the Trent at Fiskerton. Following tracks across waterlogged meadows, they marched via the village of East Stoke, bivouacking 'upon the brow or hanging of a hill' beside the Nottingham to Newark road. Henry's vanguard confronted them next day. A near contemporary account of the coming battle claimed Lincoln's army was drawn up in a single massed body, with Swartz's men in the front rank. From his hilltop vantage point, Lincoln watched with growing unease as Henry's larger army came into sight. Sometime in the mid-morning, the Tudor vanguard came under missile fire from Swartz's crossbowmen, but soon Henry's more numerous archers gained fire supremacy. The ill-protected Irish in particular suffered heavily. Accounts of the battle describe them as appearing like 'hedgehogs, shot through with arrows' – a grim replay of the Battle of Mortimer's Cross and a sight which is said to have sorely disheartened the rest of Lincoln's army. Perhaps because of this high level immediate of casualties, or because Henry's main force was by now arriving on the battlefield, the order was given to advance down the slope of the hill to fight 'upon the plain'. Hand-to-hand fighting suited Swartz and Fitzgerald's men better than trading missiles. Fighting is said to have raged for three hours, but then a great shout went up as the Yorkist line wavered and broke. The leaders of the rebellion – Lincoln, Swartz, and Fitzgerald – were all killed in the final bout of fighting. Many Irishmen were trapped and slaughtered in a series of gullies traversing the northern slopes of a ridge, today covered by Stoke Wood. Aptly named 'the red gutter,' the deepest of these lies just beyond the place where Henry is said to have planted his standard after the battle.

It is hard to exaggerate the desperate circumstances the common Irish kern found themselves in. With nowhere to run, trapped between the broad Trent and the sharp bills of the English, death was certain. Reports tell of the Irish being denied quarter and slain in the manner of 'dull and brute beasts' – the harbinger of equally uncompromising ethnic bloodshed to follow in coming centuries. None survived the carnage. Such casual slaughter reflected brutal violence common to colonisers and those fearful of outsiders. A mass grave at Stoke Hall beside St Oswald's Church entombed whole rows of dead Irish soldiery. Swartz's mercenaries fared better. Being professionals, they received quarter and were later freed and allowed to return overseas. Lambert Simnel was quickly apprehended after the battle. Henry was lenient with him: the one-time impostor later became the king's falconer. The real Warwick continued to languish in the Tower, until executed in 1499 after a failed escape bid. Tradition has it that Lincoln, with a stake driven through his heart in the manner of a vampire, was buried on the battlefield. The renowned Martin Swartz lived on in folklore: 'Martin Swart and his men, sodledum, sodledum, Martin Swart and his men, sodledum, bell' are lines from a popular sixteenth-century ballad.

*

Around thirty years of age when Lincoln departed from Dublin, Gerald Fitzgerald, 8th Earl of Kildare – known henceforth in the narrative as Kildare – was described in the *Book of Howth* as being 'without great knowledge or learning, but rudely brought up according to the usage of his country'. As we have seen, Edward IV for the most part had been content to allow the Anglo-Irish nobility to govern Ireland without undue interference. Other than the ill-fated despatch of Tiptoft, the only other time the king intervened was in 1478, after the rise of Kildare, who some were then calling 'the uncrowned king of Ireland'; modern historian Michael Bennett agrees with them, stating that 'none since Brian Boru, the last high-king, had [ever] wielded such power and authority in Ireland [as Kildare].' The earl certainly had strong backing at Dublin. When Edward's newly appointed deputy in Ireland, Henry Grey, attempted to assert himself, he was cold-shouldered by the ruling class at Dublin and refused access to the castle and the use of the Great Seal. Impotent in the face of such widespread opposition, Grey was recalled by Edward in 1479, leaving Kildare in almost unfettered control of the country. Edward formalised the arrangement by making him his deputy lieutenant, detailing him to ensure the maintenance of good rule and that the king's interests were protected. They were tasks carried out to the best of his ability until Edward's death, in 1483.

Kildare gained from Edward grants of land in Carlow, Wexford, Westmeath, and south Dublin. Though Crown lands, these often had to be acquired and retained by force. The bulk of the Irish dispossessed were likely kept on as tenants, so this process was by no means as draconian as might be assumed. Reliance on military means to achieve his ends saw the build-up of a standing force at his disposal: several hundred soldiers, kern, Gallowglass and cavalrymen. He later added a company of handgunners to their ranks. It seems he had admired Swartz's handgunners when marching through Dublin in 1487, so appropriated some of his own. Some historians have detected in Kildare a wish to establish himself at the head of an Ireland free from the shackles imposed by the English Crown; the promise of home rule may have been the lure used by John of Lincoln to gain his support during the Lambert Simnel episode; but the facts of the case are unknowable – nothing incriminatory was recorded at the time, for obvious reasons. Indeed, much about the business remained mysterious to even high-placed contemporaries; Tudor historians were reliant on government-supplied information, which of course can be misinformation, then as now.

After the disaster at East Stoke, Kildare entrenched himself and his family at Dublin for several months before submitting to Henry's commissioner, Sir Richard Edgecombe. Oaths of allegiance to the Tudor king appear to have been made with fingers tightly crossed. In 1491, another imposter arose to challenge Henry. This one was named Perkin Warbeck, a man claiming to be none other than Richard, Duke of York, the younger of the two princes who disappeared in the Tower in 1483. Sponsored by Margaret of Burgundy, the pretender landed at Cork and was taken in by Kildare's cousin, the Earl of Desmond. It seems Kildare himself was more cautious this time, fully realising the desperate nature of the conspiracy, but was nonetheless implicated. Henry acted with vigour by despatching the illegitimate brother of the Earl of Ormond, Sir James Butler, with 200 men-at-arms to prevent the Fitzgeralds from combining their forces. This precipitated the hurried flight of Warbeck to the Continent. Kildare was stripped of office for the next four years. Henry supported Ormond as a counterweight to Fitzgerald power, and this in turn fuelled outbreaks of violence between the two factions.

In September 1494 Henry appointed Sir Edward Poynings to the lieutenancy of Ireland. Poynings landed at Howth in October and kept the two rival earls – Ormond and Kildare – at his side when he led a punitive military expedition into Ulster. His small, well-trained and equipped army proved an effective deterrent against the more numerous but ill-led rebel groups. He presided over the Dublin parliament, which strengthened English rule. This has been said to mark the culmination of the demand for autonomy of the Old English in Ireland. It also resulted in the first official use of the term 'Pale of Dublin', a geographical and political construct that, as we have seen, had existed in a practical sense for some time. The first reference to the Pale occurred in a document that dealt with plans for fortifying the perimeter of the enclave by digging defensive ditches. An earlier parliament of 1310 had mentioned the three terms 'land of peace', 'land of war' and 'marcher lands'. A parliament of 1462 had directed the Irish living in Meath, Louth, Dublin and Kildare to adopt English surnames. Legislation later to become known as 'Poynings' Law', passed by Sir Edward, limited ministers in Ireland to passing laws only if approved in advance by the English king. Its immediate purpose was to prevent an imposter like Simnel from ever again securing a foothold. Reinforcing earlier royal dictates, it was also decreed that all statutes made in England should apply equally in Ireland. Additional clauses made it treasonable to incite the Irish to war. The custody of all royal castles was limited to men born in England. From then on, no battles fought in Ireland were deemed lawful but the king's battles.

Much from this time is obscure. Kildare was charged with plotting Poynings' murder, but on what evidence remains unclear. Nonetheless, the accusation carried sufficient weight to see Kildare arrested and shipped off to England. Henry VII kept him under lock and key in the Tower for a time. Poynings meanwhile drove the incorrigible Perkin Warbeck from the walls of Waterford. But it was not until September 1497 that the threat from Warbeck was finally snuffed out, when Henry's forces defeated the pretender's army of Cornish rebels at Taunton in Somerset. Warbeck gave himself up, later to be executed. Despite the problems he had caused the Crown, Henry VII, always a reasonable man, only agreed to Warbeck's execution after the pretender's second unsuccessful escape bid from the Tower. The young Earl of Warwick died with him, having been a party to the escape plot.

After a judicial process of sorts, which cleared Kildare of any involvement in the recent troubles, Henry VII allowed the earl to return to Dublin. As a precaution the English king took Kildare's eldest son, Gerald, known more usually as Garrett Og, hostage to guarantee his father's good behaviour. Prior to his departure, the earl had sworn to uphold Poynings' law, to oppose the king's enemies, and to make peace with the Butlers. Relations between Henry and Kildare from then on improved. It was clear to the former that he needed someone with the prestige of Kildare, a direct descendant of one of the earliest Normans to set foot in Ireland, to oversee governance at Dublin. The English king is alleged to have stated, '[Kildare] is meet to rule all Ireland, seeing all Ireland cannot rule him.' Kildare repaid the king by rebuilding towns on the frontiers of the English Pale that had earlier been laid waste by Irish insurgents. He replenished them with colonists. A number of broken-down castles were also renovated by him and garrisons installed. Enemy castles were battered into submission using state-of-the-art cannon. Four castles in the west (Athleague, Tulsk, Roscommon and Castlerea) fell to Fitzgerald forces in 1499. On only one occasion did Henry VII consider intervening in Ireland in person, and, after consultation with his ministers, it was decided wiser to continue to delegate to Kildare. Lack of money may also have been a factor. The five years between 1491 and 1496 had already cost the Crown a considerable sum, assessed at £23,000. Henry was probably unable to spend more without borrowing. Ireland would therefore, of necessity, have to police itself. Kildare made this happen by gathering around him at all times a permanent body of armed men. This was not just in response to Henry's parsimony. Since the Bruce invasions, the 'Old English' and Gaelic lords had heeded the need for better military preparedness and had as a consequence sought to attract professional fighters. Among these were a steady supply of Gallowglass from the Hebrides and the west of Scotland. Kildare's was the largest force. He is said to have mustered such an army of English and Irish 'as would have conquered the Pale in twenty-four hours', but had the good sense to keep quiet about it.

The greatest clash between opposing Gallowglass occurred a few miles to the north-west of Galway at Knockdoe on 19 August 1504. Kildare and his son-in-law Ulick de Burgh of Clanrickard had fallen out over the latter's ill-treatment of Kildare's daughter, Eustacia, and the custodianship of his grandchildren. But a deeper issue may have been de Burgh's constant feuding with Kildare's allies, the O'Kellys. Prior to the clash at Knockdoe, three O'Kelly castles had fallen to de Burgh and were demolished by him. De Burgh forces had then occupied Galway in breach of a royal charter that forbade armed entry to the town. The renegade earl levied punitive tolls on the citizens, resulting in urgent calls for intervention from Dublin. Both Galway town and the nearby town of Athenry were highly anglicized – extensions in the far west of the Dublin Pale. De Burgh's actions therefore represented a direct challenge to English rule. This was something Kildare could not countenance.

Kildare mobilised his forces east and west of the Shannon. They comprised an army from the Dublin Pale bolstered by forty spearmen and eighty archers from the Dublin garrison. He could also count on the support of the O'Kellys of Connaught as well as strong contingents from the north of Ireland, including fighters from clans O'Neill, O'Donnell, MacMahon, O'Hanlon, O'Reilly, MacDermott, O'Farrell and O'Connor. His forces from the Pale were drawn from counties Dublin, Kildare, Meath and Louth: a 'fraternity of arms' paid for by public money, including demi-lances (lightly armoured horsemen), billmen and bowmen. As attested at East Stoke in 1487, a potent mix of billmen and archers had become the mainstay of the English infantry.

Ulick de Burgh, sometimes known as Ulick Finn, could also call on many allies. They comprised clans ever ill-disposed to the Earl of Kildare: the O'Briens, the Macnamaras, the O'Carrolls and the O'Kennedys; a concentration of forces described by the chronicler Holinshed as 'all the rebels of Ireland'. In the past, these clans had supported the Butlers against the Fitzgeralds, so were akin to companions in arms. In this sense the coming fight might be seen as a continuation of the longstanding rivalry between the affinities of the Fitzgeralds and the Butlers, even as an aftershock of the quake that had been the Wars of the Roses. De Burgh's main ally, Turlough O'Brien of Thomond, was, in particular, a man to be feared, described by the Earl of Kildare as 'the most maliciously disposed of men and a mortal enemy to all Englishmen'. The competing musters have been described as the greatest of their kind that ever took place in Ireland. The stage was set for one of the island's fiercest and most brutal battles.

The low but locally prominent hill of Knockdoe remains a striking feature in the flat, patchwork landscape of the modern-day parish of Lackagh/Turloughmore, co. Galway. There is little or nothing, however, to alert a casual visitor to the fact that just over 500 years ago two sizeable armies, perhaps 10,000 men all told, squared up to one another and fought to the death here. The slowly meandering River Clare still maintains its unhurried course to Galway Bay, south and east of the hill, and there has been little urbanisation during the intervening five centuries. Nothing has really changed, only the addition of a few loose stone field boundaries and modern roads in place of tracks. In the small village of Carnoneen, on the slope of Knockdoe Hill, an old church and a ruined castle are among buildings still extant from the day of battle.

Kildare's army approached Knockdoe in mid-August 1504. The Old English divisions of the earl's army were placed under separate commands: Viscount Gomanstown and Baron Killeen with the archers, St Lawrence of Howth with the billmen, and Lord Delvin with the cavalry. Kildare also had with him a few men wielding firearms; we know this because at some point during the coming battle a German handgunner reputedly clubbed to death one of de Burgh's cavalrymen with the butt-end of an arquebus. Kildare's Gaelic forces comprised a number of further divisions for which the command structure is not known. What is known is that the Gallowglass operated in battalions of eighty fighting men, each with two retainers who carried their master's weapons and themselves fought with light javelins. More numerous kern probably skirmished from the flanks. Kildare's army arrived at the battlefield first, probably the day before the battle. They occupied the hill facing south-west, where the distant, blue-tinged mountain ranges of Connemara would have been visible through the early morning haze. De Burgh and his allies probably approached later in the day or evening, from the direction of Galway.

Next day, 19 August, Kildare called forward his grim captain of Gallowglass, saying it was he who would first meet the enemy attack. The leader flourished his axe and proudly exclaimed, 'You can do me no more honour, by God's blood!' Historians have since argued whether Kildare's order to the captain of Gallowglass represented a desire on the earl's part to place his trust in his Gaelic allies because of their martial prowess, or because he was happy to see them bear the brunt of the fighting and take losses. Kildare's exact words are alleged to have been,

'Call to me the captain of the Gallowglass, for he and his shall begin this game, for it is less force of their [lustiness, or losses] than it is of our young men.' Kildare's own Gallowglass command probably fronted the centre of the earl's line. Behind them would have been arraigned the fighting men of the Pale, probably drawn up in the manner of English armies of the time – each billman backed by a bowman, with a flanking body of archers. The earl's Gaelic command (yet more Gallowglass and their supporting kern) formed up separately, probably on the right wing. Historians have postulated that the Gaels and the Palesmen were mistrustful of one another, so this might explain the separation, but it may also have been the normal practice to place the proud Irish on the right of the line, it being 'the station of greatest honour'. Both sides fielded cavalry, and at some point de Burgh's horsemen succeeded in looting Kildare's baggage train – something of a victory for the impoverished Gaelic men. A small mounted reserve under the command of Kildare's son Garrett Og, who had newly returned to Ireland from the court of Henry VII, remained to the rear, but failed to prevent the baggage from being overrun.

The main body of de Burgh's army formed up opposite the earl's, down the slope of Knockdoe Hill, facing into the rising sun. The low sun in their eyes, if visible, like the slope may have disadvantaged them. Also telling against the men of Connaught was the fact they had spent the night before carousing into the early hours. On first spying the enemy, Kildare wrote them off as a rabble, saying, as related in the *Book of Howth*, 'A great number of them hath but one spear and a knife … without wisdom or good order they march to battle as drunken as swine to a trough.'

To attempt to describe the course of an ill-documented battle, fought over 500 years ago, is impossible. Suffice to say that a fierce hand-to-hand struggle ensued. It was a fight 'terrible and bold': the numbers engaged at Knockdoe rivalled or exceeded the forces which had clashed at Clontarf in 1014, with weaponry more varied and lethal. In particular, the hand-to-hand clash between opposing Gallowglass must have been a terrifying spectacle. De Burgh attacked up the hill into combat 'in one battle', shoulder to shoulder, coming under fire from Gormanstown's and Killeen's archers and being threatened from the flank by Lord Delvin's cavalry. The battle may have swung this way and that, but how long it really lasted is not known. Chroniclers focussed on individual combats, abjuring the broader struggle. An unnamed MacSweeny captain of Gallowglass, fighting on de Burgh's side, is said to have clashed with one of Kildare's followers, named Sir William d'Arcy, killing him before being himself killed by Baron Nagle of Navan. Other fights between opposing noblemen were also remembered. In themselves they probably did not decisively influence the course of the battle; a frightful level of attrition would be the main arbiter. De Burgh's losses piled up at a greater rate than did Kildare's. With the battlefield soon littered with corpses 'cross-thrown', de Burgh's surviving foot soldiers fled. Of his nine battalions of Gallowglass, numbering 1,800 men, only the remnant of one battalion escaped alive. Estimates ranging from 2,000 to 6,000 men are claimed for the fallen on both sides, but, because casualties were routinely over-estimated at this period, the lower figure is the more likely. Whatever the true figure, the killing is said to have continued all the way to Claregalway and the banks of the Clare, where the ruins of a castle and abbey still stand. De Burgh and Turlough O'Brien managed to escape the slaughter.

After the battle, Kildare occupied Galway town, much to the relief and joy of the inhabitants. His coat-of-arms adorned Lynch's Castle (now a bank) within the town, and two sons and a daughter of de Burgh were seized as hostages for their father's better behaviour; Kildare also gained the custody of his grandchildren. After some hesitancy on the part of Henry VII, who had at first been dismayed and shocked at the scale of losses, Kildare was well rewarded with grants of land and the Order of the Garter. Many at court considered the battle to be the outcome of a private row, the type of fighting outlawed as part of Poynings' reforms; forces of the size which clashed outside Galway were heavily proscribed. This explains why not everyone at Dublin or Westminster considered the battle to have been in the lordship's best interest.

From then on, Kildare energetically carried on the fight against the king's rebels. In 1510, six years after Knockdoe, he pursued Turlough O'Brien back into modern-day county Clare and broke down the bridge across the Shannon that his enemy had built. The earl's forces then suffered a reverse when counter-attacked by O'Brien's men. Two years later, Kildare captured the castles at Belfast and Larne and again ravaged Connaught. Predictably, his end came while campaigning. He was shot and mortally wounded while watering his horse near Kilkea Castle, co. Kildare, one of several Geraldine strongholds in the area. His attackers were the O'Mores of Laois, an ever troublesome family. He died on 3 September 1513, and was buried with great ceremony at Christchurch Cathedral, Dublin, in a now destroyed chapel he had built two years earlier.

Known now as 'the Great Earl', Kildare remains among Ireland's most prominent historical figures. In his later years he excelled all previous governors at Dublin by energetically defeating the king's enemies in Ireland and by reconstructing fortifications previously reduced by the Irish – all of this being, it was said, 'to the great profit and defence of the English'. Even the native Irish recognised his worth. The *Annals of Ulster* proclaimed that, 'in power, fame and estimation', he exceeded all the lords of Ireland. He probably came the closest of all the Anglo-Irish lords since Strongbow's conquest to gain regal ordination. He had the military wherewithal and support in Ireland to have rebelled, but, after the alarms caused by the two imposters, sensibly ignored any who might have encouraged him to do so. Instead, he made his mark by sound governorship. It was said that the Geraldines gained under Kildare a popularity in Ireland such that 'they covet more to see a Geraldine to reign and triumph than to see God come among them'. English kings took a risk in placing their trust in him, so powerful was he, but were in the end well rewarded. The great earl's death can now be seen to mark a watershed in the history of English affairs in Ireland. The imminent English break with Rome and a looming Spanish threat meant that English kings and queens could not in future tolerate a sometimes largely unsubdued and periodically hostile neighbour cheek by jowl – the threat of Ireland becoming a springboard for invasion was considered too great. The struggle for control of Ireland would be raised another notch in the coming years, under the weight and scrutiny of England's most famous king, Henry VIII.

9

DETESTABLE AND ABOMINABLE TREASONS

A summary of how Ireland appeared to the English at the beginning of Henry VIII's reign is contained in a report commissioned around the year 1515. The report stated that those inhabitants who willingly subjected themselves to the king's laws all lived in the Pale of Dublin and its immediate hinterland (Galway and other loyalist enclaves are not mentioned). Elsewhere, the king's Gaelic enemies controlled the North and West of Ireland, as well as occupying outposts in the Wicklow Mountains and the Cork and Kerry mountains. Beyond the Pale were also Henry's Old English rebels, whose obedience to the Crown was at best ephemeral. The report provided a sobering assessment of Irish Gaelic-speaking society in the early sixteenth century. It claimed the Irish 'live only by the sword'; that constraining them was envisaged as requiring a wholesale militarisation plus additional immigration. The proviso was that newcomers introduced into the country must be English speaking and willing to accept English customs. Resorting to force of arms alone was never really considered viable. The report stated, 'An army that is moving [only] ... for a season and not perpetual, shall never profit the King in Ireland without the King's subjects of the land be put in order, for as soon as the army is gone, the obedience to the King goes too.'

The distances involved and other more pressing priorities meant that successive English kings since Richard II had taken a laissez-faire stance to the problems presented in Ireland, relying, with the exceptions of Richard, Duke of York, and 'the Great Earl', on a series of often lukewarm or ineffective justiciars and lieutenant-governors to keep the peace. Henry VIII, however, was a strong, centralising king, who baulked at having a warring Gaelic society, hardly changed since early medieval times, on his doorstep. The man Henry looked to at Dublin to enact his policies was Garrett Og Fitzgerald, 9th Earl of Kildare, who had succeeded his father to the earldom of Kildare and the governorship of Ireland after his father's death. Described as bookish, Garrett later became an important sponsor of Irish cultural development. He played a prominent part at Henry VII's eldest son Prince Arthur's funeral in 1502, and was held in sufficient regard by Henry to be allowed to marry the king's kinswoman Elizabeth, the granddaughter of Elizabeth Woodville, the king's mother-in-law.

Garrett was at first given very much a free hand in Ireland, but was later criticised by Henry VIII's government for not doing more to prop up the defences of the ever dwindling English Pale against inroads made by insurgents. Irish support for pretenders after the death of Richard III had highlighted the risks of an unpacified Ireland and had made the Tudor monarchs decidedly uneasy about a repeat conspiracy. Spurred to action at the king's urging, Garrett trounced the O'Mores and O'Reillys in Laois and East Breifne, and then partially destroyed an O'Carroll castle at Leap, near Roscrea, co. Offaly. A year later, in 1517, he moved against the O'Donnells in Tyrone, capturing Dungannon Castle. To observers in England, however, this round of purges was nothing new – what is more, it did not promise to make significant, lasting inroads against the rebels. Henry summoned Garrett back to court in 1519, relieved him of the governorship and replaced him with Lord Thomas Howard, Earl of Surrey – a fierce and warlike man, who, two years earlier, had scattered rioters in London 'like sheep at the sight of a wolf'. He came to Ireland with an army reckoned as 1,100 strong and soon confirmed the king's worst fears that only in the Pale did the Crown have sufficient control for sheriffs to act, elsewhere Irish law prevailed. Howard's method of taming Ireland was through extreme violence. He said on one occasion,' 'Ireland will never be brought to obedience without compulsion and conquest.' But when he asked the king for men and money (6,000 soldiers were requested), Henry demurred and recalled him. The king wanted firm governance, but only on the cheap. Short of money, Henry now expressed a royal desire to see 'Ireland brought under control by sober ways, politic drifts and amiable persuasions' – a policy switch that hardly played to Surrey's strengths.

For the next six years or so, the deputy lieutenancy of Ireland see-sawed between Garrett and his family's long-term rivals, the Butlers, now led by Piers Butler, 8th Earl of Ormond. Raiding of the Pale, however, continued largely unabated. By the summer of 1529, Henry had had enough. He appointed his illegitimate son Henry Fitzroy, Duke of Richmond, as lieutenant-general of Ireland, and placed him in control of the Irish council. It was rumoured the king planned to raise Fitzroy to the lordship of Ireland (much as Henry II had once done with his son John), but Richmond, like others before him, failed to meet the king's exacting objectives in the realm. Within a year, with funding again curtailed, Garrett was reconfirmed as the king's deputy.

The earl would have been safer remaining in England. While campaigning against Mulroney O'Carroll at Birr Castle, co. Offaly, he was shot in the body by a handgun and nearly killed. He never fully recovered. He lost the full use of his limbs and suffered impaired speech from then on. Forced to rely on others less politically skilled than himself to enforce royal policy, a number of military reverses followed. Garrett's standing with Henry, ever a hard taskmaster, again plummeted.

*

These were turbulent times in Britain too. They witnessed the fall of Cardinal Wolsey at the hands of the Boleyns, the king's marriage to Anne Boleyn, Henry's marriage to Queen Katherine of Aragon made null and void, Rome's angry response, and Henry's making himself head of the Church in England. By the mid-1530s the break with Rome was all but complete. This created complications with regard to Anglo-Irish relations. Catholicism was deep-rooted in Irish and Old English society; the Reformation was opposed by the vast majority of the Irish and Old English. The dissolution of religious houses not only shocked the masses but served to undermine the development of an urbanised Ireland: the great monasteries of Ireland had acted as important foci for settlement. Unlike in England, with its established towns, villages and manors, Ireland in the sixteenth century was relatively undeveloped outside of major centres like Dublin, Drogheda and Kilkenny. The vandalism of the agents of Henry's dissolution proved 'a terrible blow' for the Irish. Most shocking perhaps was the deliberate policy of relic burning, which sought to undermine deep-seated Irish traditions and their religious legitimacy. The most venerated relic to be destroyed was the *Baculum Jesu*, alleged to be the staff of Christ and St Patrick's crosier, by tradition used to banish poisonous reptiles from Ireland and later said to have been borne aloft by Malachy when confronting Turlough O'Brien, King of Thomond, in the year 1080. In 1180 it had been moved from Armagh to Christchurch Cathedral, Dublin, where it was 'preserved with the greatest care, and held in the highest veneration'. Its destruction took place in 1538. After all gems and golden ornaments from it had been removed, it was burned, along with other relics, in the High Street – an act carried out by order of George Browne, Archbishop of Dublin. Other victims of this iconoclastic purge were the famous statue of the Virgin Mary at Trim and a revered image of Christ crucified at the Abbey of Ballyboggan, co. Meath. The abbey was dissolved the same year and the land made over to the Berminghams.

Garrett had been among those who had lobbied the Pope to support Queen Katherine when the 'great matter' of the king's divorce from Katherine of Aragon had first come to light. As a result, he had become distrusted by both the Boleyns and by

Henry's chief minister, Thomas Cromwell, a calculating man with fingers in many pies. Cromwell's aim was to place 'new men', English immigrants, firmly in the seats of power at Dublin (alongside loyal Old English) to counteract reactionary elements. By the spring of 1534 these measures had gained broad acceptance. Garrett was recalled to England, but, pleading ill health after his wounding, he ignored the demand, sending his wife instead. When categorically ordered to appear in person, fearing the worst, he left his son and heir, Thomas, lord Offaly, to deputise for him, ceremoniously handing Offaly the sword of state. Critics expressed surprise at Garrett's choice of deputy. They considered Offaly to be 'young and wilful, and most of the time ordered by light counsel'. A contemporary described him as a 'headlong hotspur ... soon carried where he fancied'. Warning his son to make no decisions without first gaining advice from men and women he could trust, Garrett set sail for Anglesey, and from there to Westminster. Cromwell meanwhile lost no time in appointing the septuagenarian Sir William Skeffington, known as 'Gunner' Skeffington, a one-time Master of Ordnance, to oversee Henry's Irish interests from Dublin. Skeffington had previous experience of service in Ireland. In 1529 he had served as a commissioner at Dublin, charged with compiling a report on the military situation in the country. The following year he had been appointed deputy governor, launching raids into the Irish midlands against the usual suspects: the O'Mores, O'Reillys and O'Connors. In the company of Garrett, he had also led a punitive expedition into war-torn Ulster. He captured an O'Neill stronghold at Kinard, co. Tyrone, and burned a number of O'Neill settlements.

It seems Garrett and Skeffington at first worked well together, but Skeffington was soon complaining that Garrett treated him no better than a commoner. Others in Ireland, like Piers Butler, were also at loggerheads with Garrett, part of the longstanding family feuding previously noted, which still caused rifts serious enough to risk armed confrontation. Skeffington may have encouraged Butler to make his misgivings regarding Garrett's so-called 'pretensions' known to Thomas Cromwell. Skeffington's own efforts to undermine Garrett were, however, met with counter-accusations designed to humiliate the Englishman. This led to a terminal breach in relations and Skeffington's recall to London in the autumn of 1533. Given past performance, and antipathy to the Fitzgeralds, it is little wonder Skeffington's reappointment to the position of Lord Deputy of Ireland after Garrett's recall in the spring of 1534 was met with disquiet by many in Ireland. Skeffington's objectives, dictated by Thomas Cromwell, were to lead a military campaign against popish insurgents, to resist any Catholic backlash to the king's 'great matter' in the council at Dublin, and to extract as much money from Ireland as possible. The council at Dublin had consistently overspent its budget and had therefore become a drain on royal coffers. Underlining the paucity of funds available for such a venture, Skeffington was given just 150 men-at-arms to travel with him. This was a force he knew to be wholly inadequate for the task ahead. It is little wonder he tarried in Wales, blaming the weather and contrary tides for his delay.

Even before Skeffington's proposed departure, the mood in Dublin had darkened. Henry VIII's order for Piers Butler to convene a council at which the king's pleasure would be declared coincided with an instruction from Garrett to his son Offaly, advising him to do nothing untoward but to keep his head down and avoid placing too much trust in any of the king's councillors – Garrett clearly feared that his hot-tempered son would be led astray and goaded to rebel. Garrett's arrest while in London is dated to 29 June 1534. As early as 11 June, however, Offaly had openly defied the king by denouncing royal policy. News of his father's arrest, then the false news of Garrett's death, was the spark needed for Offaly to set Dublin aflame. Having been giving sufficient rope, the headstrong lord soon found ways to hang himself.

Archbishop Alen became the rising's first notable casualty. He was one of a dozen men who had sought Garrett's arrest and removal from Dublin to London. Having anticipated trouble, it seems the archbishop tried to make a run for it. He knew he was a marked man. Embarking for England from Dublin's Dame Gate, his barque ran aground on the sands near Clontarf. Offaly's men then dragged him from hiding from a fortified house in Artane, now a northern suburb of Dublin. Despite the archbishop's description as a pugnacious man, when brought before Offaly he at once fell to his knees and pleaded for his life. Offaly's brusque retort was to 'take the fellow away'. Though not a direct execution order, the archbishop's fate was sealed. On 28 July he was executed. Many of his chaplains and secretaries died with him. To add to the ignominy of his death, the archbishop's body was buried in a pauper's grave.

It may have been the news of these killings, and his son's part in them, that so shocked the ailing Garrett as to prematurely hasten his death. The rising in Dublin was the most serious for a generation, and its instigators could expect nothing less than the full force of the law to be applied. Speeded by the bad news from Dublin, Garrett took to his death-bed in the Tower of London. Although it was alleged that manifold enormities had been proven against the earl, Garrett was too ill to stand trial and answer the charges levelled at him. He died on 2 September 1534, a broken man, and was buried in the Tower's grim church of St Peter ad Vincula, where corpses lay so thick the flagstones sometimes buckled. Two years later he would be posthumously attainted and his titles and lands made forfeit to the Crown.

Meanwhile, Dublin Castle was laid siege to and stormed by Offaly's insurgents. The attack was widely rumoured to be a precursor to the rebels gaining full political control of the English Pale. It appeared to observers that the whole of Ireland would soon be up in arms. When riding through the streets of Dublin, to the terror of its inhabitants, Offaly and his supporters, including 140 heavily armed Gallowglass, sported silken fringes on their helmets, the source of the lord's enduring sobriquet, Silken Thomas. Offaly had earlier burst into the Council Chamber at St Mary's Abbey, flung down his sword, and repudiated his allegiance to the English crown. Denouncing Henry VIII as a heretic, he had demanded that all Englishmen in Ireland pledge an oath to himself, the Pope and the Holy Roman Emperor.

Skeffington remained obstinately immovable in Wales. He blamed desertion and bad weather for his delay. This may have been a cover for a more general reluctance to intervene against the rising tide of revolt in Ireland until better provided for. Military reforms in England had seen the establishment of substantial county militias, and it was from these that Skeffington now hoped to benefit. Men from nearby counties were summoned to bolster his numbers to around 2,300 men. With the crisis escalating in Dublin, money may also have been found to hire well-trained mercenary handgunners and pikemen from Germany and Italy. His army also boasted a sizeable artillery train. Although Henrician ordnance was said to have been sufficient 'to conquer Hell itself', it would play little part in Ireland, where roads were often little better than trackways, making the cartage of heavy guns, ammunition wagons and siege trains problematic.

Irish military manpower was organised on a much less well-regulated basis than in either England or Wales. Surveys carried out by Skeffington in the 1520s established that the sixty to eighty or so Gaelic chieftains of Ireland could muster around 20,000 men, but these came in penny-packets. Hardly changed from earlier centuries, the bulk of Irish soldiery comprised light horse and ill-accoutred and poorly armed kern, bolstered by units of axe-wielding Gallowglass. The latter were still the mainstay in any pitched fight.

Not until mid-October did Skeffington depart. Waterford rather than Dublin was selected as a safer disembarkation point for the English army. The intelligence from Dublin was contradictory, or at best uncertain. Skeffington was right to act cautiously, but at some point, either before leaving or while en route, he changed his mind and opted for Dublin. He might have done better to have kept to his original plan. Upon arriving in Dublin Bay on 24 October, he was met by a furious fusillade from cannon sited by Lord Offaly along the shore at Howth. Forty Englishmen lost their lives. Skeffington's ships were at first driven off and scattered. But it was to be a temporary setback. When the fleet finally managed to regroup and dock, the rebels dispersed inland. Lord Offaly then became little better than a renegade, a man almost immediately marginalised within the Pale and with few committed allies outside of it.

Styling himself the 10th Earl of Kildare, but increasingly desperate, Offaly threatened to lay siege to Drogheda. His men wasted crops outside the town and set upon Skeffington's patrols, but were not strong enough to confront the main English army advancing against them. The *Annals of the Four Masters* for the year 1535 records how Offaly 'plundered and laid waste all Fingall ... and all Meath was made to tremble'. Yet, when marching north, Skeffington easily set the rebels to flight before occupying Drogheda. At the high cross in the town centre, he formally proclaimed Offaly a traitor. He also swore the local notables to maintain their allegiance to King Henry VIII. Many did so half-heartedly, concerned that Offaly would later gain a pardon and return to wreak revenge on them. For a time Skeffington became too sick to make further inroads against Offaly's ever smaller band of miscreants. Being of a choleric temperament, prone to dysentery (and old), he relied more and more heavily on his son Leonard, who was soon engaged in a series of fierce skirmishes with rebel outriders. Some of these clashes occurred in the depth of winter, well outside the normal campaigning season. How seriously they were contested is unclear. By the 1530s, javelins and bows and arrows were giving way to gunpowder, and it seems likely Skeffington's forces were well provided with companies of men using it. In driving rain and drizzle, neither the rudimentary handguns employed by English nor Irish bowstrings would have been of much use on campaign: damp powder would cause misfires from handguns, while wet bowstrings severely limited arrow range. Targets, moreover, were often obscured by the low visibility – the 'fine mist' which Ireland remains famous for.

Unable to make decisive inroads in open battle against an elusive foe, the English resorted to terror tactics. They torched a number of Fitzgerald properties and laid siege to Offaly's headquarters at Maynooth Castle. Maynooth was a strongly defended edifice, located just inside the western perimeter of the Pale. The castle fell after a five-day siege in March 1535. In accordance with strict sixteenth-century military practice, having failed to submit when first summoned, Skeffington ordered the garrison to be put to the sword; a bloody act that would become known as 'the pardon of Maynooth'. Although littered with corpses and battered about, the castle cannot have been too badly damaged, since Skeffington chose it as his headquarters, perhaps as a snub to the Fitzgeralds. The severe treatment meted out at Maynooth persuaded garrisons elsewhere still holding out – at places like Carlow, Athy, Woodstock, Ley and Offaly – to surrender. Worse from a rebel standpoint, attempts by Lord Offaly to inveigle the O'Neills of Ulster in his quarrel with the English came to nought when the northerners signed a peace accord with Skeffington at Drogheda in July. Earlier than this, Offaly had sent envoys abroad to Rome and Spain requesting assistance, portraying himself as a defender of the Roman Catholic faith. No help was forthcoming, merely encouraging words. It became simply a matter of time before the rebel earl, by now probably regretting his precipitate behaviour, was apprehended.

Increasingly desperate, he and his last allies laid down their arms and surrendered on 24 August 1535. Offaly's supporters in the Dublin council later claimed accommodating words had been spoken to the earl on Skeffington's behalf. Skeffington insisted no terms had been set, that Offaly's capitulation had been unconditional. Another version of events claimed the Dublin government resorted to subterfuge to reel the rebel leaders in by supporting a rising in the midlands against Offaly's ally, Brian O'Connor. Faced with enemies on all sides, Offaly's position soon become untenable. By this time Skeffington was in the process of being replaced as military commander by the forty-five-year-old Lord Leonard Grey, a soldier of some considerable experience, who arrived in Ireland in July and quickly assumed command of the army. It was in fact Grey, not Skeffington, who apprehended Offaly, and it was also he who escorted the rebel and his five uncles back to London to stand trial. Skeffington, still formal deputy governor of Ireland, again fell ill. Friends remarked that the knight appeared almost dead. A planned sortie to put down a rising in Munster had to be curtailed. When Skeffington requested to be relieved of the deputy governorship, Henry VIII, with characteristic insensitivity, refused, declaring himself perfectly content the knight should remain in post. Skeffington died shortly afterwards, on 31 December, at Kilmainham Castle, Dublin. He was buried with great ceremony before the steps to the altar in the north wing of St Patrick's Cathedral. Offaly along with five uncles was arraigned on charges of high treason at Westminster. Their final acts were played out on the scaffold, where all six were drawn on hurdles from the Tower to Tyburn and executed as traitors.

The shock in Ireland when news reached Dublin was acute. The executions more starkly than ever before demonstrated the unforgiving nature of the English Crown. Skeffington's death and the Fitzgerald executions marked a new, more aggressive phase in Anglo-Irish relations. Thomas Cromwell's intrusive policies, aimed at balancing the books in Ireland and encouraging immigrant planters to settle, became widely resented at Dublin. Under Cardinal Wolsey, whom Cromwell had replaced, Ireland had been left very much to run its own affairs. Even though Wolsey openly mocked Kildare, calling him the 'king of Kildare', a balance of power existed across the Irish Sea. But this equilibrium was wrecked by the Lord Chancellor's myopia and lack of conciliatory dialogue. The Silken Thomas rebellion had shaken the Tudor regime by proving how extensively held was the opinion among Irishmen that Ireland remained a papal fief, held by the English Crown by virtue of Pope Adrian's donation during the reign of Henry II.

Lord Leonard Grey proved to be a much more energetic man than Skeffington. He led a series of punitive raids against insurrectionist Gaelic chieftains and rebel English lords, achieving a degree of success. In 1536, he forced the Earl of Desmond's submission. The following year, he campaigned against the O'Connors, Cavanaghs, Nolans and O'Maghers. Grey's aggressiveness was not just restricted to the battlefield. Colleagues

1. Drombohilly stone circle overlooking the Kenmare River, co. Kerry. Prehistoric Ireland was most probably an integral part of the European scene, linked to Britain and the Continent by regularly traversed sea routes, a relationship which facilitated cultural interchange.

2. The Giant's Causeway, co. Antrim. In legend, Finn McCool clashed here with a Scottish giant named Benandonner. When routed, the latter tore up the causeway to prevent Finn from chasing after him. At Staffa, in the Hebrides, identical basal columns at Fingal's Cave are from the same ancient lava flow.

Above: 3. Gougane Barra, co. Cork. St Finbarr built a monastery here in the sixth century. Monks like St Finbarr led a straitened existence. They practised the most severe penances in an attempt to emulate Christ.

Left: 4. Map to show the likely extent of Dalriadan influence. Dalriada's royal remit may have been delineated to the west by the River Bann in Ulster, and to the east by the Drumalban mountain range, today the eastern boundary of Argyllshire.

5. Replica Viking longship moored at Roskilde, Denmark. These sleek, seaworthy ships enabled Viking raiders to bypass mountain, bog and forest and strike deep into the interior of Ireland through the country's many waterways.

Right: 6. Viking sword, with spread-eagle patterning. Anglo-Saxon King Aelle of York was allegedly 'blood-eagled' by Dublin-based Vikings under the command of Ivar 'the Boneless', progenitor of Clan Ivar. Aelle's lungs were drawn out after death in a cruel parody of an open-winged bird.

Above: 7. Defensive ditch-line at Baginbun. To secure their bridgehead into Ireland, the Cambro-Normans constructed fortifications across the narrow, windswept neck of Baginbun Head, discernible here.

8. The Baginbun beachhead, co. Wexford. The Battle of Baginbun and its bloody aftermath was a decisive moment in the attempted Norman Conquest of Ireland.

9. Round Tower. These trademark Irish constructions are thought to be bell towers; their doors are set well above ground level for better security. Ireland does not have a monopoly on them. This one is in Scotland, located beside the cathedral at Brechin. There are just two in Scotland, but around sixty altogether in Ireland.

10. Aughnanure Castle, co. Galway. This is a good example of a walled castle, comprising a six-storey tower built by the O'Flaherty's around 1500. The O'Flaherty motto was 'fortune favours the strong'.

11. The mountains of Kerry. The Irish had an intimate knowledge of the mountainous and forested terrain which the Norman invaders lacked. This negated any advantage the Normans had in heavy cavalry, boosting the effectiveness of the fleet-footed Irish, armed with spears, knives, bows and slings.

12. Landsknecht ensign. The Yorkist mercenary army that arrived in Dublin in 1487 contained flamboyantly attired landsknecht troops. They were armed with long pikes, halberds (bladed pole weapons) and two-handed swords. Their ranks also boasted well-drilled handgunners and crossbowmen.

Above left: 13. Three English kings who adorn the outer wall of Canterbury Cathedral, and whose policies had a profound effect on Ireland during the fifteenth and early sixteenth centuries. From left to right, Henry VII, Edward IV and Henry VI.

Above right: 14. The battlefield of Knockdoe, co. Galway. The low but locally prominent hill of Knockdoe remains a striking feature in the flat, patchwork landscape. There is little to alert a casual visitor to the fact that two sizeable armies, perhaps 10,000 men all-told, squared up to one another and fought to the death here.

15. Irish warriors, *c.* 1521. This group is a mix of Gallowglass and kern from a wall display at Ross Castle. Churchmen referred to such soldiers as 'a shower from Hell; sons of malediction, beyond salvation'.

16. Renvyle Castle, co. Galway. A number of Grace O'Malley turret castles, like this one, remain standing along Ireland's 'wild Atlantic way', windswept sentinels that hark back to troubled times. The O'Malley motto was 'powerful by land and by sea'.

17. Aerial view of the Rathlin Island, Antrim and the Kintyre Peninsular. The Rathlin Island massacre of 26 July 1575 is remembered as a war-crime of heinous proportions, but was at the time applauded by the English Crown.

Above: 18. A ruined outpost on the Antrim coast, looking north. Clan Campbell incursions into the Western Isles triggered an upsurge in MacDonald migration across the North Channel to Antrim in the 1540s.

Below left: 19. Prince Rupert of the Rhine. When parliament ordered no quarter be given to Irish Catholics in the service of the Royalists in 1644, Rupert claimed the English nation was 'in danger of destroying itself and degenerating into such an animosity and cruelty, that all elements of charity, compassion, and brotherly affection shall be extinguished'.

Below right: 20. Oliver Cromwell. Upon arriving in Ireland in the summer of 1649, Cromwell spoke of his army as being akin to Israelites, setting out to 'extirpate the idolatrous inhabitants of Canaan'.

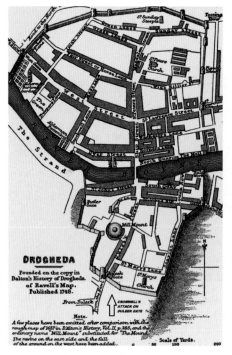

DROGHEDA

Founded on the copy in
Dalton's History of Drogheda
of Ravell's Map.
Published 1748.

From Duleek

Note.
A few places have been omitted after comparison with the
rough map of 1657 in Dalton's History, Vol. II, p.285, and the
ordinary name "Mill Mount" substituted for "The Mound".
The ravine on the east side and the fall
of the ground on the west have been added.

Scale of Yards.

21. Drogheda, 1649. Cromwell's cannonade opened a great rupture in the south wall beside the Duleek Gate, bringing down the south-east corner tower and the steeple of St Mary's Church. Ten or more companies of infantry burst through the gaps at five o'clock in the evening, but were driven back with loss. Cromwell personally led the final assault which carried the town.

22. Macroom Castle, co. Cork. On 10 May 1650, 500 Irish confederate soldiers lost their lives in a fight outside the town. The ornately castellated Macroom Castle had earlier been set ablaze by the confederates to deny it to the Parliamentarians.

23. Ross Castle, near Killarney, co. Kerry. A local legend prophesied that 'Ross may all assault disdain, till strange ships sail on Lough Laune'. When the castle fell to a lakeside attack in 1652, almost 1,000 men marched out from behind its walls.

24. The lake at Killarney from one of the high passes over the Kerry Mountains. After the fall of Ross, a further 3,000 men, who had taken refuge in these highland fastnesses, capitulated to the Cromwellian forces.

25. The River Garry and the Pass of Killiecrankie, near Blair Atholl in Perthshire – a forbidding geological feature, described in the nineteenth century as 'a dark and profound abyss'. According to tradition, Bonny Dundee vetoed the idea of laying an ambush here with his Irish troops because of a time-honoured Highland maxim never to attack someone who could not defend himself on equal terms.

26. Bonny Dundee's breastplate and helmet. The Jacobite general was killed by a random musket shot at the very commencement of the battle. The ball entered his brain through the left eye. His body was taken back to Blair Castle and later interred in a vault at nearby St Bride's Kirk. (From the collection at Blair Castle Perthshire)

Left: 27. British Grenadier from the late seventeenth century. With no time to fix their bayonets, and assailed by Highlanders wielding axes and broadswords, men like this were quickly overwhelmed at Killiecrankie in July 1689.

Below: 28. The relief of Derry. This old illustration shows the *Dartmouth*, *Phoenix* and *Mountjoy* navigating the five-mile river passage to the city. While the *Dartmouth* engaged the Jacobites, the two other ships headed downriver to break the boom (shown on the right of the picture) erected by the Jacobites north of Foyle Bridge.

29. Londonderry walls. These walls were completed by 1618, turning a once open town into one of Ireland's most prominent fortresses.

30. James II on parade in 1685. When Charles II died on 5 February 1685, his brother James gained the throne unopposed. It was said that 'after grim apprehensions [of Civil War], James' accession came as something of an anti-climax'.

31. Lundy, traitor or scapegoat? Rumours that Lundy was intent on surrendering the city raised the fear he might be lynched. With four others, he fled Londonderry. Each year, his effigy is burned by Protestants in memory of these dangerous times.

32. Patrick Sarsfield. The French ambassador at the court of King James II described Sarsfield as 'greater than that of any man I know … brave but above all he has a sense of honour and integrity in all that he does'. James called him a blockhead.

33. The River Boyne at Oldbridge. Because the Boyne is a tidal river, there was just a short two-hour window for the Williamites to make their crossing. Orders went out for every man to wear a green bough in his hat to distinguish friend from foe, and for the flanking columns to set off at first light, when mist from the river would hamper Jacobite onlookers on the south bank, the foreground in this picture.

34. A coin bearing the likeness of William III, minted in 1695. The reverse of the coin shows a harp, denoting, presumably, his kingship over Ireland.

35. Aughrim Village. The position on St Ruth's left flank. Nearby is a small museum dedicated to the battle.

36. The Aughrim battlefield, looking toward Kilcommodan Hill. For some considerable time after the battle, passers-by noted large flocks of sheep on the hill, only to be told by locals that what they took for sheep was in fact an extensive mass of human bone.

37. Keimaneigh, the scene of an ambush in 1822, where three Whiteboys and a member of the Crown forces were killed. Named for their white smocks, the Whiteboys had become radicalised by agrarian issues: rack-rents, tithes, excessive priestly demands and evictions.

38. The memorial stones at Keimaneigh, laid in 1999.

39. Hands across the divide, Londonderry.

complained about his uncontrollable temper at council. Some remarked, too, on his acquisitiveness, noting that the lord's main priority appeared to be to make himself wealthy at the expense of others. In this respect, the justiciar may have been taking his lead from his boss, the even more rapacious Thomas Cromwell, a man well known for feathering his own already substantial nest. The Butlers of Ormond were specifically targeted by Grey and obliged to pay large cash sums to prevent their castles being searched or confiscated by the crown. An exasperated James Butler, 9th Earl of Ormond, alleged, 'My Lord Deputy Grey is the Earl of Kildare newly born again.'

The powerful Thomas Howard – when last featured, Earl of Surrey, but now elevated to the dukedom of Norfolk – had by this time become Cromwell's arch-rival. Norfolk remained a religious conservative, un-enamoured of the Reformation, a man always more likely to side with the status quo in Ireland. The Butlers were his allies in Ireland, and this perhaps explains Grey's targeting of them. Other than hounding the Butlers, fortification of the Pale became the number one priority for Grey. It seems that wider ranging, expensive and potentially disastrous expeditions against the Gaels and the king's Old English rebels remained prohibited by the fretful Henry. Bolstering the Pale's defences had therefore become essential. The hope was that revenue would amass through the Dissolution of the Monasteries and that this might help make inroads into the deficit being incurred in Ireland. Henry, as ever, did not want money spent on wasteful campaigning. Disappointingly for Cromwell, actual income continued to fall well short of expectations – this despite a remorseless attack on the Catholic Church.

One Fitzgerald who managed to avoid capture during the round-up of his relations was Offaly's twelve-year-old half-brother Gerald, later to become the 11th Earl of Kildare. Though too young to personally threaten Tudor rule in Ireland, the focus he supplied for those opposed to Henrician policy was of great concern to the king. The English made every effort to capture the youth, but Kildare's extended family, led by the formidable and comely Lady Eleanor McCarthy (a woman who had recently accepted an offer of marriage from Manus O'Donnell in order to secure the powerful support of the O'Donnell clan), refused to budge. Malcontents like Conn Bacach O'Neill also joined the growing coalition to promote the interests of young Gerald Fitzgerald. It was rumoured abroad that the so-called Geraldine League stood ready to rise in revolt against the Crown. The O'Donnells and O'Neills coming together attracted other families to the cause of freedom. Among them were the O'Briens of Thomond, descendants of the great Brian Boru; others included the Cavanaghs and the ever rampant O'Mores. Had the risings been supported by an influx of continental troops, as was for a time feared, the Pale might have been overrun. State papers betray the apprehension felt in England, describing the situation in Ireland as 'much to be doubted'. No wonder that pro-English elements in Ireland, the Butlers in particular, continued to lobby for the whole 'sept of the Geraldines' to be wiped out.

Together with elements of clans O'Donnell, Magennis, O'Kane, O'Hanlon, MacWilliam and others, Conn Bacach invaded the English Pale, burned the towns of Ardee, co. Louth, and Navan, co. Meath, and plundered all the country through which they passed, until they came to the Hill of Tara, where they reviewed their forces with great display and spectacle, a targeted provocation to the regime at Dublin. These overt acts of war risked the fabled reawakening of Finn McCool and his restless Fianna, but before the caves of Antrim could yield up the ghostly reinforcements, Lord Leonard Grey marched out against the insurgents. In the summer of 1539, he crushed them at the decisive Battle of Bellahoe Ford, fought on the borders of modern-day counties Meath and Monaghan in Monaghan's most southerly parish, an outpost of the fierce MacMahons. Strengthened by a 250-strong contingent of Cheshire troops under the command of Sir William Brereton, Grey is said to have pursued the Geraldines northward into a land of ancient pathways and gloomy raths before defeating them. According to one near contemporary history, the Irish lost nearly 400 men slain, together with Magennis, lord of Iveagh, one of their commanders; as many English may have fallen, in what by all accounts was a sharp conflict. Irish Attorney-General Lawyer Sir John Davies later said of the battle, 'that prosperous fight at Bellahoe, on the borders of Meath, the memory whereof is yet famous'. The setback threw the Geraldines into disarray. Tradition has it that a great treasure was hurriedly thrown into a nearby lake to prevent it being seized by Grey's men; when a true Irish Gael on a white steed rides by – the re-awakened Finn McCool perhaps – he will swoop into the lake and regain it.

The following year, Grey advanced to Dungannon, co. Tyrone, and ravaged the O'Neil lands. His proximity forced Gerald Fitzgerald's protectors to hurriedly evacuate their young charge from Ireland to St Malo in France, then on to the French court at Paris, pursued all the while by English envoys desperate to undermine him. He proved too hot for the French king to handle, and was promptly hurried eastwards to Austria, where he briefly visited Charles V's court. Both the French king and the Emperor granted Gerald a pension: the young man's future potential as a diplomatic asset was not lost on either of them. Heading south, Gerald then placed himself under the protection of Cardinal Reginald Pole, a die-hard English Catholic and a mortal enemy of the Henrician regime in England. With help from such allies on the Continent, it was feared Gerald might mount a return expedition to Ireland.

In England, meanwhile, Thomas Cromwell was rounding up Catholic intriguers, among them the sixty-six-year-old Margaret Pole, Countess of Salisbury, Reginald's mother and a niece of the late King Edward IV. She was accused of openly aiding and abetting her staunchly Catholic sons in perpetrating 'detestable and abominable treasons'. Her end was unusually gruesome: a blundering youth is said to have hacked her neck and shoulders to pieces in a most pitiful manner, while she attempted to parry the blows. Her corpse joined other victims of Henrician fury, and perhaps paranoia, beneath the yawning flagstones at the Church of St Peter ad Vincula. In parallel, Grey's enemies worked round the clock to incriminate him, claiming, with some credence, that he had connived in the escape of the elusive Gerald Fitzgerald. Described as diseased and aged, Grey was by now keen to retire to England. He was eventually recalled the same month Margaret Pole faced her executioner. He might have done better to stay in Dublin and keep his head down. Within a month of his return, his mentor, Thomas Cromwell, had been indicted on charges of treason unrelated to Ireland. Grey nevertheless was soon dragged into the same wide net which encompassed many of the ill-fated chancellor's allies and confidants.

Cromwell's incarceration in the Tower dates to 10 June 1540. Underlining the swiftness of the round-up, Grey was imprisoned just two days later. At his trial the lord was charged with a host of misdeeds. Many of these were probably conjured up by his enemies. They included private dealings with the Geraldines, untoward leniency in his dealings with the O'Connors, inciting insurrection, abuse of authority, going against the advice of the king's council at Dublin, and doing unsanctioned deals with unspecified Gaelic chieftains. A document held at Lambeth Palace library lists the scores of names of those said to have been questioned. Among them were John Allen, Chancellor of Ireland, George Browne, Archbishop of Dublin, James Butler of Ormond and Alexander McTirlogue, a captain of Gallowglass. Henry's Privy Council found Grey guilty of all charges. Perhaps world-weary by this time, Grey admitted his guilt. On 28 June 1541, the same year Henry VIII assumed the title King of Ireland, Grey was beheaded at Tower Hill. Cromwell had met a similar death the year before. Although the Lord Chancellor had extended Tudor power in Ireland and had introduced religious reform, escalating costs had undermined his efforts. His centralising policies did not long survive his death.

Grey's successor, Sir Anthony St Leger, was given more freedom to act than his predecessors. A gifted diplomat and administrator, St Leger, with the backing of the Duke of Norfolk, proved adept as an intermediary between his sovereign and the proud chieftains of Gaeldom. His development of an earlier attempted policy known as 'surrender and regrant', whereby acceptance of Henry VIII as king of Ireland would lead to a reciprocal recognition on Henry's behalf of a chieftain's titles plus the refutation of onerous feudal claims, established a workable formula upon which to base his diplomacy. Under this scheme, title to Gaelic territory was substituted for new titles under English law. In return, Irish landowners would be protected by a strong standing army from the Pale, and also be enabled to set up their own local law courts and to attend the parliament at Dublin. Henry VIII meanwhile laid down the maxim of an Ireland 'united, annexed and knit forever to the imperial crown of the realm of England'. That many in Ireland continued to look to the Pope as the supreme arbiter of Ireland's fate encouraged Henry to assert his own primacy. A parliament was convened at Dublin in the summer of 1541, where Henry was formally proclaimed holder of the 'Crown of Ireland', a title designed to win over naysayers by flattering their pride. The hope in Dublin and London was that this confirmation of overlordship and the simultaneous introduction of the policy of 'surrender and regrant' would turn Irishmen, who had once been enemies of the Crown, into loyal subjects. Previously rebellious Gaelic chieftains and a number of entrenched Old English lords were actively encouraged to surrender their lands to the king, then have them returned as freeholds. They would then be brought within the English polity and their lands would be secured under English common law rather than the ancient Brehon law. Those who submitted were also expected to adopt the English language as their first language, to wear English-style dress, remain loyal, pay rent, repudiate Rome, and also recognise Henry as supreme head of the Church in England and Ireland.

The result was a large number of decorously attired chieftains and their entourages marching through London to be presented at court and make their submissions to the king. In return, those who submitted were formally reinvested with their lands.

The submissions were to some extent political theatre, but were effective nonetheless. Long-running feuds went to arbitration. Where successful, this freed up Gaelic soldiery for service to the Crown, and Henry was able to draw on Irish manpower for wars closer to home during his rough-wooing of Scotland. All of this was to the credit of St Leger, the architect of what was seen at the time as the making of a 'new Kingdom of Ireland'.

10

BEARS AND BAND-DOGS

Henry VIII's death in January 1547 led to a rapprochement between the Crown and Gerald Fitzgerald. Edward Seymour, the most powerful man in England during the boy-king Edward VI's minority, made allowance for Gerald Fitzgerald's earlier misbehaviour and by 1549 had secured for him a full pardon. Yet only after Seymour's execution three years later did Fitzgerald regain some of his lost lands in Ireland. Knighted that year, he was then created Earl of Kildare and Baron Offaly. By the mid-1550s, during the reign of the staunchly Roman Catholic Mary I, he had regained all his forfeited lands and with her blessing set sail for Ireland. The return of a Fitzgerald, long given up as a forlorn hope, was greeted with as much rejoicing by the Irish as if Finn McCool had made an appearance at the head of the phantom Fianna. There was everywhere felt a keenness for change, but, perhaps inevitably, as in the past momentum for a wider political franchise in Ireland stalled. Real power remained vested in a small clique.

James Fitz John Fitzgerald, 13th Earl of Desmond, became St Leger's most important supporter among the Old English of Munster. He had wisely held back from supporting the Silken Thomas rebellion, gaining Henry VIII's thanks for doing so, and had later campaigned against the king's rebels in Cork. Thereafter he embraced 'surrender and regrant'. Others who submitted to the English and accepted the changes were the O'Tooles and the MacGeoghegans. The warlike O'Donnells from the north-west of Ireland offered their submission as well, but their old enemies the O'Neills of Tyrone proved less tractable.

Open internecine warfare had first erupted between the O'Donnells and the O'Neills in the north of Ireland in the early 1520s. The O'Neills had captured the O'Donnell castle at Ballyshannon, co. Donegal, but had then been defeated at the Battle of Knockavoe, beside Strabane, c. 1522. Nine hundred men died when the O'Neill camp was surprised at night. Only after a disastrous winter campaign against St Leger did the veteran O'Neill leader Conn Bacach reluctantly accept Henry VIII as his sovereign lord. He not only gained an audience with Henry VIII for doing so, but was also handed the prestigious English title Earl of Tyrone. A number of other lords came into the fold at around this time. Barnaby mac Gilla Padraig took the name Fitzpatrick and gained a peerage as Baron Upper Ossory. The O'Briens of Thomond were created lords Inchiquin. The de Burghs (or anglicized Burkes) formally gained the earldom of Clanrickard. Others remained out of the system: the MacMahons for good, the mac William Burkes of Mayo and the O'Donovans of Cork until the 1590s. It seemed that Ireland's long-running rebellion might finally be checked, but, a few months prior to Henry VIII's death, open rebellion once again broke out across the Irish Sea. The warlike O'Connors and the O'Mores were the protagonists. Both clans were accused by the Lord Justice of Ireland of acting like 'bears and band-dogs' (large guard dogs in need of 'bands' to restrain them), tugging at each other so that no-one really cared who came out on top. The O'Mores had been regranted their lands in 1543. Rebellion was therefore for them a lapse. Fighting became so protracted and vicious that St Leger's policies appeared dead in the water. With their O'Byrne and MacGeoghegan allies, the O'Connors, led by their chieftain Brian O'Connor (of whom more to come), ravaged the frontiers of the Pale, burning several towns. Only with great difficulty, and by calling on the support of Desmond from Munster, did St Leger bring the situation back under control. Another flashpoint in Ireland was the south-east, where the Cavanaghs fought an internecine war within the clan. Cahir mac Art Cavanagh had earlier been involved in the Silken Thomas revolt, albeit which side he was on is difficult to determine with confidence. Disagreements over the partition of land led to the inter-clan feuding. The result was a fight near Hacketstown, co. Carlow. Cahir gained the victory. The slaughter was said to have been immense. But since only rivals within the same family were involved, casualties cannot have been as high as suggested. There was, however, a worrying lack of royal oversight, explaining much of what was to follow.

Brian O'Connor was an out-and-out Irish rebel. His father Cahir O'Connor had been assassinated by the 'Great Earl' of Kildare in 1511. The subtext for the murder was the promotion of Geraldine influence in the midlands. During the period of Garrett Fitzgerald's confinement in England, the O'Connors made a comeback. Described by a contemporary as 'more like a beggar than a captain or a ruler of a country', Brian re-established himself as the clan chieftain in Offaly. Putting past differences behind him, he swore allegiance to Garret on the latter's return from England. When Garrett was again recalled to London, he launched destructive raids on the Dublin Pale. This may have been at Garret's behest, to persuade the English the situation in Ireland would quickly become ungovernable should Fitzgerald not be reinstated. Brian's daring and disdain for Henry VIII's authority was such that on one occasion he made a point of stopping to brazenly shoe his horse on the Hill of Tara, an act designed to impress fellow dissidents by hearkening back to heroic times gone by. Later he seized and held captive the English king's vice-deputy, Richard Nugent, lord Devlin. Orchestrating a reign of terror worked. Garret was hurried back to Ireland to put down what was described at the time as 'the great rebellion that O'Connor had made with [the support of] diverse Irishmen'.

Brian married Garret's daughter Mary in 1527. They had nine sons and two daughters. Only Brian's support kept his brother-in-law Lord Offaly's revolt going as long as it did. When, however,

Offaly and his uncles faced the full weight of Henrician justice, Brian was merely fined the loss of 800 cattle. Had the fine been paid off, all might have been well; but it was not. Brian's continued intransigence saw him for a time hounded from his home and forced on the run. Described as Henry VIII's most rank traitor, he only regained his standing because St Leger needed a man of influence to exert control over the unruly Irish midlands. St Leger was happy to overlook minor infractions so long as Brian kept his distance and did not threaten the Pale. As soon as St Leger returned to London, however, Brian widened the scope of his banditry. His attacks on the Pale in 1546 marked a tipping point. No more could the English rely on untrustworthy men of his ilk. Returning to Ireland the following year, St Leger devastated the midlands, but failed to apprehend the miscreant. Raiding by the O'Connors and the O'Mores continued throughout the winter and early spring of 1548, but under increasing pressure from St Leger's military build-up – funded by the government to the tune of £12,877 – Brian fled into Connaught, leaving lands in the midlands unprotected. His allies were soon cowed by the English and his standing in the region was weakened. He sought an accommodation with St Leger, but was instead arrested, shipped to England and incarcerated in the Marshalsea Prison at Southwark. He remained there until 1554. Upon eventual release, Brian returned to Ireland and made some attempt at re-establishing himself, but to no avail. The daring rebel died in the end a broken man at Dublin Castle sometime after 1559.

St Leger had been recalled from Ireland at much the same time as Brian's imprisonment, but returned two years later in the August of 1550, by which time preparations were underway for an influx of new soldier-settlers into the Irish midlands. It was hoped that such an intervention would support a more widespread acceptance of 'surrender and regrant' and also extend the frontier as a staging-post for the reduction of still-outlawed Irish. In expediting all this, not only were military agencies to be employed, but there was also the hope that diplomacy and patronage would win over the recalcitrant Irish. Men like Desmond, Thomond and the O'Donnells were to be showered with gifts and goodwill, 'whereby they shall the more diligently be inclined to serve the king and not to embrace foreign arguments'.

The first of several new towns outside the Pale, at places like Philipstown (now Daingean) and Maryborough (now Port Laoise), were soon being settled by what the Irish called planters. Brian O'Connor's former territories in modern-day counties Offaly and Laois were split up and renamed the King's and Queen's Counties, after Philip of Spain and Mary of England. These powerful, married monarchs were keen to see Ireland become a more vibrant and integrated part of their joint Catholic domain. Confiscation went hand in hand with plantation. The lands of the turbulent O'Mores and O'Connors were first on the list. Many formally regranted clan chiefs switched their religious adherence back to Rome during Mary's reign. Anglo-Irish landowners in Ireland deserted Protestantism in droves. Sons of Irish noblemen were withdrawn from English universities and sent instead to Catholic seminaries on the Continent. Unlike in England, where the drift back to Catholicism after the Reformation remained relatively insignificant, in Ireland it engulfed the whole country. Mary was even more interventionist in Ireland than her father had been, viewing colonisation as mutually beneficial. Settler plantations she sponsored have been described by modern historians as extensive. Under Mary and, later, her sister Elizabeth, it became a common occurrence in Ireland to declare vast tracts of land forfeit. Ireland was seen by Mary and Philip of Spain as a valuable colonial asset that required close attention. Had Mary fallen pregnant and born a son, this conjectural future king might have inherited a Catholic empire comprising Spain, Portugal, the Netherlands, England, Wales and Ireland. Instead, after two phantom pregnancies she succumbed to a virulent bout of influenza, which killed her. From then on, instead of an adjunct of empire, Ireland became a pawn in a power game between Protestant England and Catholic Spain.

Another drawback to the anglicization of Ireland – other than religion – was the clash of English with Brehon law; in particular, with regard to primogeniture. Brehon law allowed for literally dozens of men within a clan to stand for election as clan chief, whereas English law relegated them to tenants of the main line of the family and also allowed women to claim rights over land. Such rights for women were disallowed in Brehon law. The inter-clan feuding that ensued was exploited by cynical English officials at Dublin as a way of weakening the clan system. The so-called Irish pirate queen, Grace O'Malley, once explained face-to-face to Henry VIII's daughter, Elizabeth I, that in Gaelic law she enjoyed no rights to her husband's land, whereas in English common law she did. When her husband died, Grace gathered together her followers and with 1,000 head of 'cows and mares' occupied her ex-husband's lands. She asserted her dower rights to these lands based on English common law. The president of Connaught, Sir Richard Bingham, was ordered by Elizabeth to grant her demands, but the Irish administration proved slow to take up Grace's case. Bingham would later became infamous for his merciless treatment of the Irish. His massacre of Irish and Scots at Ardnaree, the 'hill of the kings', co. Mayo, is remembered to this day. On a summer's night in 1586, Bingham's forces attacked a rebel Irish/Scots encampment after surrounding it, so that none might escape. Not only were all the soldiers within killed, women and children were also slaughtered. Irish landowners implicated in supporting the rebels were later hanged by order of Bingham and their lands allocated to new settlers.

Whereas Elizabeth was receptive to the notion of a woman like Grace O'Malley speaking on behalf of her family, the harsh and intractable Bingham and his associates were not. Other than fascination at meeting such an outlandish subject, and putting to one side any heartfelt sisterly support, Elizabeth had a practical need for allies in the west of Ireland. Grace O'Malley controlled naval assets that could be placed at the Crown's disposal. The O'Malley motto was 'powerful by land and by sea'. Bingham, however, feared the Irishwoman was playing both ends against the middle and distrusted her to the last, this despite the O'Malley clan being among those who most ruthlessly enacted Crown policy of slaughtering Spaniards in droves as they struggled ashore from their wrecked galleons when the ill-fated Armada was battered by storms in the Atlantic. One positive outcome of Grace's stand was to underpin the future establishment of her son Theobald, created Viscount Mayo by the English in 1627, as the greatest ever Mayo landowner. It also cloaked her life in a veil of myth and legend, the subject of later buccaneering tales. Today, a number of O'Malley turret castles remain in situ along Ireland's 'wild Atlantic way', windswept sentinels that hark back to these troubled times.

*

Prior to the Catholic resurgence under Philip and Mary, Edward VI's government had for a time all but suppressed Catholicism in England, or at least its outward display. Archbishop Cranmer's brazen policy of stamping out idolatry had made extensive inroads: candles and shrines were banned, religious images proscribed, stained-glass windows were re-glazed, and church walls daubed in lime. A rich medieval, pictorial heritage was destroyed or hidden. Cranmer later paid a heavy price for his vandalism. Although, allegedly, willing at the last to recant his Protestantism and embrace Rome after Edward VI's death, Mary had the churchman, one of many, burned alive. Popular culture was also hard hit under the youthful Edward. Religious processions, mystery plays and pageants became things of the past. When the common people revolted, they were put to the sword. Risings in England in 1549 dealt the country what has since been termed 'a staggering demographic blow', likened proportionately to around 200,000 deaths in a single year today – in other words, pandemic levels. Such unyieldingly hard-line policies enraged Catholic onlookers from abroad. The emperor Charles V, Philip of Spain's father, considered declaring war on England; the downtrodden Catholic Irish would have been natural allies. Under international pressure, Edward VI's ministers were of a mind to backtrack, but were prevented by the reforming ardour and rhetorical skill of the young king. Only Edward's death, at the age of sixteen, prevented a more draconian Reformation, and, possibly, a costly foreign war.

Mary's accession turned everything on its head. By promising not to coerce her subjects back to Catholicism she hoped for the assistance of an upswelling of popular sentiment for the old religion. Rather than a small cabal of Protestant die-hards, however, acceptance of Edward's reform agenda proved to be more deep-rooted than she imagined. Matters might have stabilised had her announcement of impending marriage to Philip of Spain not reawakened fears of foreign domination and Catholic reprisals. Risings occurred in Kent, Hereford, Devon and Leicestershire. Most serious was one in Kent, from where, early in 1554, approximately 3,000 insurgents, led by Sir Thomas Wyatt, reached the western outskirts of London, threatening the city. Wyatt had promised to match the government 'pike for pike', but his men proved no match for the Earl of Pembroke's army who faced them at Charing Cross. Mary bravely refused to quit the city, having earlier declared Wyatt a traitor, promising if necessary to shed her royal blood to defend 'this Common Weal'. The Londoners held firm, Wyatt hesitated and the danger passed. Four hundred rebels lost their lives. Wyatt's execution occurred in the spring of the following year. Two potential focal points for future Protestant revolt, Lady Jane Grey and the Princess Elizabeth, were secured in custody. The former was later executed.

In Ireland, the marriage of Philip and Mary meant a restoration to the pre-Reformation status quo. Pope Pius IV invested the newly-weds as joint monarchs of Ireland on 7 June 1555. The tireless Sir Anthony St Leger was confirmed for third time as Ireland's Lord Deputy, but this time charged to restore Catholicism and to reduce the military establishment down to just 500 men. This in the end proved impossible to achieve. The O'Connors and O'Mores were once again in the field, and rival factions were clashing openly in Munster and Ulster. By the summer of 1554 the Crown's standing army remained at over 1,000 effectives, twice what was budgeted for. The following year, Pope Paul IV issued a papal bull, raising Thomas Cromwell's old enemy Cardinal Reginald Pole as papal legate in Ireland and confirming Ireland's status as a kingdom. Mary was then formally proclaimed Queen of Ireland. The by now ailing and financially compromised St Leger was replaced for the last time on 21 April 1556. He died three years later, his reputation tarnished by claims of 'partiality and corruption'. Historians have portrayed him since as an able, conciliatory and pragmatic governor, despite ruling during a period of tumultuous change. His last year in post saw another upsurge of violence in the midlands. Once again it was the O'Mores, under the leadership of Connell MacConnell, causing the problems. From the trackless wastes of western Laois, they raided the new Marian settlements. For a time the situation became sufficiently serious for martial law to be imposed. Connell, when caught, was hung in chains from Leighlin Bridge, co. Carlow, but not until 1564, after the death of more than thirty leading O'Mores, did the situation stabilise. The lord deputy at the time, Henry Sidney, once exclaimed he would 'bare such a hand upon the whole name of the O'Mores as I trust the Queen's county shall be a quiet county'. He would be as good as his word.

Although Philip and Mary never travelled to Ireland, the former took a close interest in the island's defence. On one occasion, he praised the Anglo-Irishman, Thomas Butler, 10th Earl of Ormond, for his military successes against the Scots of Antrim. He knew a talented soldier when he saw one. Known as Black Tom for his complexion, Thomas Butler had served at the Battle of Pinkie in the autumn of 1547, considered to be the first modern battle fought in the British Isles. The victory had proved a hollow one. The hope of establishing an equivalent Pale in lowland Scotland to match the one at Dublin came to nought in the face of later stiff Scottish resistance. Thomas had also rallied to Mary's side when Thomas Wyatt marched on Westminster, distinguishing himself by his gallantry. Mary granted him extensive lands in Kilkenny and Tipperary, probably on the condition that he back her policies of military subjugation and colonisation.

Elizabeth I, on her accession to the throne, was also well disposed to Thomas Butler. On one occasion, she flirtatiously encouraged him to remain by her side at court, rather than travel back to Ireland. The queen made no secret of her affection for the dashing Irishman. Unsurprisingly, he used his growing influence to lobby her for lands and titles. As well as additional landholdings, over and above those ceded by Mary, he gained the position of Treasurer of Ireland. In return, he enthusiastically executed government policy. Assize courts were convened by him at Kilkenny and Clonmel. Musters of troops, known as shire levies, were organised and funded by him. Thomas also sought ways to finally put an end to the 'lingering [and] horribly devouring system of Coign and Livery', aided in doing so by the adoption of St Leger's alternative system of 'surrender and regrant', which by this time had made important inroads into stamping out the practice. When, however, Thomas was challenged militarily by the Fitzgeralds of Desmond, in 1560, it became clear to him he could not readily abandon 'Coign and Livery' whilst others did not, since raising an army by commission of array in the English manner was too slow. This brought him into conflict with the authorities at Dublin, who considered the earl to be backtracking on his commitments. Black Tom's Athassel estates in modern-day county Tipperary were at some point ravaged by the Geraldines, but he got his own back when overpowering his enemies at the Battle of Affane, fought on 8 February 1565.

Affane has been described as the last private battle fought on British or Irish soil. Each side could muster sizeable support. The Fitzgeralds are accounted as raising fifty-six horsemen and perhaps twice as many foot, as well as an unknown number of ill-equipped 'rascals'. Their cavalry and the professional foot soldiers – mainly mail-bedecked Gallowglass and supporting horse-boys and kern, some of them O'Connors and O'Brians – could be relied upon, but itinerant hangers-on, the majority, could not. Black Tom's force, of which there are no details other than that they comprised Gaelic and Old English levies and that they outnumbered the Geraldines, crossed the Knockmealdown Mountains and advanced upon the Fitzgeralds from the north. The battle took place at the ford of Affane (literally, the middle-ford) on the Blackwater River, a short distance from Lismore, co. Waterford. Thomas later confirmed that his enemies gave the first charge 'with red banners displayed'. The *Relation of the Fitzgerald's of Ireland* recounts how 'Gerald Fitzgerald gave a violent charge into Ormond's battle of horse, wherein being far entered and having few [supports] about him, he was overthrown from his horse by Ormond's brother [Sir Edmund Butler of Cloughgrenan] who broke his [Desmond's] thigh with a shot from his pistol'.

Desmond became Thomas' prisoner. The rest of the Geraldine army scattered. Overall casualties are not known, but excavations near the battlefield in 1908 uncovered human remains besides the Affane crossroad, four miles east of the village of Cappoquin, on the modern-day N72. As the badly wounded Desmond was being carried, piggy-back, from the field, an Ormond commander rode up and jubilantly inquired, 'Where is now the great Lord Desmond?', whereupon Desmond shouted back, 'Where but in his proper place, on the necks of the Butlers'.

Elizabeth continued to favour Thomas, even after the earl's brief imprisonment in the Tower because of so openly feuding. Upon release, he quickly re-established himself at court, and acted as the queen's chief male escort on state business in 1566, just a year after Affane. The couple's relationship developed to the extent that the queen referred to him, to the scandal of eavesdroppers, by her pet name for him, 'Tom Duff' – even on occasion as her 'black husband', a reference to Thomas' dark complexion, black eyes, hair and beard. If more than simply part of an elaborate court ritual, how intimate they became stayed closely guarded behind bedchamber drapes.

Another serious Irish revolt broke out in April 1569. The rebels (with Geraldine support?) first attacked Clonmel, killing a number of men loyal to Thomas, before switching their attention to Kilkenny town and a number of neighbouring Butler fortresses. By September the rising had been suppressed, but the news of these attacks arrived almost simultaneously with damning reports that agents of Philip of Spain had approached Thomas in order to facilitate a Spanish landing in Ireland. A year later, in 1570, a papal bull would absolve all Englishmen from allegiance to Elizabeth and would legitimize plots to kill her, so the threat from Catholic Ireland was at the time very real. Although implicated, Thomas' reputation remained undimmed in the queen's eyes. She took the Irishman's word that he had given the Spanish messenger short shrift and that the charges against him were malicious, spread by his many enemies. In a letter to her deputy governor in Ireland, she described her favourite as 'a dutiful noble personage, in whom we have ever found trust and fealty towards us and our crown'. She was probably right to do so. Further disturbances in Ireland were crushed by Thomas in 1570 and 1572. To show her appreciation, Elizabeth bestowed on him new estates in eleven counties, as far apart as Dublin and Roscommon.

By now the dominant and favoured peer in Irish politics, Black Tom nevertheless retained a sense of patriotic zeal. He had no brook with English captains who executed Irishmen without trial under the umbrella of martial law. Many thousands of Irishmen may have died in this manner, a number of them probably on the borders of Thomas' estates. Unlike the new English lords, Thomas only ever put to death men who had risen up in arms against him. Tensions between Old English and New English would dog Irish politics in the coming years. Typically, the latter viewed the Gaelic Irish and the Old English as dangerous, making scarce any distinction between them. All were suspect as far as Elizabethan adventurers and colonists were concerned. The English, moreover, persuaded themselves that the Irish were unequal to the task of tilling and manuring the land. They considered them lazy, drunken and heretical. Reports made to Elizabeth's famous spymaster-general, Francis Walsingham, in 1580, likened Ireland to 'an old sock which had been so often mended to now need urgent replacing'. Puritan Thomas Churchyard, in his book *A General Rehearsal of Warres*, applauded 'fear and terror' as a necessary way to handle the Irish. Such views would later serve to dehumanise the Irish in many Englishmen's eyes, an outcome that reflected the way indigenous peoples have been targeted elsewhere in the world when beset by conquerors of a different ethnicity and stronger economic base.

Hostility to the Irish had become official state policy. Well-grounded politically, it is little wonder it festered culturally. A more aggressive colonialism was afoot. Finn McCool might have wakened and reacted with rage had not the Irish anticipated him, stirred to action by the ambitiously ruthless and proudly partisan Shane O'Neill.

*

After the Battle of Faughart, in 1318, having supported Edward Bruce, the MacDonalds of Islay found themselves at odds with the Scots, who viewed the clan as a 'wild and untamed race, primitive and proud, given to plunder and the easy life'. The MacDonald lords disregarded efforts made by successive Scottish kings to integrate them into a mainly law-abiding, tax-paying society. Being remnants of a now defunct Irish heroic age, they also continued to pose a serious security threat to the opening up of the western highlands. By the 1540s, the honorific title Lord of the Isles was formally annexed to the Scottish crown. Further undermining MacDonald authority, loyalist Clan Campbell were allowed to extend their territorial control to incorporate the Western Isles. This triggered an upsurge of migration westward across the North Channel to Antrim.

Despite such reversers, the last great pretender to the lordship of the Isles, Donald Dubh MacDonald, retained his feisty spirit. During England's war with the Scots and the 'rough wooing' of the infant Mary Queen of Scots, Donald sought English support in a bid to recover his patrimony. As late as 1545, he was reported as harrying and slaying Scottish subjects on the west coast of Scotland, assisted by Henry VIII's navy. So successful was he that a reconstituted council of the Isles, comprising his own leading supporters plus the chiefs of the Macleans, MacLeods, MacNeills, Mackinnons and MacQuarries, was reconvened with English support. Meetings were held by the chiefs of these clans on the Isle of Islay, as well as at Carrickfergus Castle, still described throughout the sixteenth-century as 'a garrison of war'. Oaths of allegiance were sworn to Henry VIII by the clan leaders and plans were progressed to assist an English invasion of Scotland. If successful, Donald Dubh would have been rewarded financially with an annual pension and a formal regrant of lost MacDonald lands. With such support he might have restored a semi-independent Gaelic kingdom in the Western Isles: a new Dalriada. He had the wherewithal to back up such an ambition, being credited with bringing 180 war-galleys and 4,000 armed men with him to Ireland and leaving another 4,000 men behind to counter any threat from the Campbells. Had it not been for his sudden death at Drogheda in the winter of 1545, such an aspiration might have been fulfilled.

The establishment of a strong MacDonald presence in Antrim and the upsurge of westward migration from mainland Argyll and the Isles created an inevitable backlash among the more dominant O'Neills. While the Butlers were feuding with the Fitzgeralds in southern Ireland, the O'Neills of Tyrone were flexing their muscles in the north to resist this influx of newcomers from across the North Channel. Had the northerners been united in their efforts, they might have done better in confronting the threat. Rival O'Neill and O'Donnell factions, however, continued to contest the lordship of the north. In a letter to Conn Bacach O'Neill, the Archbishop of Armagh urged that he desist from feuding, saying, 'No longer take delight in wild and barbarous manners [since] it is much better to live in a civilized fashion, than to seek a living by arms and rapine, and to have no thought beyond pleasure and the belly.' As we have seen, Conn Bacach took the archbishop's advice and later submitted to English rule, but his subsequent elevation to an earldom made him widely distrusted in the north of Ireland. The English found it easy to foster discord between him and his sons, in particular Matthew O'Neill, who was elevated by the English to the lordship of Dungannon. A bloodless contest for control of the clan then ensued between Conn, Matthew and a number of his brothers, the most famous being Shane O'Neill. When Conn was later seized and imprisoned by the English, it left the field open for Shane to confront Matthew more openly. Other brothers sided with Shane, a turnaround which allowed the latter to briefly exercise rule in his father's name. Still wary of Matthew and his relations with the English, Shane cosied up to the MacDonalds by marrying Katherine, the daughter of James MacDonald. This had the immediate effect of alerting the English authorities to the threat of a more explosive revolt brewing in the north of Ireland.

In the spring of 1552, Shane marched on Dungannon Castle and seized £800 of treasure, claiming it rightfully belonged to him, igniting the fuse. Sir Thomas Cusack, Ireland's Lord Chancellor, travelled to Ulster to parley with Shane, but, having perceived in the young chieftain an unwarranted level of pride and stubbornness, came away more concerned than when he left. Cusack declared Shane to be a dangerous man, 'bent to do all he could to destroy the poor country'. In the hope that Shane would bow to his father's authority and assist the English in expelling the MacDonalds and their unruly allies from Ulster, the aged and infirm Conn Bacach O'Neill was released from confinement, but conflicting inheritance laws hindered closer cooperation between father and son. Conn Bacach recognised his elder son Matthew as his successor, as did the English, resulting in Shane being sidelined. When Matthew and Conn raised an army in 1554 to attack the MacDonalds, Shane backed the clansmen. With their support, he repelled his father's and brother's attack. The stand Shane took evinced a nationalistic upsurge in the north of Ireland. The young warlord gained widespread support from men long incensed by English colonising encroachment.

Shane's first objective was to overawe and dominate the O'Donnells. By 1557, he had assembled a large army with which he sought to confront them. His camp was described as hero-thronged. Calvagh O'Donnell's opposing army of just thirty horsemen and two companies of Gallowglass managed to storm it nonetheless. Chroniclers spoke of 'killing, destroying, slaughtering, hacking, mangling and mutilating', with weapons 'polished sharp, well-tempered, and keen-edged'. A now desperate Shane managed to escape the bloodbath, swimming across three rivers – the Deele, Finn and Derg – to safety. He left behind his prized warhorse, named the Son of the Eagle (*Mac an Iolair*). No less than the remorse over his lost horse was the dent received to Shane's pride. He might have been toppled from the lordship altogether had not his enemies been at odds. The English government of the ailing Queen Mary was focussed on repelling the encroaching Scots, not to punish inter-clan feuding. Nevertheless, when Shane failed to support the English against ever increasing incursions of Gaels from across the North Channel, they twice burned his capitol at Armagh. The threat posed by the Scots against Ireland was real. In 1558, an army of Scottish adventurers penetrated as far west as Connaught, before being brought to battle beside the River Moy by the Earl of Clanrickard. On this occasion, the earl's mail-clad men-at-arms and artillery made short work of the interlopers. Shane in the meantime orchestrated the assassination of his brother Matthew, and forced his father, Conn Bacach, to flee to Leinster, where he died in the summer of 1559. The English government agreed to recognise Shane's claim to the chieftainship of the O'Neills, but only on condition he bow to the authority of Elizabeth I of England.

The new English queen was of necessity a thrifty woman. She was also wary of undertaking so formidable a task as the military subjugation of the north of Ireland. Her instinct was to fete the northern Irish and charm them into submission. Invited to an audience in London, Shane arrived at the beginning of January 1562, flanked by a bodyguard of Gallowglass. Londoners stood agape at the spectacle of this fierce Gaelic warrior chieftain draped in all his finery and his retinue of tribesman, the latter sporting long, ash-coloured hair trailed over shoulders, clipped short above the eyes, clothed in rough yellow shirts with loose sleeves, short tunics and shaggy lace, armed to the teeth. The English are said to have received them with as much wonderment as if the newcomers had arrived out of China or America. Whether the queen was in such awe of her visitor is unrecorded, but it may be guessed that she could not have been other than attracted to the tall, proud specimen of manhood confronting her, even if she at no time attempted to understand the forbidding and war-wracked world he inhabited.

News reaching court that the Spaniards might seek to come to terms with Shane if the English did not helped the talks run smoother than they otherwise might have done. Realpolitik demanded Elizabeth recognise Shane as *the* O'Neill and accept him as an ally. By direct descent from the Mortimers, Elizabeth could claim the title Countess of Ulster. The old province of Ulaid, where the great John de Courcy had first planted his standard, was hers by right without recourse to any native claim. Nevertheless, Shane boasted that his claim to all Ulster was better than anybody's, saying that he was 'better than the best of them' and that his ancestors were the true kings of Ulster, exclaiming, 'Ulster is mine and shall be mine.' At that moment, the extent of his control in Ireland was indeed quasi-imperial: three counties in Ulster, plus 'the vassalage' of the Maguires, MacMahons and O'Reillys, among others. Although it seems he was willing to accept Elizabeth as sovereign, it was to be on his terms, without the imposition of English laws or foreign norms. The Crown's policy of conciliation with Shane was therefore, with hindsight, always doomed to fail. The proud chieftain was never going to agree to any break-up of the time-honoured O'Neill lordship of the north or to relinquish authority over subsidiary lords who paid him rents. Coercion would become the only practical answer to ridding Ireland of its remaining proud Gaelic lords, of whom Shane was the most dangerous. Intellectuals at London and Dublin toyed with radical solutions, sometimes akin to wholesale ethnic cleansing of the north of Ireland. To help sweeten the pill, when such schemes were presented to the queen, Irishmen like Shane were portrayed as from a primitive race, with 'faces of men, but hearts of beasts'.

The stage was set for a major struggle for control of the north. Shane's immediate enemies were not the English but the neighbouring O'Donnells and the now burgeoning Scottish clans. By the 1560s the Scottish highlanders had re-established a maritime lordship extending from the Mull of Kintyre in the east and across the North Channel to Antrim. Much of the coastline between Coleraine and Louth was occupied or targeted by them. Signal fires on Tor Head could summon MacDonald reinforcements from the Western Isles within a matter of hours. Writing in 1586, the soldier Sir Henry Bagenal confirmed the Scottish clansmen in Ulster were supplied with all they required from their homelands. The queen shared these concerns, concluding, 'If time and other opportunities might serve us, [we should]... suffer no Scot to have any habitation or abode in Ireland.' This was not mere racism: being at loggerheads with her neighbours in the north and on the Continent, Elizabeth had every reason to fear a second front against England arising in Ireland. Encouraged by emissaries of Elizabeth's, Shane attacked the MacDonalds first. By 1 May 1565 he had pinned down a lesser force of Scots under the command of Sorley Buide McDonnell, a man known as Sorley Boy (not for his youth, but his fair hair). Shane confronted McDonnell in Antrim's most northerly glen, Glenshesk. Shane had approximately 2,000 men under arms, and was faced by about half this number.

A new type of fighting man had emerged by this time, known as the Bonnaught; roughly translated, it meant 'billeted men', mercenaries. The Bonnaught emulated the Gallowglass in weaponry and deportment, but were essentially Irishmen, not Hebrideans. In Ulster, the Bonnaughts and Gallowglass are said to have 'thronged from every mountain passage'. Freelance Hebridean mercenaries known as redshanks (a shorthand for Scottish kilted infantry) were also abroad, taking advantage of the rich pickings to be had in the troubled province. Like the Gallowglass, the redshanks were in the main of mixed Gaelic and Norse stock. Gaels called them *Gall-Gael*, or foreign Gaels. Most hailed from Argyll, Lennox and the Hebrides, but a sizeable contingent must also have originated in the Scottish borders, where lowland Scots had been involved in warfare against the English for generations.

Being much sought after during the Elizabethan wars in Ulster, these fighting men commanded a high wage, the equivalent of four pence a day in the 1550s, but this had doubled ten years later. Pay would have been received in kind: cattle, grain, cloth and other goods and services. There was no set uniform for a redshank warrior, nor was there for an equivalent Bonnaught or Gallowglass. Gaelic warrior dress code in the sixteenth century was as much a reflection of climate as of military necessity.

Redshank communities in the north of Ireland wore heavy kilts. The earliest eyewitness account of this, a description of a company of redshanks in the service of the O'Donnells, dates from 1594. An improvement in looms in the sixteenth century had allowed for more elaborate patterns and density of wool than hitherto. The original name for the weave was Clo-Mor, or 'big cloth'.

Of the Battle of Glenshesk, Shane later wrote, 'Early the next morning [22 May] we advanced upon them in battle array, and the fight was furiously maintained on both sides.' Shane's secretary added that the battle commenced just after dawn, around five o'clock, and that his master's forces overthrew the MacDonalds and captured many of their standards, enough for some 900 Gallowglass. Between 300 and 500 MacDonald clansmen may have fallen in the fighting. The victors claimed 700 killed, but English commentators considered this to be an exaggeration. Twenty-three gentlemen of quality were captured, including Sorley Boy McDonnell. More noteworthy was the mortal wounding of Sorley Boy's father, James MacDonald of Dunyvaig, who died while captive. Rumours would spread that Shane had had James murdered; a damning claim, since no Scot worth his salt could ever forgive the killing of so great and respected a man. Glenshesk halted further Scots inroads into Ireland by immobilising the survivors in Antrim. The Scottish recovery was further hampered by Shane's decision to colonise the Glens and drive off those settled there, an unprecedented tactic for a Gaelic chieftain; one that emulated the English and Scots at their worst, but was in tune with Shane's high ambition.

Shane's success did, however, have the unwarranted effect of reducing his immediate usefulness to the English government, which, cynically, ceased supporting him. In response, Shane attacked English garrisons at Newry and Dundrum. He then turned on northern Connaught to reassert his overlordship there. By the turn of the year 1565/6, Shane's fame had reached its high point. The Scottish and French governments saw him as a potential ally against Elizabeth. Shane in turn felt assured enough to request troops from Charles IX of France to help him expel the English from Ireland.

It was this threat of foreign intervention which finally persuaded Elizabeth to work towards Shane's destruction. A letter dated to early 1566, from Lord Deputy Henry Sidney to the Earl of Leicester, read, 'I believe Lucifer was never puffed up with more pride nor ambition than that one [O'Neill].' Sidney is quoted as saying Ireland was a place 'cursed, hated and detested' by him because of Shane. He railed at Shane's growing military strength. At the time of writing, this comprised a bodyguard of 600 Gallowglass and Bonnaught and a field army of 1,000 horse and 4,000 foot; an increasingly armed and equipped peasantry backed them up. Sidney reported that Shane 'furnished all the peasants and husbandmen of his country with armour and weapons, and trained them up in the knowledge of the wars'. Historians have drawn from this that Shane was making a major departure from normal practice, since in the past the tillers of the soil and the drovers of cattle had remained unarmed, rarely joining in hostings.

Opinion differs over Shane's standing as a general. Sir George Carew saw him as a 'prudent, wise captain, while others claimed he was 'the last to charge and first to flee' (which is not necessarily a contradiction in terms). Against Gaelic opposition, Shane was ready for a fight in the open, but when against government forces he either backed down or relied on methods more redolent of the Irish against the Normans, relying on traps and ambuscade. Elizabeth was convinced that O'Neill – described by her now as a 'cankrid, dangerous rebel' – must be eliminated. She reinforced Sidney with newly levied men from Somerset, Devon and the Scottish borders and ordered the commencement of offensive operations against Shane at harvest-time 1566. Timing was calibrated to inflict maximum damage on the O'Neill economy.

Sidney's army comprised 300 horse, 1,200 archers and arquebusiers, 300 Gallowglass and 92 gunners. Although Shane could not be lured into the open to fight, his lands and crops were razed and his forces dispersed. Sidney also installed Shane's rival, Calvagh O'Donnell, to rule in modern-day Donegal, garrisoned Derry with a strong force, and then marched into Connaught. Attempts by Shane to retake Derry Town were rebuffed. Although ultimately successful in neutralising the English threat, Shane was severely weakened, having lost a number of his best foot soldiers to battle, disease and desertion. Laden down with booty, many Scots are said to have left his service. Undeterred, Shane sought a showdown with the O'Donnells. By this time, Calvagh had died and had been replaced by his brother Hugh, a man who appears to have remained unintimidated by Shane, despite being outnumbered. The civil war in the North showed no sign of slacking. In the spring of 1567, Hugh O'Neill harried the region around Strabane, on the east bank of the River Foyle. Shane tracked him back to Letterkenny, co. Donegal. Nearby, on the west bank of the River Swilly, Calvagh O'Donnell drew up his small force on boggy ground to await attack. Shane's army drew up on the east bank of the river, beside a fording point at Farsetmore, the place the coming battle would be named after. O'Donnell cavalry disputed the O'Neills' crossing, but were driven back by superior numbers. The Irish horsemen were armoured in mail with iron helmets, described as 'hardy men on small horses'. They rode on pads without stirrups and held their lance overarm when charging. The Irish infantry at Farsetmore can have differed little from those who fought to the death at Knockdoe more than half a century earlier. Commentators who wished to glorify the O'Donnells claimed just a few hundred fighting men mustered on the boggy ground north of the Letterkenny to Dunfanaghy road, and that they faced a much more numerous foe.

Rather than a battle, Farsetmore was little more than a rout. In a repeat of the surprise attack launched by his brother ten years earlier, Hugh's small army, described as a 'venomous phalanx', fell upon Shane's forces on 8 May and slew most of those in camp. The choice made to fight by Sir Hugh was said to have been, in the circumstances, 'bold, daring, obdurate, and irrational'. Military historian Cyril Falls has seen the action as 'not so much a battle as a killing', implying surprise followed by a massacre. An English observer on the day reported 613 dead bodies. Many of Shane's fighters who fled the fight were overcome by the tide when attempting to cross the Swilly Estuary. Other bodies may have been swept away by currents. Adding credence to the claim Shane was first to flee when disaster threatened, he managed to escape. Presumably he had a horse waiting at the ready. Having now twice been surprised in camp and forced to run surely undermined any claim of military acumen on Shane's part. That he became little better than a desperado, rapidly running out of luck, is better attested. When seeking refuge among the MacDonalds, they repaid him for the suspected murder of their leader James of Dunyvaig by cutting him down with their 'slaughter-swords ... mangling him cruelly'. His head was cut off and sent, pickled, to Dublin. Many men later claimed to have finished off the outlaw. One man who might have known the truth, Sir John Davies, the Irish Attorney-General, considered Shane's death a mere accident, the result of a drunken brawl. Sidney succinctly summed up by saying Shane's end was hard enough 'but not sufficient for his deserts'.

II

THE GALL AND MISERY OF
ALL EVIL MEN

Before his death, Shane had eliminated his brothers and anyone else he considered a threat. One person he failed to eliminate, however, was his cousin, Turlough Luineach O'Neill, a direct descendant of Niall of the Nine Hostages and also of Brian O'Neill, the high-king aspirant killed at the Battle of Downpatrick in 1260. Not until Shane's defeat at the hands of the O'Donnells at Farsetmore did Turlough dare to fully assert himself. Shane's murder then quickly propelled him to the O'Neill lordship. The out-of-favour Elizabethan Sir Henry Sidney may have backed Turlough as part of a proposed establishment of an Ulster presidency, but this is by no means certain. One of Turlough's first acts upon gaining the lordship was to contract a new alliance with the O'Donnells. Elsewhere, intermarriage smoothed acceptance of his title. One of his daughters was presented in marriage to Rory, chief of the MacQuillans. Turlough himself gained the promise of betrothal to Agnes Campbell, the wife of the late James MacDonald of Dunyvaig. The match served to ally the thirty-seven-year-old Turlough with a network of important men in Antrim, Argyll and the Isles. Already twice or thrice married, the formidable Agnes commanded the services of 'multitudinous redshanks'. The marriage ceremony took place in August 1569. Shortly afterwards Turlough was credited with an army of 3,000

Scottish mercenaries plus thousands of Irish kern and Gallowglass. Although difficult to maintain, this military build-up proved sufficient to deter English colonists from making unwarranted inroads west of the River Bann.

Turlough sought to agree a territorial settlement with the English from a position of strength. Unfortunately for peace in Ulster, the English prevaricated. Making matters worse, Sidney had returned to Ireland in 1568 determined to abolish once and for all the practice of 'Coign and Livery' in the north of Ireland. Its demise would deprive Gaelic warlords of their wherewithal to make war on the Crown, and was therefore a direct attack on the by now powerful Turlough. The bill to outlaw the practice in the north of Ireland was presented at the first parliament to be convened at Dublin since 1560. Other bills dealt with the raising of new taxes to fund the implementation of government policy. Another outcome of Sidney's return was the forcing of Turlough to accept a resurrected fiefdom on his doorstep, that of the barony of Dungannon, to be occupied by the teenaged Hugh O'Neill, the brother of an earlier baron, murdered on Turlough's orders while Shane was still alive. This was a serious reverse for Turlough, who had aimed to maintain a discrete overlordship. His fiefdom would now be demarcated in the south by the River Blackwater. All these measures when taken together (albeit not all were passed) have since been described as a series of policies designed to advance the anglicization of the north of Ireland. This may be true; they also led to renewed warfare.

It seems members of the Irish parliament distrusted Sidney not to favour English adventurers at the expense of the Irish in both the north and south of Ireland, fearing it to be the prelude to a large-scale 'sponsored takeover'. One such adventurer was Sir Peter Carew. His attempted seizure of extensive estates in Meath, Cork and Carlow, some of which are said to have comprised the most 'pleasant, sweet and fruitful land' in all of Ireland, resulted in an upsurge of warfare in the region. A fraught conveyance of lands in direct contravention of Gaelic custom resulted in an unnatural alliance of Butlers and Fitzgeralds against him. Carew's horsemen sacked the Butler castle at Clogrennan in Carlow. Garrison troops, women and children included, were massacred. The castle still stands today, a grim, ivy-smothered ruin, with gaping windows gazing sightless on cloud-wreathed mountains to the east. Too long a stay, especially on a day of blustery winds and chasing clouds with shapes redolent of the banshee Morrighan, will, it is claimed, leave a lasting chill on the heart of any visitor.

Elizabeth I became gravely concerned when hearing news of this upsurge in violence across the Irish Sea. Carew was recalled to court in 1570 to answer charges that his too-vigorous pursuit of private gain had damaged relations between the Crown's justiciar and the native Irish elite, but by then the damage had been done. The ante was raised two years later when an upsurge of militant Catholicism on the Continent resulted in the St Bartholomew Day massacre of French Calvinist Protestants, known as Huguenots. Fear of a similar upsurge of violence in England speeded plans to colonise Ulster. Private entrepreneurs, like Walter Devereaux, Earl of Essex, were in the vanguard of these efforts. Essex described his objectives in the north of Ireland to settle a province up until then oppressed by 'the gall and misery of all evil men' in the country. He portrayed his mission in the manner of a social crusade, claiming that the plantation of English families would be both economically and ethically beneficial. Essex was allocated much of Antrim, all save for the great fortress at Carrickfergus, which remained under the queen's control. The economic incentive for carpetbaggers like Essex was a substantial tax-free period while these lands in Ulster were secured, plus trade with England free from tariffs and duties and Crown support in fortifying the region. In Essex's case, to kick start the scheme Elizabeth loaned the earl £10,000 against the security of his English landholdings. Essex reckoned on an annual profit of £5,000 from plantation rents. He felt comfortable that the debt could be repaid within the three-year term set. Another man at the forefront of these affairs was Thomas Smith, who earmarked lands between modern-day Belfast and Strangford Lough in Down for settlement. He and Essex employed soldiers with previous experience of warfare in

Ulster. The thirty-three year-old pirate, Francis Drake, captain of the warship *Falcon*, was among them. His earlier raids on Spanish outposts and shipping had already yielded booty worth in excess of £100,000, so he was a very rich man by this time. Some of this looted wealth was now planned for investment in Ireland.

The expedition had an inauspicious start. Essex's fleet of ships suffered a battering when setting sail from Liverpool on 19 July 1573. Many craft became dispersed. Some were driven by winds as far south as Cork. Essex managed to make landfall at Carrickfergus. He then summoned the Ulster chieftains, promising them that his sole objective was to oust the Scots not to encroach on the chieftains' own lands. Given the network of alliances between Gaelic Irish and the Scots, this approach was hardly likely to succeed. The spirit of the Fianna had by this time been awakened. A fierce attack on the English made by the Irish in mid-October resulted in the death of Thomas Smith; the Irish are said to have later boiled his body and fed it to their dogs. Fear of further raids – and perhaps a similar fate – soon drove Essex's men to desert, a problem compounded by outbreaks of plague and an uncertain supply chain. Essex was forced to press-gang men into his employ and also to plead for additional funding from the queen. He recklessly backed up his request by promising never to abandon the enterprise while he had lands in England to mortgage.

Among those at Dublin who opposed the Ulster plantation was Elizabeth's Lord Deputy in Ireland, the ague-wracked William Fitzwilliam. Fitzwilliam had good reason to appeal for caution. In the spring of 1568 he had led an unsuccessful sortie into Ulster, so knew the difficulties involved. He once described Ireland as 'a disease which grievously eats inwardly to the waste of all the stuff applied unto the same'. He supported colonisation and what we might term social engineering but was wary of private enterprise projects over which he had little control and for which he might bear responsibility if things went wrong. Like other Englishmen of his generation, he believed that only 'fear and force' could bring such 'rebellious people' as the Gaels to heel, but recognised that the limited resources available to him made this virtually impossible to achieve. Fitzwilliam's attempts to downsize Essex's plans were countered by the queen, who instead rewarded Essex with the promise of the governorship of Ulster and ordered Fitzwilliam to make men available. Only a miserly handful of Gallowglass were in the end provided. Essex nevertheless mustered what forces he could. He then carried out a murderous offensive against the Clandeboye O'Neills in Down. From there he raided Tyrone, burning crops and harrying the populace. But without permanent fortified outposts Essex was powerless to make lasting inroads. More worryingly, while at Carrickfergus his soldiers were dying of disease at the rate of more than fifteen a day. Essex shared his men's suffering. His methods and morality can be questioned, but his personal courage cannot.

Forced to resort to subterfuge, Essex invited the heads of the Clandeboye O'Neills, including Brian mac Phelim O'Neill, his wife Anne and brother Hugh, to a conference. He also held out an invitation for his guests to spend the Christmas of 1574 with him at Belfast. At the time Belfast was a small hamlet, clustered beside a fording place on the River Lagan. The O'Neills must have been sufficiently confident that their past misdemeanours had been set aside to attend, but they were wrong. At some point during the banquet, Essex signalled his troops to pounce. Many of Brian's retainers were slaughtered where they sat. Brian, his wife and brother were seized and later executed at Dublin Castle. Each suffered hanging and quartering. These judicial killings are referred to today as 'the Betrayal of Clannabuidhe'. Essex boasted that he had succeeded in breaking the resolve of those opposing him, but the infamy the murders attracted hardened resolve among native Irish to oppose future colonising programmes.

An even more appalling episode followed when Essex sent a naval force, comprising 300 foot soldiers and 80 horsemen in three frigates under the command of Sir John Norris and Sir Francis Drake, to Rathlin Island, off the north coast of Antrim. A one-time home of St Columba, Rathlin Island was also the site of an early Viking attack. Today, the island has around 150 inhabitants, but in the sixteenth century it is thought to have been more densely populated, mainly by members of Clan Donald and their affiliate septs. A two-day siege of the castle on Rathlin resulted. Fifty defenders and an unknown number of civilians were put to the sword; an outcome, arguably, within the bounds of sixteenth-century military protocol, since a fortress which refused to yield to reasonable terms when offered was considered fair game for retribution. The subsequent hunting down and slaughtering of around 300 non-combatants (old men, women and children) from caves around the island was, however, carried out with inhumane disregard for the rules of war. Sorley Boy McDonnell is said to have witnessed the killing of his wife and children, remaining all the while powerless to intervene. In retaliation, Sorley sacked Carrickfergus, seized cattle, and killed one hundred of Essex's soldiers.

*

The Rathlin Island massacre today is remembered as a war-crime of heinous proportions, but was at the time applauded by the English. Elizabeth wrote to Essex in September 1575 to relieve him of any anxiety he might have harboured regarding his conduct in Ulster. Even a cultured Renaissance monarch like Elizabeth appears to have condoned draconian measures when eradicating enemies she may have considered barbarous. When Essex complained of the emotional and physical toll the expedition was taking on him, she replied, 'You may think it has been a dear [an expensive] conquest to you, in respect of the great care of mind, toil of body, and intolerable charges you have sustained ... but you have invested yourself with immortal renown.' She was wrong on a number of counts: the massacre and Sorley Boy's retribution marked the conclusion of Essex's attempt to pacify and settle Ulster and left an indelible stain on his reputation. What is more, his campaign had proved a costly failure – the Crown had sunk in excess of £100,000 in the venture. By raising finance, the earl had lost much of his patrimony. Far from becoming a fast-growing plantation of settler families, Sir Henry Sidney, the queen's Lord Deputy, reported the province remained largely uninhabited. Sorley Boy's territories, on the other hand, were described as full of ripe corn and fattened cattle. Sorley Boy himself was said to have remained very haughty and proud.

At some point it seems the ever pragmatic Sidney came to terms with McDonnell and returned Rathlin Island and the Glens of Antrim to his charge. This was done despite concern at Dublin and London that the Gaelic warlord would seek to expand his control by bringing across from the Isles and from mainland Scotland a further influx of redshanks. Partly for this reason, after a spell back in England, Essex was once again despatched to Ireland, now with the title Earl Marshal. That Essex resented the appointment is indicated by his plea to the queen not to wear out his youth in such a place as Ireland. His appeal was more prescient than he can have imagined. He died at Dublin, aged thirty-seven, two months later, on 22 September 1576. It was said his natural strength had become much diminished by dysentery, known in the sixteenth century as the bloody flux. His career had ended early and in failure, his schemes had proved ill-judged and under-resourced. Insufficient cognisance had been taken by him of the fierce resistance likely to be faced from displaced Gaels. Essex had also been badly served by the queen, who had chopped and changed her mind, and by Fitzwilliam, who consistently denied him material support.

A year later, another massacre in Ireland was perpetrated, this time of Irish gentry by the English army. Members of leading Irish families from modern-day county Laois were summoned by Sidney to the Rath of Mullaghmast, co. Kildare. Most were then slaughtered. Little is really known of the affair. The *Annals of the Four Masters* speak of 'a horrible and abominable act of treachery', adding that the victims were, 'surrounded on every side by four lines of soldiers and cavalry, who proceeded to shoot and slaughter them without mercy, so that not a single individual escaped'. By tradition, rain or dew would never again fall on the Rath of Mullaghmast. The killings are said to have irreparably damaged the trust of the Irish in the English and in Sidney specifically. Sidney had by the time of the killings in Kildare come to an accommodation of sorts with Turlough O'Neill in the north. The two men met at Armagh and agreed a treaty whereby Turlough would disband his private army, save for his Campbells, in return for an English peerage as Earl of Clan O'Neill and Baron Clogher, albeit only for life. It seems Turlough was a heavy drinker and in Sidney's estimation was not likely to live long. In the end, nothing came of these promises. Sidney was recalled to England in the autumn of 1578. Complaints about the Lord Deputy's brutality and intransigence may have hastened this. He is said to have left a land united in anger against him.

In 1582, the dyed-in-the-wool rebel Sorley Boy McDonnell amassed a 2,000-strong army of redshanks to support a Gaelic rising in Connaught. Finally out of patience with him, the decision was made at Dublin to crush him and his clan once and for all. First, however, the Clandeboye O'Neills and the MacQuillans, supported by seventy regular English soldiers armed with muskets, were tasked to fall on the remaining Antrim Scots in Sorley Boy's absence and to kill or drive them back to Scotland. In the face of this attack, Sorley Boy's nephew, Angus of Dunyvaig, shepherded what refugees he could back across the North Channel. In the spring of the following year, having returned from Connaught, Sorley Boy assembled a small army and confronted the invaders, drawn up on a broad ridge at the base of Slieve-na-Orra (modern-day Slieveanorra) in Antrim, a mountain which rises to almost 1,700 feet.

The traditional account of the battle envisages the McDonnells luring the O'Neills from the hillside by spreading a carpet of rushes across the bog to allow the ingress of their own light horse. When the McDonnells feigned retreat back across the artificial causeway, having launched a half-hearted attack, the heavier O'Neill horsemen pursued them and became bogged down. Trapped in this way, Hugh McFelim is said to have begged for his life, saying to his assailant that he would give him all the young horses of Clandeboye as a ransom, to which the other replied, 'I would rather go on foot.' Leaders of the small Anglo-Irish force were hunted down and killed near the summit of Slieve-na-Orra; others sought refuge on a crannog in Lough Gile, but were slaughtered by men who pursued them by swimming across. All seventy English musketeers and two of their captains died during the fighting. Sorley Boy took no part in the battle. He was probably well into his seventies by this time. Not only were his days numbered, so too was the toehold of independence he and his men had strived to maintain for so long.

The following year, Sir John Perrot, Ireland's new Lord Deputy, recommenced hostilities against the McDonnells. Perrot was said to closely resemble Henry VIII in height, looks and temperament and was rumoured to be the king's unacknowledged bastard son. Inheriting also his natural father's massive ego, rather than deport himself as a mere knight, he posed as a man of much higher rank, having in train thirty-four servants, all kitted out in his family's distinctive livery: a parrot with a pear in its claw. He himself was a fierce, clawed creature too. Over a decade earlier, while campaigning in Munster, Perrot had intimidated the Irish insurgents by having the heads of fifty rebels affixed to the market cross at Kilmallock, co. Limerick. During Perrot's presidency of Munster, not only did he crush rebellions, he also authorised over 800 hangings.

Adding to Perrott's problems with the McDonnells, in the summer of 1584 several thousand Scots, mainly Macleans, invaded Donegal in an attempt to reassert the overlordship of one of the sons of the late Shane O'Neill. Turlough's son Art joined the rebels in an attempt to salvage something from the shipwreck of his father's lordship. Having fallen into an alcohol-induced coma the year before, inaccurate reports of Turlough's death had encouraged Hugh, Baron Dungannon, to cross the Blackwater with an armed force and to occupy the seat of the O'Neill's at Tullahoge. Although Turlough, after a heavy hangover, briefly reasserted himself, the Maclean/McShane incursions and his own predilection for beverage forced him to cede much of his authority and rely on Perrot's Elizabethan forces to break the back of the invasion. A much diminished Turlough would live on until 1595, before dying, an outcast, at the age of sixty-five.

Against this growing tide of change and Perrott's superior army, Sorley Boy was both disheartened and outmanoeuvred and forced to retreat back across the channel to Scotland. He did return on two separate occasions to renew the fight, but by the spring of 1586 was reduced to seeking terms with Perrot. Queen Elizabeth was by then pushing her Lord Deputy hard to quickly come to an agreement in the north of Ireland. Her orders were for Perrott to make 'some reasonable composition' with the McDonnells. Both Sorley Boy and Angus of Dunyvaig submitted soon after this on favourable terms. Entering Dublin Cathedral, Sorley Boy is said to have thrown his sword at the feet of a portrait of the queen, then kissed the picture and sworn his allegiance. He knew his day was done. For his pains, he received a grant of lands between Ballycastle and Coleraine and the constableship of Dunluce Castle. One of his sons was left behind at Dublin as a hostage, to ensure his father's continued good behaviour. This was hardly necessary. Sorley Boy's death occurred in January 1590, aged eighty-plus. His warlike spirit and example to others had ensured that, despite the Crown's best efforts, the McDonnells and other Antrim Scots from Ulster managed to retain their foothold there. In great numbers their forebears attest to this fact to the present day.

Elsewhere, Elizabethan reaction after two failed risings in Munster, known as the Desmond Rebellions, resulted in the first great mass plantations of settlers in Ireland, far outstripping the early settlement efforts made in the Irish midlands during the reign of Mary Tudor. The risings occurred in two phases: the first between the years 1569 and 1573, the second six years later. Attempts to restore the Catholic Mass in towns captured by Crown forces may have been the catalyst for the violence. The south-west of Ireland was set aflame, Protestants were roughly handled and many expelled from the region. Sir John Perrot complained that for every white hair he had brought to Ireland he now had fifty. Perrot's resulting 'reign of terror' in Munster would, as previously mentioned, yield a crop of 800 hanged corpses, not counting those who died of hunger or wounds. Much of the fighting centred on the area around Kilmallock, co. Limerick. Assaulted on numerous occasions, the town was finally burned to the ground by the English. The castle at Castlemaine, situated on the south-west coast of modern-day county Kerry, fell in the summer of 1572, but only after the sacking of Derrinlaur Castle, on the River Suir, where the rebel garrison was put to the sword, did the insurgents finally seek terms.

Englishman Sir Philip Carew summed up the context of the animosity, declaring, 'This realm was never so dismembered, owing to the quarrel upon religion.' He was one of Ireland's foremost roughnecks, who backed up his land grants with his sword. Carew's claim to half of the county of Cork (which had been Desmond territory from time immemorial) had sparked the first Desmond rebellion.

In the autumn of 1580, during the second so-called Desmond Rebellion, when England was at war with Spain, 600 Catholic troops from Spain, Portugal and Italy, commanded by Sebastiano di San Giuseppe, landed at Smerwick, co. Kerry. The invasion was the precursor of future, larger Spanish expeditions designed to support the Catholic Irish against the colonising Protestant English. The mission had been paid for and sent by Pope Gregory XIII. English warships blockaded them upon landing and put ashore forces, which bottled them up in a nearby fort at Dún an Óir. The fort proved to be a deathtrap for the invaders, who, lacking firewood, suffered dreadfully from the biting cold and wet and were eventually forced to burn their ships to keep warm. Heavy guns landed by the English belched fire upon them at the beginning of November, demoralising them further. The bottled-up invaders surrendered a week later. Four hundred Italians, Spaniards, Basques and others were then put to the sword. The English are said to have fallen to revelling, despoiling and killing, even though a white flag had been raised by their victims. All the Irish taken, including women and children, were hanged. Among the executioners was Sir Walter Raleigh. Only one English soldier is known to have died during the siege, but many more likely succumbed to disease and the inclement weather.

It is estimated that several thousand Irish died in battle during the two Desmond conflicts. Worse, a scorched earth policy enacted on Irish lands and cattle in Munster became a harbinger of famine and pestilence. Food stocks were soon exhausted and the harvest remained unreaped in Munster for lack of labour. Famished people were described in gruesome detail by an early supporter of Irish genocide, the author Edmund Spenser:

> Out of every corner of the wood and glens they came creeping forth upon their hands, for their legs could not bear them; they looked like anatomies [of] death, they spoke like ghosts crying out of their graves; they did eat of the carrions, happy where they could find them, yea, and one another soon after, in so much as the very carcasses they spared not to scrape out of their graves; and if they found a plot of water-cresses or shamrocks, there they flocked as to a feast for the time, yet not able long to continue therewithal; that in a short space there were none almost left, and a most populous and plentiful country suddenly left void of man or beast.

Modern estimates reckon on an overall death toll in Ireland approaching 50,000 from these times. Queen Elizabeth's spymaster-general Francis Walsingham declared it a just outcome, brought on by the Irish themselves. Depopulated Munster became a draw for colonists from England and Wales. Half a million acres of land were allocated. The target was for 15,000 new arrivals, but as late as 1589 only 700 tenants had taken up the offer. Reports dated to that year estimated 3,000 men, women and children. All had to be protected by militia, but by the 1590s, for reasons of economy, such protection was abolished. When warfare again erupted, most new settlers were chased from their lands without putting up a fight. They either sought the protection of the few walled towns under English rule or took ship back to England. A later report described the planters as plain country gentlemen, the implication being that they were unable to defend themselves and therefore easily scared off when threatened by the Irish. Not until the early seventeenth century did the plantations in Munster again get under way. Rather than respectable, hard-working pioneers, those attracted to come were more often rogues, misfits and vagabonds. Because of this, of the area designated for planting in Munster by 1611, onethird was reallocated to native farmers, not newcomers. Intermarriage between settlers and the native Irish served to dilute the impact of the planting even further.

The man who was to lead the revolt that most nearly succeeded in stemming the tide of English encroachment for good was Hugh O'Neill, 2nd Earl of Tyrone, who, when last mentioned, was merely Baron Dungannon, Turlough O'Neill's neighbour and rival. He had by this time succeeded his drink-afflicted cousin to the earldom of Tyrone as part of the more extensive political reforms undertaken by Sir John Perrot. That such a man as Hugh O'Neill (known henceforth in the narrative as Tyrone) should be driven to revolt against a status quo that should have favoured him underlines the incompetence of the English administrators and the clumsiness with which they sought to achieve their ends. Tyrone through judicious manoeuvres held 'a palatine jurisdiction' over his domains, in a manner only enjoyed elsewhere by the likes of the Ormonds in Tipperary. Gaining favour from the Elizabethan authorities, he dealt harshly with enemies of the Crown: men like the MacShanes and Macleans, who, as we have seen, had for a time made problems for the Crown by introducing a steady influx of redshanks into the north of Ireland. In another display of loyalty, when a number of the warships from the great Spanish Armada were beached or wrecked by storms along the Irish coast in 1588, Tyrone executed as many as 500 of the survivors, gaining the plaudits of the queen.

Elizabeth, on the advice of her ministers, had declared it treasonable to offer any survivor of the Armada aid. She feared any

Spanish landings on the west coast of Ireland to be a vanguard of invasion and likened the island to an albatross around England's neck, stating, 'The like burden and charge is not found in any place in Christendom.' In the spring of 1586, Francis Walsingham, Elizabeth's spy-master, had provided a copy of an official Spanish memorandum to Elizabeth, which detailed an earlier Spanish invasion plot against England. A fleet of 206 warships, 60,000 troops and 200 landing craft (barges) had been projected for the directive. They would sail from a variety of Spanish ports to Ireland, where they would be bolstered by the rebels. The plans were not taken seriously but perhaps should have been, since they were, if nothing else, an indication of Ireland's strategic value to a foreign invader. On this occasion Philip of Spain's attentions were diverted when dynastic union with Portugal gained a higher priority on his 'to do' list.

The following year, however, overwhelming evidence of Spanish intent to invade heightened tensions at Westminster, and there was renewed focus on Ireland's defences. Walsingham, despite ill-health, was at the centre of these preparations. But not until the Armada's actual arrival off Land's End in late July could Walsingham be sure that, in his own words, '[Spain's] whole plot and design was against the City of London', not a landing in Ireland.

With respect to Elizabeth's orders to allow no beached Spaniard in Ireland to live, not all Irish grandees obeyed. One man who ignored Elizabeth was the Irish chieftain and rebel Sir Brian O'Rourke. Captain Francisco de Cuellar of the wrecked *San Pedro* later spoke of the Irishman as a very good Christian and an enemy of heretics, and Philip of Spain wrote to O'Rourke thanking him for the succour he had provided to his subjects at great risk. Sir Henry Sidney claimed O'Rourke to be 'the proudest man I have ever dealt with in Ireland'. Bingham referred to him as 'a proud beggar', so out of touch with reality that he thought the queen of England to be frightened of him. Another description of O'Rourke pictured him as 'learned, but indolent'. Once, when having come across an image of a tall woman in a church, he scrawled the name Elizabeth across the breasts, assaulted it with insults, and called the queen an 'old calliagh hag'. He then had his McCabe bodyguard drag the panel through the mud.

Captain de Cuellar saw at first hand the way the indigenous Irish lived in Mayo, describing their lifestyle as primitive in comparison with the peasantry of Spain, but praising the men as big, handsome, well-built and fleet as the deer. He mentions them being dressed in 'short, loose coats of very coarse goat's hair'. In inclement weather, 'they wrapped themselves in blankets and wore their hair long, down to their eyes … they eat but one meal a day [bread, of an oaten kind, and butter] and drink sour milk; on feast days, half-cooked meat, without salt.' He described the women as 'pretty, but poorly dressed, wearing nothing but a shift and a cloak over it [and] a linen cloth, much folded, on their heads, tied in front'. He enjoyed the spectacle and company of O'Rourke's 'comely wife', perhaps in the manner a man who had spent months at sea well might. He also commented on the Gaelic penchant for robbing their neighbours, a competitive outlet for aspirant warriors; the objective being to carry off by night as many of their rivals' cattle as they could, leading to fights which at times proved fatal. He added, 'When the English learn of the whereabouts of the rustled cows, they swoop down, drive them off and seize the spoils.'

Despite isolated examples of cruelty, such as when a huge Gallowglass warrior named Melaghlin McCabe allegedly hacked eighty defenceless Spanish sailors to death while they struggled to wade ashore, the Irish typically treated their uninvited guests with kindness, sometimes at great risk to themselves, but also on occasion for a price. One account from a small group of officers from the *Valencera*, which ran aground off the Donegal coast in mid-September 1588, mentions them being confronted by 'twenty savage people', the vanguard of many more inquisitive natives, who systematically stripped the Spaniards of their possessions in return for food, water and the promise to provide boats to ferry those still aboard the *Valencera* to safety. Four hundred soldiers and sailors were saved before the stricken ship broke in two on the rocks. Captain Francisco De Cuellar witnessed the devastation. At Streedagh Strand, co. Sligo, he watched ravens and wild dogs feeding on Spanish corpses. At a nearby church he discovered the bodies of twelve hanged Spaniards littering the stalls, killed by the English or their Irish enforcers. Sorley Boy McDonnell was one who risked the wrath of the predatory English and a traitor's death to help survivors of the Armada. He proudly made good his promise not to barter Christian lives by shipping boat-loads of men washed up in Ireland to Scotland. Approximately 3,750 Spaniards, Greeks and Italians and upwards of sixteen ships were lost at sea during this period of intense autumn storms sweeping in from the Atlantic, and this may not include the 1,500 or so killed outright by Tyrone and English forces.

Meanwhile, growing distrust at Westminster of the Earl of Tyrone echoed earlier fears felt by medieval kings toward men like Strongbow, William Marshal and John de Courcy. The earl had become too big and powerful in the north for the Crown's comfort. What is more, he was proving to be a difficult man to deal with. He has since been represented by historian R. F. Foster as the 'Janus-face of Ireland'; both ambivalent and elusive; a Gaelic hero on the one hand, and a 'temporising politician' on the other. Tyrone's English contemporary William Campden once declared himself to be tired of pursuing Tyrone 'through all his shifts and devices'. Elizabeth's Lieutenant-General in Ireland, Sir Henry Bagenal, described by a contemporary as 'a greedy, restless, rapacious and unscrupulous adventurer', more damagingly for Tyrone complained that the earl was all the while in covert communication with the Spanish. There were also personal reasons for the Englishman's antipathy to the earl. A serial womaniser, Tyrone had eloped with Bagenal's twenty-year-old sister Mabel. The distraught knight is said to have cried out, 'I can but accurse myself and fortune that my blood should now mingle with so traitorous a stock and kindred.' Tyrone, in turn, claimed Bagenal ever sought to undermine him, yet the two men somehow managed to rub along together and keep the peace in Ulster – until October 1593 that is, when a great battle was fought at Belleek, co. Fermanagh. At Belleek, Tyrone's pikemen and musketeers, fighting alongside Bagenal's similarly armed English forces, defeated more traditionally armed and equipped kern and Gallowglass of the rebel Sir Hugh Maguire, lord of Fermanagh. Sir Hugh Maguire was Tyrone's son-in-law. He had married one of Tyrone's daughters the year before the battle. It was a match since described as one strand in a tight and complex network of family connections created by Tyrone.

Maguire's rebellion followed several years of predatory encroachment into the north-west by Sir Richard Bingham, president of Connaught. Maguire may have been acting as a frontrunner for Tyrone, perhaps a stalking-horse for his father-in-law, set loose to test English resolve. Tyrone's involvement in the early phases of the war remained marginal. Sir Philip Holles described Maguire's decision to entrench himself on an indifferently fortified island on the River Erne as surprising. The ford beside the island was broad enough for cavalry and infantry to cross unmolested. Maguire suffered approximately 400 casualties in the resulting action, almost half his army strength. Bagenal's and Tyrone's losses were slight. Leaders suffered disproportionately. Tyrone incurred a pike-thrust to his thigh; Bagenal emerged from the battle badly bruised from the flat blade of a Gallowglass axe.

In a reversal of fortunes, on 7 August 1594 Maguire ambushed an English column at Drumane Ford and killed or wounded in excess of 120 English soldiers and wagon-masters. Provisions were seized, earning the battlefield the name 'the Ford of the Biscuits'. The following year, Maguire and his allies raided south into Breifne, part of which comprised modern-day county Longford, an area sometimes referred to as 'the Gap of the North'. Through it, Redshanks and Bonnaught travelled southward into wild Connaught in search of paymasters. English-held Enniskillen Castle was recovered by Maguire in May. Tyrone's momentous decision to switch sides away from the English and back his son-in-law can perhaps be dated to this event. From then on fighting a defensive war, Tyrone hoped to undermine further colonising efforts. Elizabeth I was by now an old woman, described unkindly as grown prematurely old with 'a goggle throat and a great gullet hanging out'. Her advisers were also old and worn out through years of service. The queen's death could not be long away. James, king of Scots, her likely successor, described as a pacific man, might have come to terms with Tyrone. Spanish intervention might have also been a factor, something doubtless counted on by the now rebellious earl.

12

A HAPPY VICTORY, UNLOOKED FOR

Tyrone was declared a traitor at Dundalk on 24 June 1595, just after a major defeat of arms for the English at Clontibret in Monaghan, on 13 June, where Bagenal's army was attacked on all sides by Tyrone's more numerous forces. The account written of the action by Sir Francis Stafford tells how the English vanguard and rearguard came under attack simultaneously, and how the flanks of the English army were assailed by musketry and bowshot. Tyrone's men were described as 'ready shots', trained by Spaniards and levied into well-organised companies. The English force came under such pressure that they failed to advance above a quarter of a mile in the space of three hours. A quarter of all English combatants, some 420 men, lost their lives. Irish losses amounted to 130 killed or wounded. Bagenal might have been numbered among the slain had not forty of his cavalry troopers mounted a counter-charge that unhorsed Tyrone and threw the Irish horse into confusion. This allowed the remnants of the English army to press eastward along the Newry Road, all the while 'boggered on' by the victorious Irish.

Three years later, the English suffered their worst defeat ever at the hands of the Irish. At the Yellow Ford, a few miles to the north of Armagh, on 15 August 1598, Sir Henry Bagenal finally met his death when 4,500 Irishmen under the command of Tyrone, Maguire and the twenty-six-year-old Hugh Roe O'Donnell crushed his army and inflicted 50 per cent losses on them. Almost 1,000 Englishmen may have lost their lives at the battle for just the loss of a few hundred Irishmen. Bagenal was mortally wounded; some accounts say he fell into the hands of the enemy, others that he was carried from the field with those who fell back to Armagh.

The English routs at Clontibret and the Yellow Ford encouraged Tyrone to proclaim himself lord of all Ulster and to champion the old religion. His stock was running high: in Spain and Italy he was cast as another Hannibal after Cannae. Philip II of Spain was already close to dying when the news of the English reverses reached his ears. Closer to home, the disaster posed a crisis of epic proportions. Other Gaelic lords, including the wild O'Mores, arose. Plans for the plantation of Ulster disintegrated. Ireland might have been lost to the English forever, or so it was feared at the time. Lord Burghley, Elizabeth's closest adviser, had died just over a week before the battle, so the ageing queen could no longer rely on his council. Burghley had often in the past been at odds with Elizabeth, but the queen was wise enough to keep him close and place her trust in him. She knew he served God first. Even though a vain and jealous woman, she did not allow this to impair their relationship. Famously, Burghley once told his son, 'Serve God, for all other service is indeed bondage to the devil.'

It was Walter Devereux's son, Robert, 2nd Earl of Essex, a veteran of the war waged on the Continent against Spain, who would be tasked with bringing the Irish to heel and usher in a new, even more aggressive tranche of enforced colonisation. By 1587 he had established himself as the queen's favourite. He was handsome, well formed, dark eyed and fiery tempered; and, as importantly, willing to flatter and flirt. One of the queen's servants observed ruefully, 'My lord is at cards or one game or another with her; and he comes not back to his own lodging till the birds sing in the morning.' By the 1590s Essex was openly seeking advancement. He likely speculated there might be an opportunity to mount a bid for the throne outright or a protectorship over the queen when in her dotage.

He suffered a blow to his ambitions, however, when his kinsman Sir John Perrot, the man we last tracked in the mid-1580s when accepting the submission of Sorley Boy McDonnell, was arraigned for treason. Perrot was charged with consorting with the queen's enemies in Ireland, in particular with Sir Brian O'Rourke, who was suspected of being in cahoots with the Spanish. On 3 November 1591 O'Rourke was hung, drawn and quartered at Tyburn, a fate he is said to have faced quite unmoved. The *Annals of the Four Masters* described his gruesome demise as just 'one of the [many] mournful stories of the Irish'. O'Rourke had been arraigned for 'inciting the queen's deposition, giving succour and aid to the queen's Spanish enemies, and corresponding with the king of Spain', all of which was undoubtedly true. After his execution, his privy members and bowels were consumed by fire, his heart was removed from his chest and cast into the flames. His head was then struck off and his body quartered.

Despite lack of any credible witnesses, the case against Perrot gained traction. The knight was first placed under house arrest, then taken to the Tower. He knew his enemies were conspiring against him. On one occasion he was noted as saying, 'Nothing has so much hurt me as wind whispered in corners.' In a letter written in April 1592, he complained that his memory had become impaired because of the trauma of his imprisonment. At his trial he agreed he might have said some words which reflected badly on him, having once called the queen 'a silly woman', adding, 'she will not curb me [being but] a base bastard pissing kitchen woman'. Agitated throughout the trial, he took comfort that Elizabeth had already six times stayed judgement on him. Perhaps this was at Essex's pleading – but, unknown to Perrot, the ever affable Lord Burghley, the queen's chief fixer, was numbered among those who sought his destruction. A guilty verdict was passed. Fortunately for Perrot, he died in the Tower before his execution could take place. He cheated the headsman's axe or an even worse fate, and cheated, too, men who would have gloated to see him brought to the scaffold.

It might have been the case that Elizabeth would have in any event pardoned Perrot. Another possibility, mooted at the time, was that Perrott was poisoned while in custody. If true, the culprits might be identified among the men who worked toward his destruction, fearing his retribution if he were pardoned.

A famous falling out between Essex and the queen later occurred when the pair argued over who should be placed in the post of justiciar in Ireland. When the queen scorned Essex's choice he petulantly turned his back on her. She in turn struck him on the back of the head, enraged by his insolence. Essex may have instinctively grabbed for his sword and is alleged to have had to be restrained by the Lord High Admiral. Essex exclaimed, 'He neither could nor would put up with so great an affront and indignity, neither would he have taken it at King Henry the Eighth's hands.' He then strode from court. A month later, after the news broke of the military reverses in Ulster, the opportunity to make amends offered itself. The earl had been taken ill. This allowed Elizabeth to make matronly moves in seeking his welfare by despatching her own physician to attend on him. When the two again met, on 12 September 1598, Essex had recovered sufficiently from his tantrum. Elizabeth forgave him, and entrusted him with the lieutenancy of Ireland. 'By God,' he cried, 'I will beat Tyrone in the field or die in the attempt,' or words to that effect.

One of the largest armies ever to leave England's shores up until then departed for Waterford in the spring of 1599. Its strength has been assessed at 16,000 foot soldiers and 1,300 horse, an extraordinary rejoinder to a military setback overseas. Whether Essex's heart was ever really in the enterprise is a moot point. After arrival in Ireland, he consistently failed to engage the enemy. He promenaded his army well out of striking range of the main rebel army, making a wide sweep of Leinster, following this up by moving south into Munster rather than north into Ulster. After having a detachment of his army mauled by the voracious O'Mores, described as 'men in strong leathern jacks with bare legs', in the Pass of Plumes near Maryborough (now Portlaoise), he captured the strongly built but indifferently defended Cahir Castle and relieved the English outpost at Askeaton, on the banks of the River Deel, co. Limerick.

When Elizabeth heard of Essex's success at Cahir she taunted him that the task of driving out the Irish had been too easy, saying the defenders were merely 'a rabble of rogues'. The purpose of Essex's southern thrust was to safeguard the south of Ireland from the threat of future Spanish landings. Such a strategy, however, ran down his resources and also served to enrage the queen, who fretted at the expense involved. She railed at the £1,000 a day it was costing her for Essex, as she saw it, to 'strut his stuff'. The danger of a Spanish invasion was nevertheless real. A second great Spanish Armada had set sail for Ireland in the autumn of 1596. Battered by 'Protestant' storms off Cape Finisterre, seven galleons, twenty-five merchantmen, a number of lesser craft and 2,000 men had been lost, but this did not mean the ageing and terminally ill Philip II of Spain would not try again. A letter from Tyrone and Hugh Roe O'Donnell to the Prince of Asturias had spoken of the Irish desire to assert Catholic liberties and to free themselves from 'tyrannical evil', and snatch loyal Irishmen from the 'jaws of Hell'. It was ever Ireland's fate to be both England's neighbour and in religious affinity with the Catholic powers.

The Irish did their best to make good Tyrone's wish, and English forces in Ireland suffered a series of defeats. Essential ingredients of warfare in Ireland had hardly changed since the time of Clashacrow in the twelfth century; the fear of being cut-off in difficult terrain, better known to the Irish, gave a psychological advantage to the natives. The first of these defeats occurred on 29 May 1598, when Phelim mac Feagh O'Byrne's pike blocks crushed forces under the command of Sir Henry Harrington. The fight occurred close to the spot where Sir Philip Carew had been killed eighteen years earlier, on the road connecting Rathdrum and the coast, in county Wicklow. The terrified English are said to have 'never offered to turn [against the enemy] nor speak, but as men without sense or feeling, ran upon one another's backs'. English leaders who survived the debacle were cashiered, and an ensign hanged. The men who fled were reduced from regulars to ancillaries, and may have faced decimation. In mitigation, they claimed 'the rebels had come up on us very fast, and charged us in the rear with push of pike'. At the Battle of the Curlew Mountains, near Boyle Abbey, co. Roscommon, just over a year later on 5 August 1599, 400 Irish musketeers advanced unseen over difficult terrain and peppered an advancing English column, commanded by Sir Conyers Clifford, from flank and rear, causing mayhem. Only the presence of English cavalry prevented a massacre. Under leaden skies, the horsemen navigated boggy and boulder-strewn ground beside the trackway and faced off the Irish pursuit. In doing so, they allowed the surviving infantry to gain the security of Boyle Abbey. Clifford lost his life in the action. His corpse was decapitated on the Irish commander's orders, his head taken as a prize in much the same manner as Dermot mac Murrough would have done in the twelfth century.

Essex was at Dublin resting from his earlier exertions when news of Clifford's death reached him. Exhausted, sick and disillusioned, he foresaw a long, costly campaign ahead of him. This was something he had never bargained for when accepting his commission. He knew his enemies to be conspiring against him at court; he feared a backlash from the queen. He was right to be concerned. Reports of his alleged inaction, and his overly generous bestowing of knighthoods and honours on men as if he were a prince regent, had exasperated Elizabeth. Her anger was further stoked by his demand for more men and supplies. The planned launch of a three-pronged attack on the north of Ireland was in the end abandoned. Splitting his forces would, in any event, have been to invite defeat in detail, piece-meal. Only a long-term war of attrition now seemed likely to succeed, but that required more men and time than Essex had at his disposal, and was exactly what Tyrone was hoping for.

To explain what occurred next requires insight far beyond the available facts. That Essex resolved to return to England at the earliest opportunity appears self-evident from what later transpired. An impromptu meeting with Tyrone on 7 September, at Bellaclynthe ford, near Drumconragh, co. Monaghan, led to a series of concessions made by Essex. If not exceeding his authority, it was claimed as such by his critics. The concessions included an agreement to build no further garrisons on Tyrone's frontier and a six-week truce. This was time needed by Tyrone to allow requested Spanish reinforcements to reach Ireland, so favoured the Irish. Essex is also said to have spent time alone with Tyrone with no witnesses present. The two men conversed for an hour on horseback, knee-deep in muddy water. It was the incautious act of a desperate man, one who may have been considering initiating a pre-emptive strike on his enemies at home. He is reported as once saying he needed but 'two hundred resolute gentlemen to take control of the queen's person'. Essex would later declare the queen's mind to be 'as crooked as her body', so he clearly held her in contempt. The earl had the forces to mount a revolt but lacked the resolve. Tyrone later told a Spanish priest that he came near to persuading Essex to turn against Elizabeth, but that Essex had demurred when it became clear he would need to ally himself with the Spanish. This may have been an empty boast on the part of the Irishman, but, if true, Essex's behaviour was clearly treasonable.

The queen had earlier written to her one-time favourite, making it clear that his first priority should be to bring Tyrone to battle, saying, 'If we meant that Ireland, after all the calamities in which they have wrapped it, should still have to be abandoned, then it was very superfluous to have sent over a personage such as yourself.' It was this withering rebuke that had set in motion Essex's march north to the fateful meeting with Tyrone, The queen then censured the earl for spending time alone with Tyrone outside of anyone's hearing, saying 'such an action was uncomely', adding that she 'marvelled he had not shown better sense'. Elizabeth referred to Tyrone as 'a devil and a traitor', and now worried that Essex sought to come to a compact with him. Shakespeare in his play *Henry V*, first performed at the Globe theatre in May 1599, makes an indirect allusion to the concern felt that Essex might become too powerful, and perhaps threaten the peace of England:

> Were now the general [Essex] of our gracious Empress,
> As in good time he may, from Ireland coming,
> Bringing rebellion broached on his sword,
> How many would the peaceful city [London] quit,
> To welcome him!

On 24 September Essex sailed with a small retinue for England to make his case in person to the queen. His homecoming has been likened by Catherine Arnold, author of *Life in Shakespeare's London*, to a 'hollow mockery of Henry V's triumphal entry into London'. Four days later, the returning general set formal protocol aside by bursting in upon Elizabeth while she was still dressing; the queen was wigless and unpowdered, her wrinkles exposed. He arrived much in the manner of a petulant lover with his mistress. Elizabeth patted Essex's head and told him to retire; that they would convene more formally later that morning. All at first seemed well, but after lunch the queen's demeanour darkened and her reproof of Essex, after asking him to explain his actions in Ireland, left none in doubt that they were witnessing the Icarus-like fall of one undone by hubris. Stripped of his offices, Elizabeth had Essex placed under house arrest. This was to be their last ever meeting. Essex suffered a nervous collapse. The months of campaigning in Ireland and his several blunders had drained him physically and emotionally. Two months later, he was rumoured to be close to death. Churches in London rang their bells to call well-wishers to pray for him. Essex recovered, but his political career was over. Charles Blount, 8th Baron Mountjoy, a man described as 'courtly, grave and tall', succeeded him in Ireland.

*

It was Baron Mountjoy who faced the unenviable task of rejuvenating a demoralised army in Ireland. He also faced Tyrone and his allies. Mountjoy's strategy was to act aggressively and open up new theatres of war. He anchored his front line on two strongly defended garrisons, one at Ballyshannon on the Donegal coast and another at Lough Foyle. Wrangling with the Dublin authorities over resources at first tried Mountjoy's patience. He wrote back home, 'If I were aided by a council of Solomons, I think this kingdom and this army, as they now are, would afford them matter enough to try their wits.' When news broke in Ireland of the Earl of Essex's last rebellious toss of the die, he is said to have panicked. Mountjoy had been complicit in corresponding with Essex regarding the accession of James VI of Scotland to the throne after Elizabeth's death. Just imagining the death of the sovereign was a treasonable offence, so Mountjoy was right to be concerned. Whereas Essex's tragedy ended in a failed rising and his execution, by retaining the queen's favour Mountjoy had all evidence against him suppressed. Even so, he knew that only by making a success of the Irish venture could he fully redeem his reputation.

In the autumn of 1600 Mountjoy advanced part of his army to Faughart Hill, co. Armagh, the site of Edward Bruce's demise in 1318. The Irish were positioned to the north, their strength obscured by heavy woods, skirting the much fought over Moyry Pass, the strategic defile through which the old Newry – Dundalk road then ran. From higher ground, the Irish could observe the English while they themselves remained hidden. The Spanish had earlier landed 1,000 muskets at Donegal Bay and had promised troops would arrive in the near future, so morale in the Irish camp was high. A lesser man than Mountjoy might have baulked when faced by the prospect of mounting an offensive against the Irish position. The Moyry Pass was 'fenced' with cliffs and thick bushes and trees. Three barricades or trenches, a musket-shot distance from each other, flanked the position from higher ground. The pass was 'hard enough for swine to pass through, let alone men'. A three-week campaign fought in the torrential rain followed, but neither frontal attacks nor manoeuvring against the flanks proved successful. Every attack was beaten off by the Irish. Mountjoy had at least confronted Tyrone on equal terms. He afterwards ravaged the Irish countryside with what was described as 'cold precision and fixity of purpose', destroying stores of butter, corn and meal, slaughtering and driving the Irish from their homes. A winter famine resulted. Tyrone nevertheless remained intractable; Mountjoy could not lure him to fight on open ground.

It was the arrival of just over 3,500 well-armed and trained Spaniards on the south coast led by Don Juan D'Águila with thirty-three ships that unlocked Tyrone from his Ulster fortress. Arriving at Kinsale, co. Cork, aboard his flagship the *San Filipe*, D'Águila contrived to concentrate his forces as far away from Tyrone's stronghold in Ulster as possible. His decision not to risk his fleet on the northward leg to Donegal was made because of the threat of bad weather, *'malos temporales y tempestos'* – unsurprisingly, considering the fate of earlier armadas. The Spanish numbered far less than had been hoped for by Tyrone. Few fighting men could be spared from the Spanish Empire – plague had killed half a million men, women and children between the years 1596 and 1602 in Castile alone. Perhaps a quarter of the population of Europe died of bubonic plague at around this time, creating what has been termed 'moral, religious and political disintegration'. Moreover, for the Spanish other theatres of war, the main one in Europe being the Spanish Netherlands, were of a higher priority; the empire's attention to Ireland might be likened, it has been said, to a painter applying a small brush to a very broad canvas.

In advance of Mountjoy's main force, local English forces under Sir George Carew, President of Munster, besieged Kinsale, bottling up the invaders. But after several months of close siege Carew's and Mountjoy's soldiers were falling like flies, the result of a lack of fresh food and insanitary conditions in deep, mud-soaked trenches. The men are said to have 'daily died in dozens', leading Carew to lament that never before had a siege been so miserable, 'nor so great mortality [suffered]'. Conditions within Kinsale were also acute. The Spanish were reduced to eating their horses, plus any dogs and cats they could find. An impasse might have been reached had not Tyrone, at the head of 6,500 men, described by Carew as 'all the rebels of Ireland [and the] greatest part of the Irishry of Munster', sought to relieve his Spanish allies. Tyrone's feat in traversing Ireland from north to south was all the more remarkable given the dreadful weather and parlous state of the roads. For better security, the Irish army split in two. Tyrone travelled down the eastern seaboard; his ally, Hugh Roe O'Donnell, moved southward through Connaught.

Hugh Roe O'Donnell, who we last met at the Battle of the Yellow Ford, had once been imprisoned by the English at Dublin Castle but had escaped in the winter of 1592 when aged just twenty. After a long trek in icy conditions across the Wicklow Mountains, his big toes had had to be amputated. His companion on the trek, Art O'Neill, son of the late, great but unlamented Shane, had perished. O'Donnell's escape and epic getaway was said to have 'sent a thrill through all of Ireland', and gained him the title of *the* O'Donnell. Evasion now necessitated another long and arduous trek over the mountains. In early December, without big toes, he and his men made a memorable thirty-two-mile night march over the frozen Slieve Felim Mountains. Sir George Carew claimed it was 'the greatest march with carriage that hath [ever] been heard of'.

Tyrone preferred to avoid a set-piece battle. His plan was to besiege the besiegers and deny them food or fodder, but such a passive course of action was rudely rejected by O'Donnell and the Spanish commander, D'Águila. Both men favoured the merging of the Irish and Spanish armies and attacking the English without delay. O'Donnell's biographer, John J. Silke, describes the Irishman as a strong and handsome man, and a leader who had 'advanced far beyond the traditional hit-and-run methods of Irish warfare'; yet 'hit and run' might have better suited the Irish, rather than risk a set-piece battle.

We only have later mutually recriminating reports to go on, so exactly what transpired when Tyrone, O'Donnell and D'Águila met before the battle remains speculative. We do know that on the night of 24 December 1601 Tyrone drew up the Irish army to the north-west of Mountjoy's siege-lines and advanced on Kinsale in three dense columns. Tyrone led the vanguard, at the head of 1,500 men. Behind him marched a body of pikemen and supporting musketeers led by Captain Richard Tyrrell. The division commanded by Hugh Roe O'Donnell brought up the rear, supported by the Irish cavalry. The 2,500 or so fit and able Spanish in the town may have been expected to sally out in support, but, if that was the case, they failed to do so. Tyrone's commanders may have lost track of their precise location in the dark; by veering westward across the English front, they presented their flank and rear to assault. Military historians speculate they were making for safer ground across two streams, putting a bog between them and the English. Rain squalls, however, made such a manoeuvre highly dangerous, presenting Mountjoy with an opportunity he must have prayed for. Seeing the enemy advance across his front, he exclaimed, 'This kingdom is lost today.'

The initial English attack, launched with cavalry, was repulsed, but a second attack broke Tyrone's lead column. Tyrell's and O'Donnell's supporting columns were not engaged, but nevertheless gave ground before disintegrating. An eyewitness, Sir Edward Wingfield, considered the clash 'but a skirmish' and 'a happy victory, unlooked for'. Approximately 1,000 Irish dead strewed the battlefield over two miles of ground, a pitiful sight for onlookers in the clear light of day. Almost all the dead were Irishmen. The English are reputed to have lost but a single man. Many more Irishmen perished on the long march home, picked off by the pursuing English cavalry and sometimes by their own people, who turned on them in desperation to protect scant food and belongings.

Mountjoy's outriders offered the fleeing Irish no quarter. Those who eluded them often starved. The English relentlessly pursued the broken army back to Ulster. To mark their victory they destroyed the O'Neill inauguration stone at Tullahoge near Cookstown, co. Tyrone, seized in the past, as we have seen, by Tyrone when making his move against Turlough O'Neill in 1583. The depleted Spaniards fared better. Having not been engaged and by surrendering on terms, they were permitted to return home.

One Irish commander, the princely Donal Cam O'Sullivan Beare, Chief of Dunboy, resolved to continue the struggle. He based his forces at Dunboy Castle, near Castletownbere on the Beara Peninsula in south-west Ireland. Even with a small garrison the castle was considered impregnable, but a concerted cannonade, followed by a storming, soon overcame the defenders. All fifty-eight Irishmen who survived the onslaught were later executed as rebels. Donal Cam was away at the time, attending on Tyrone. His clan having been outlawed, he moved many of the women and children to Dursey Island, off the south-western tip of the Beara Peninsula. When the island was eventually assailed by the English, no quarter was offered. According to Donal Cam's brother Philip, the whole community was massacred. The rest of Donal Cam's soldiers and dependants, 1,000 strong, had prior to this set off northward from Glengariff, co. Cork, an event dated to 31 December 1602. By the time they reached Knockvicar, co. Roscommon, only thirty-five remained; the rest died en route.

Elizabeth wrote to Mountjoy to congratulate him on his victory and for so very nearly capturing Tyrone, the 'villainous rebel', adding, 'We see no reason why so great forces [now under your command] should not end his days.' One of Mountjoy's commanders rightly claimed, 'The axe was now at the root of the tree.' Tyrone submitted to Mountjoy in December 1602 after a period in exile. He did so on his knees – a humiliating end to a potentially epochal endeavour. It marked the conclusion of what has become known as the Nine Years War (1592–1601). Elizabeth did not live to hear of it: she had died a week before.

Historians have argued ever since about what caused this remarkable defeat of Irish arms, described as the Irish Culloden. The seventeenth-century historian Geoffrey Keating (Seathrun Ceitinn) blamed the Irish leaders for arguing among themselves over 'petty claims'. But the march across the English front in battle columns, a formation more suited to the Spanish, suggests military incompetence of the first order. The unorthodox formation of lines of columns implies they must have been on the move or attempting to redeploy when attacked. Military historian Richard Brooks has suggested that Tyrone's advance may have been intended as 'a demonstration to cover the introduction of Irish reinforcements into Kinsale [that went wrong]' but adds 'the answers are lost in rumours and recrimination'. The seventeenth-century Irish historian Lughaidh O'Clerigh summed up the loss as not simply a military setback, but one which saw the total eclipse of Gaeldom; Kinsale was therefore perhaps the most decisive battle ever in Ireland's history up until that time:

> There were lost there all the noble freeborn sons of Mil, valiant, impetuous chiefs, lords of territories and tribes ... there were lost besides nobility and honour, generosity and great deeds, hospitality and kindness, courtesy and noble birth, culture and activity, strength and courage, valour and steadfastness, the authority and sovereignty of the Gaels of Ireland to the end of time.

All agree the event to have been a watershed. Writing in the 1930s, Professor Edmund Curtis stated that, after Kinsale, Ireland entered a new phase in her history: Roman Catholic by conviction, and a mixture of English and Gael by race (in his words 'a blended race'), with a sense of common heritage. Its challenge, in the professor's view, was how such a race might now fit in with 'a greedy, intolerant and pampered Protestant ascendancy'.

*

After Kinsale, Hugh Roe O'Donnell sailed to Corunna in Spain to get fresh troops, but Spanish survivors of the battle soon disabused Philip of Spain of the idea of supporting the Irishman. Instead, they laid the blame on him for the disaster. O'Donnell was for a time placed under house arrest. He died on 30 August 1602, shortly after being released, and was buried at the Franciscan monastery at Valladolid, which has since been demolished. The victor of the Battle of Curlew Mountain's remarkable robustness had failed him. Some thought he had fallen victim to a poisoner, and it was later alleged Mountjoy had despatched an assassin from Galway named James Blake to do the awful deed, but the rigours of the Castilian climate and tainted food are more likely suspects. If not Mountjoy's work, O'Donnell's death was nevertheless a welcome outcome for the English, and did much to persuade die-hard insurgents in Ulster to lay down their arms. O'Donnell's burial in a Franciscan monastery was apt; 'Red' Hugh had, it is alleged, often promised to become a Franciscan in the event of his struggle against the English coming to naught. Professor Silke considers the Irishman's contribution to the fight for liberty as significant. He describes O'Donnell as 'resolute, courteous and affable' and believes he made the rebellion in Ulster 'one of national, international and religious significance'.

One veteran of Kinsale who managed to flourish was Randal McDonnell, lord of Antrim, fourth of five sons of Sorley Boy McDonnell. Randal had brought 400 of his men to Kinsale, but by the time he returned to Antrim they numbered just a few dozen. Facing up to defeat, he sensibly submitted to Mountjoy in August 1602 and undertook to provide the Englishman with 500 redshanks and forty horsemen at his own expense. He was knighted in the spring of 1603 at Tullahoge. He would later gain a vast land grant from the Crown of 333,907 acres. In 1620, he gained the title 1st Earl of Antrim. Randal was among the few Gaelic nobles to successfully make the transition from recalcitrant chieftain to modern landlord. Even so, he brought up his sons in 'the highland manner': they spoke Irish and were educated by bards. Like 'Red' Hugh O'Donnell, Randall favoured the Franciscans, and remained staunchly, if discreetly, Catholic. King James I of England and VI of Scotland (Elizabeth's successor) would later laud McDonnell's 'civil, orderly life' and his contribution in reforming and civilising Ulster, a place described by the king as 'the rudest part of Ireland'. It seems Randal kept an open mind on religion, even welcoming Presbyterian Scots to Antrim, families who had been previously been settled in Kintyre.

After putting down a series of potentially serious revolts – probably the result of the enforced garrisoning of Irish towns with English troops, who brought with them disease and hardship – Mountjoy departed for England. He left behind twenty-five colonels still in post. 'An iron grip' was to be maintained on Ulster. Governors at key places like Newry and Enniskillen had summary power over life and death. In June 1603, Mountjoy presented the 'arch traitor' Tyrone to James I. Perhaps better attuned than Elizabeth to dealing with Gaelic chieftains, James (the first ever king of England, Scotland, Wales and Ireland) proved to be more conciliatory than punitive. The peace terms he offered meant Tyrone would lose land to neighbours and cousins, but, by agreeing to abjure his other titles, Tyrone would then be reinvested with his earldom upon payment of rent to the Crown. Hugh O'Donnell's son Rory was created Earl of Tyrconnell. By these appointments, and by abolishing once and for all Brehon law in Ulster, known as Tanistry, and replacing it with the law of primogeniture, the English Crown hoped peace might be brought to the war-wracked region. Having 'one [earl] assured in Tyrconnell and another in Tyrone' would, it was expected, ensure each was able singly – or together – to suppress local opposition and that annual rents would replace feudal obligation. Many railed at the king's apparent leniency; one nobleman declared angrily that 'that damned rebel Tyrone' appeared not only to have been honoured by James but was also well liked.

James I's views differed from his Elizabethan predecessors. He did not fully support a wholesale displacement of the Irish and refused to treat Ireland as simply a colony. Nevertheless, the idea of settling Ireland, a country with perhaps just 750,000 inhabitants, remained high on his parliament's agenda. The difference in approach under James was that there was theoretically to be no bar on religious observance or ethnicity. Protestant and Catholic, Irish, Scots, Welsh and English were all to benefit from an extensive programme of settlement, which would not be limited to Ulster but would also include modern-day counties Wicklow, Wexford, Carlow and Leitrim.

Rory O'Donnell, the new-made Earl of Tyrconnell, had been among those who trekked back northward after the Battle of Kinsale. He had made his headquarters at Ballymote Castle, co. Sligo, a fortress described as 'keepless' – presumably this did not mean that it was weak, but that it was built without a central keep. In all other respects it was a daunting bastion, with three-metre thick walls flanked by six strong towers. Throughout the summer of 1602, probably awaiting news and reinforcements from his father, Rory had maintained the fight against Mountjoy's forces from Ballymote, evading pincer movements and beating off English sorties. But news of his father's death changed all this: Rory could no longer justify holding out and placing his men's lives at risk. Like Tyrone, the young lord had been forced to back down.

What on paper and in the mind of James I seemed an ideal outcome proved in the end difficult to put into practice. The greed of English adventurers, who after Kinsale fell like carpetbaggers on the territories of the defeated Irish, changed the dynamic. Lands targeted by Sir Arthur Chichester, James I's new Lord Deputy of Ireland, were said to have been ravaged beyond hope. Three thousand people starved in Tyrone in one year. Corpses with mouths stuffed with nettles and dock leaves littered the trackways. All Ulster west of the Blackwater was spoilt by war. In the spring of 1601, Chichester boasted of killing above 100 Irish of all sorts near Dungannon, saying, 'We spare none of what quality or sex 'soever.'

Like James, Chichester too now favoured a slow process of anglicization rather than aggressive colonization, but the discovery of the Gunpowder Plot at around the same time made it all the harder for the Irish Catholic nobility to assert their loyalty to both king and pope and be believed. Tyrone and Tyrconnell, with their family members and retainers, about ninety men and women in all, resolved to quit Ireland altogether, an event known as 'the flight of the earls'. Exile was preferable to seeing their way of life overturned. They could no longer make a dignified show of status on reduced incomes: Tyrconnell land had been wrested by government agents on flimsy pretexts; English business sharks gained control of Tyrconnell fisheries and harbour rights; the Bishop of Derry, George Montgomery, seized ancient Tyrconnell lands as Church and monastic benefices.

Tyrone and Tyrconnell were proudly practical men. Tyrone, in particular, is said to ever 'have been committed to few causes other than his own survival and the preservation of his family'. Remaining in Ireland might also have later meant imprisonment; worse, the possible loss of head, private members and innards to a masked executioner on Tower Hill. The earls and their families left Rathmullan on Lough Swilly on 14 September 1607, bound for Spain. Tyrconnell took with him his one-year-old son, Hugh, but left behind his pregnant countess; perhaps she could not face going into labour on the high seas. His sister Nuala sailed with him, perhaps a nanny for baby Hugh. The event marked another dramatic political turning point in Irish history. Whether Tyrone and Tyrconnell expected to return with a strong Spanish backing is a moot point, argued by historians to this day. Most academics doubt it. Returning to Ireland was never really on the cards. In letters to James I, the earls informed the monarch of the pressures placed on them by his ministers. At the same time they pledged their support to Spain in forming an 'Irish Catholic league'.

Meanwhile in Ulster, Irish commoners were becoming marginalised by incoming Scots, who monopolised more fertile areas of land where a deep drumlin soil would later come to favour flax production. Dispossessed Catholics in large numbers took to the roads or eked out a living in bogs and wooded hideaways. They became known as the woodkern (or woodkerne), much-feared bandits and renegades, whose alleged offences probably outran the truth. In a letter sent to Chichester, news of renewed plantations drew a degree of concern from the author, who stated, 'There is no hope of the people since the news of the plantation ... that it will shortly be their cases [the Irish] to be woodkerne out of necessity, no other means being left to them to keep a being in this worlds than to live as long as they can by scrambling.' Nevertheless, an aggressive plantation of Ulster was recommended by, among others, men like Sir John Davies, Ireland's Attorney-General; this on the basis that the province was heavily depopulated and that there were insufficient trusted natives to manure the soil. Davies added, as an afterthought, that it was also his opinion that the common Irish were, through 'fickleness and disloyalty', unfit to be tenants. A letter from Davies to Lord Cecil in the summer of 1608, a year after the flight of the earls, described the 'wild inhabitants' of the province as being aghast to meet a man of refinement like himself, as 'as a ghost might wonder to see a man alive in Hell'. Unemployed Catholic soldiers were shipped off for service overseas and whole families were transplanted into the west of Ireland. Chichester considered this a reasonable outcome, saying that the Romans had done much the same with whole nations when they built their empire. Had Agricola made good his wish to invade Ireland, the Roman general might have cut out a millennium and a half of misery.

An aggressive plantation begun in 1609 in Ulster involved the settling of an estimated half million acres of land. Looking back on this period, Sir John Temple would write that Irish natives and English and Scottish planters had 'knit and compacted', and that intermarriage was frequent, making for a kind of 'mutual transmigration into each other's manners'. Yet landless Irish clogged the roads, herding their meagre bovine wealth before them, a sorry sight for all but the most hard-hearted. Ulster had by this time been largely shired: Antrim and Down in 1570, Armagh in 1571, Cavan in 1583, Monahan in 1587, Fermanagh in 1588, Tyrone in 1591, Coleraine in 1603, and Derry in 1613. By 1618, the strong walls of what officially became Londonderry had been completed for better security, turning a once open town into one of Ireland's strongest fortresses. Catholics were barred from living there; they settled on the Bogside to the west, instead. Why there was such a divisive proscription at Londonderry is unclear, since elsewhere, in towns like Belfast, Armagh and Cavan, Protestants and Catholics appear to have intermixed, even if the latter were sometimes in the minority. The most successful planters in Ulster were Scottish Presbyterians, but there were also Londoners, many of whom were granted lands in Coleraine. That there was peace in Ireland until rebellion in the late 1630s is a measure of Stuart success in rolling out these programmes, but there was push-back on occasion. When the O'Rourkes proved a threat to the plantations in modern-day county Leitrim, Lord Falkland wrote to the Privy Council to say 'all the idlers of the area' would be likely to fight. Yet it seems diplomacy or force of arms won the day and the threat subsided.

Although the English government remained concerned that the Pope might yet become 'the keeper of the keys of our back door', there would be no further adventures into Gaeldom directly sponsored by Spain. What is more, Tyrone and the other Irish exiles, despite their pledge to work with the Spanish in reinstating the Roman Catholic Church in Ireland, found themselves unwelcome in Spanish territory, forced instead to travel on to Italy. Seen as a diplomatic embarrassment, they became, in the words of author Thomas Gainsford, 'tennis balls of fortune'. An exception appears to have been Donal Cam O'Sullivan Beare, who gained from King Philip II of Spain the title Count Bearehaven and was made a Knight of the Order of Santiago. He was later murdered in Madrid in 1618. (His murderer was John Bathe, a Dubliner in the pay of the English Crown.) Tyrone had in the meantime made his way to Rome, staying in a common inn. By then he was a charity case; his health was failing, his sight too. He died and was buried in Rome on 20 July 1616. His countess survived him by just two years, dying the same year as Donal Cam. Rory O'Donnell had passed away eight years earlier than this at Rome, aged thirty-three. Rory's last remaining brother, Caffar, died a month or so later. None of the royal O'Donnell bloodline, save Rory's son Hugh (who died in 1642, a childless soldier of fortune), survived. Rory's demise ended the long dynasty known as the Cenél Conaill, stretching back into pre-history. Ten high-kings were numbered among their progeny. Finn McCool still slept. Who might now arise and strike out for Ireland and the Irish?

13

BENEATH LISCARROL'S WALLS

James I's son, Charles I, was of a different stamp to his father. A genuinely religious man, prone to stammering at moments of stress, his overt religiosity and stubbornness would accelerate his downfall. His Lord Deputy in Ireland, Thomas Wentworth, Earl of Strafford, was an equally stubborn man, with a political philosophy fixed on the divine right of monarchs. Strafford was also described as ruthless, vindictive, and anti-Catholic; in the North of England it was said that papists 'hung their heads like bulrushes' at his approach. When offered the deputyship in Ireland, friends advised Strafford against accepting, saying the island had always proved fatal to the ambitions of Englishmen. One described it as 'a place to pack eminent men into for their overthrow'. Strafford was not to be deterred. After his arrival in Ireland, on 23 July 1633, he set himself up in a grand manner by establishing 'a quasi-royal court'. Despite a consensus at Dublin in favour of 'diluting the Catholic base', he managed somehow to alienate the land's leading lights, including the richest of the planter lords, Richard Boyle, 1st Earl of Cork. By 1640, Boyle's Irish rents yielded something like £18,000 a year, an income only rivalled by the long-established Butlers.

At first, Strafford and Cork rubbed along well: both men were fervently anti-Catholic and agreed in broad terms on policy matters. What came to undermine this relationship was Strafford's decision to challenge the earl's right of ownership to vast tracts of

Church land, misappropriated in the past. Accustomed to avoiding paying any tax, Cork complained that Strafford's financial demands would have been sufficient to ransom him had he been imprisoned by the Turks. Strafford in turn grumbled about Cork's pomposity, calling him a social upstart. No less abrupt was Strafford's collision with the Old English lords, whose promise of security of tenure, when the king had sought military aid from Ireland – an agreement known as 'The Graces' – was soon compromised. The international situation having stabilised, Charles no longer needed to rely on Irish support.

Plans to confiscate Gaelic lands in Connaught for an extensive plantation also threatened many Irish Catholics. Four thousand 'quarters of land' were to be claimed for the king in Connaught, of which 1,000 would be confiscations. Prominent for the opposition was Richard Burke, 4th Earl of Clanrickard, who during the late wars against Tyrone had fought on the English side, winning a reputation for outstanding valour and gaining a knighthood on the battlefield of Kinsale. Under attack from Strafford in the courts and aged over sixty, Clanrickard's health worsened, leading to his death in November 1635. Friends and family in England lobbied for the Clanrickard lands in Galway to be exempted from the confiscations, but not until 1639 did the late earl's son, Ulick Burke, manage to persuade Charles I that it was unwise to provoke the most powerful Catholic families in Ireland, especially now that England was on the brink of war with Scotland. Not until the autumn of 1640, however, did Strafford back down in this regard. Ulick never forgave the earl for hounding his father, swearing that 'when Parliament sits, the day will come when he shall pay for it'.

The Scottish wars, known as the First and Second Bishop's wars, were crisis points for Charles. His attempt to impose a common prayer book on both Scotland and England had been a pet project of his father's, but had been mothballed during the final decade of the late king's reign. Being the first permanently absent king to rule Scotland made Charles' task all the harder when dusting off and presenting his father's plans to his northern subjects, who regarded them as an unwarranted imposition. Rioting followed. When the Scots sought to involve foreign powers and inveigle English Presbyterians, alarm turned to anger, then war. When fighting erupted, Charles' army suffered a series of defeats. The most severe was at Newburn Ford, near Newcastle-upon-Tyne, on 28 August 1640. It was an outcome described by Lord Clarendon as 'shameful and confounding'. Drastic countermeasures were called for.

The Earl of Antrim presented a proposal to raise a Catholic Gaelic army from his clan base of MacDonalds and their sister clan the McDonnells to hold the north of Ireland, then strike against Charles' enemies. Strafford sought to undermine these plans, rightly concluding that the formation of a large Gaelic army in Ulster would prove politically disastrous. Nevertheless, after long prevarication, Charles sided with Antrim and ordered Strafford to support the earl's plans. In parallel, Stafford enforced what has been termed the 'Black Oath', obliging all Presbyterian Scottish males in Ulster to declare their allegiance to the Crown. Reluctant Presbyterian congregations came under increasing pressure to accept the oath. Strafford quartered soldiers on them, adding to the miseries suffered by an already marginalised community. Many Scots abandoned their homes and returned to Strathclyde. In Down, the population declined so fast there were problems bringing in the harvest. Moreover, the existence of a largely Catholic army in Ulster, albeit untested in war, proved of great concern to the king's enemies at Westminster, who feared Charles might use it against them as a vanguard to strike at English liberty of worship. The result was Strafford's impeachment and execution on 12 May 1641. Abandoned by the king he had served so loyally, the condemned man is said to have warned others, 'Put not your trust in princes.' Charles, it seems, could have vetoed the earl's death sentence, but chose not to.

A Catholic revolt, unrelated to Strafford's execution or the king's Scottish war, erupted in the north of Ireland in the autumn of 1641. The leaders of the rising, men like the rancorous and debt-ridden Sir Phelim O'Neill, may have acted opportunistically, taking advantage of the mayhem across the Irish Sea. The Catholic Bishop of Ossory had seen it coming, stating, 'The Irish will fight for their altars and hearths, and [will] rather seek a bloody death near the sepulchres of their fathers than be buried as exiles in unknown earth or inhospitable sand.' Flames of revolt were stoked by the Catholic priesthood, in particular the Jesuits, who feared a further bout of suppression at the hands of a resurgent English parliament. Some even feared the total extinction of the old religion. Economic woes were also at the forefront. The second half of the 1630s experienced a massive trade downturn in Ireland.

The focus of the rebellion was Ulster, where the six counties of Armagh, Coleraine, Fermanagh, Tyrone, Cavan and Donegal had been, or were again planned to be, widely planted. Castles, fortified houses and homesteads fell to the insurgents. Protestant families were driven to flee with the few belongings they could carry. Those not killed in cold blood at the hands of assailants faced death through privation in the prevailing inclement weather. Strabane fell to the rebels in December 1641. By early 1642, a spiralling war of dislocation and revenge had engulfed much of Ireland. An estimated 2,000 settlers were killed. In Armagh, the epicentre of the revolt, the death toll has been estimated at between 600 and 1,300 people: between 10 and 25 per cent of the estimated settler population. Irish peers like Ulick Burke of Clanrickard, the late Earl of Strafford's mortal enemy and now the most influential man in Connaught, were horrified by what occurred, referring to it as a 'strange madness ... a most disloyal and detestable conspiracy'. Loyalists like him looked to raise foot regiments for the king. Meanwhile, in London the numbers of Protestants killed in Ireland became grossly exaggerated, as did the manner of killing. Pamphleteers imagined an orgy of bloodletting consuming thousands of defenceless English and Scottish settlers, with babies skewered, women raped and men torn limb from limb. The way this was presented says more about the mindset of the pamphleteers and their readers than the massacres themselves, such as they were. What was new, however, was that such virulent anti-Irish propaganda gained such a wide airing from by then ubiquitous news-sheets.

The leaders of the rebellion may have hoped for a quick and beneficial outcome, but faced a countrywide revolt. The verse, 'remember the steel of Phelim O'Neill, who slaughtered our fathers in Catholic zeal', sums up how Protestants later viewed the supposed main ringleader of the revolt. A provisional government, known as His Majesty's Roman Catholic subjects of the kingdom of Ireland, was created, a forum also sometimes referred to as the Confederation of Kilkenny, its motto, 'United for God, king and the Irish fatherland'. As an alternative government to the one at Dublin it raised taxes, minted coins and passed legislation. It also provided a degree of legitimacy for the raising of another large Irish army, one that attracted substantial sign-up, causing garrisons as far distant as North Wales to be placed on high alert: Protestant noblemen at places like Conwy and Brampton Bryan hurriedly prepared for the possibility of siege; invasion was hourly expected. Refugees from the violence in Ireland flooded across the North Channel to Bute, Ayr and Irvine. Some 4,000 of them are thought to have later starved, despite attempts by the Scottish authorities to make food supplies available.

Meanwhile, surviving Protestant refugees from the north of Ireland, some of them the survivors of a massacre at Portadown Bridge, co. Armagh, where up to 100 men, women and children died, found safety behind Drogheda's strong walls. From mid-November 1641, the town became encircled by insurgent forces. Rory O'Moore, father-in-law of the more famous soldier Patrick Sarsfield (of whom more to come), crushed an English relief force at Julianstown at the end of that month. Men with pitchforks, clubs and pikes, described as 'disordered, elemental and desperate', overwhelmed better-equipped opponents. Five hundred men of the relief force lost their lives or were wounded. Motivated by the loss of his ancient patrimony, Rory O'Moore had earlier pressed for advantage to be taken of Charles I's difficulties in Scotland. It was at O'Moore's instigation that armed men gathered in villages and bands of cutthroats roamed the roads. Another outcome of the Julianstown fight was the sealing of an alliance at Tara between the Old English leadership and the Irish insurgents. It was a defensive compact made in the face of the growing Parliamentarian threat. John Pym, the opposition leader at Westminster, foresaw nothing but 'the sword' deciding the issue in Ireland. The veteran Sir William St Leger, however, made light of the rebel threat, describing the insurgents as but a company of naked rogues. Another man who did not baulk was James Butler, Earl of Ormond, Charles I's main enforcer in Ireland. In April 1642, Ormond collided in battle with the confederate Irish at Kilrush, north-east of Athy, on the Dublin – Kilkenny road. His 3,000-strong army saw off a force twice its size, described as 'a rabble of disarmed freshwater soldiers, without arms, ammunition or soldierly commanders'. Had not nearby bogs and failing light assisted rather than prevented flight, many more than the several hundred rebels slain would have met a similar fate. Around twenty English soldiers were slain and forty wounded, but in excess of 100 rebels may have been killed outright. The site of the fighting is now called the Battlemount. The victory was seen at the time as sufficiently important for the English parliament to vote Ormond a sizeable bounty.

Limerick, the only sizeable city in south-east Ireland away from the coast, fell to the confederates in the summer of 1642. A stash of artillery seized there helped subdue resistance in Munster. Galway town had earlier fallen to the rebels. The Earl of Clanrickard's estates in Connaught are said to have been despoiled by English and Irish alike; 'what one left [was] always destroyed by the other'. By the summer of 1642, the forces opposing the Catholic insurrection comprised Ormond's Royalist army, a Scottish Covenanting army, and a bewildering number of local commands, each loosely tied to the royalist cause. Irish royalists had predominance at Dublin, a city of perhaps 20,000 souls, and much of the Pale, as well as smaller communes in Carlow, Derry, Dungannon, Enniskillen, Loughrea and Portumna. The Scottish Covenanters, under the command of Major-General Robert Monro, established themselves in eastern Ulster, where they undertook a campaign of revenge against Catholics for the earlier slaughter of their compatriots. Sixty townsmen were strung up by them at Newry and several women were either drowned or shot to death while floundering in the river running through the town.

Equally draconian payback was enacted in southern Ireland. At Liscarrol Castle, co. Cork, in July 1642, General Murrough O'Brien's English foot soldiers defeated a much larger confederate army under the command General Garrett Barry (a name with Cambro-Norman resonance), a veteran of the Spanish wars in the Netherlands who had returned to Ireland in 1640 hoping to recruit Irishmen for the Spanish army. Barry had captured Limerick for the confederates, achieving this through skilled siege techniques learned abroad, in particular the undermining of the city walls. The defeat at Liscarrol and his earlier failure to take Cork ended Barry's military career. He played no further role in the conflict, dying in Limerick in 1647. The victor of Liscarrol, Murrough O'Brien, might have been killed outright on the day of battle had not his foster brother come to his aid in the thick of a cavalry melee and pistoled to death O'Brien's assailant. Fifty captured confederate Catholic officers were later hanged. Seven hundred confederate other ranks fell in the fighting, for a loss of just thirty-two English. The hanging of the officers would later provide inspiration for the poet Callaghan Hartstonge Gayner.

> Beneath its folds assemble now and fight with might and main;
> That grand old fight to make our land a nation once again.
> And falter not till alien rule in dark oblivion falls;
> We'll stand as freemen yet beneath Liscarrol's walls.

Overall English army strength in Ireland by the summer of 1642 stood at around 40,000 foot, 3,500 horse and 300 gunners, deployed half in Ulster, the rest in Leinster, Munster and Connaught. As Charles I's difficulties increased in England, so too did the attraction of bringing back some of these troops from Ireland to swell the ranks of the English Royalist armies. It was later said that

Charles I feared Presbyterianism more than he did Catholicism. Even so, he must have been aware of the deep antagonism felt by his English subjects toward the Irish confederacy and opposition to any weakening of the English army there. Now at war with his parliament, he pressed Ormond to settle the rebellion in Ireland as quickly as possible; either that or to agree a ceasefire.

The monarch's inherent vagueness when issuing instructions for a time left Ormond uncertain exactly what was required of him. Was he to sacrifice the defence of Protestant Ireland for an unlikely victory in England? The earl deliberately stalled for time. Cajoled at last to act with urgency, he negotiated a year-long cessation of hostilities with the confederates in Leinster on 15 September 1643, whereby the king might gain the use of Ormond's troops. For his efforts, Ormond was awarded the title Lord Lieutenant of Ireland. In Munster and Ulster, however, the fighting continued unabated. Regional generals could never be persuaded to down weapons for long.

Although a pragmatic solution to the king's immediate military problems (one strongly lobbied for by his German nephew Prince Rupert, a youthful veteran of the Thirty Years War), the idea of men returning from Ireland, even if mainly Englishmen and Irish Protestants, was politically inflammatory. The fear among parliamentarians was that the returning regiments would be filled with native Irish, a popish front aimed at exterminating Protestantism. Pressure to make a decisive military intervention from Ireland increased as the king's situation in England worsened. Historians now see the king's move to bring across troops from Ireland as ill-judged, a provocation of parliament which made the war in England's prosecution even more uncompromising than hitherto. Parliamentarians at Westminster had by this time opened negotiations with the Scottish Covenanters, who agreed to join them on the understanding that Presbyterianism be made compulsory south of the border. This opportunistic agreement, which resulted in 20,000 Scots crossing the Tweed at the end of the year 1643, would more than offset Charles' equally opportunistic initiatives in Ireland, and would serve to further stoke partisan passions.

Only by the autumn of 1643 did the first of Ormond's regiments arrive in England, a few thousand at a time. These soldiers were described by royalist general Sir Ralph Hopton as 'bold, hardy men and excellently well officered'. Approximately 12,000 troops would make the dangerous passage across the Irish Sea, arriving at a variety of landing places: Bristol, Minehead, Chester, Beaumaris, Weymouth and Whitehaven. The first arrivals filled royalist ranks depleted by a great typhus epidemic. Had it not been for this crippling disease, which affected both sides, campaigning in the south of England might have proved decisive one way or the other and the wars in Britain brought to an early conclusion, securing an uninterrupted Stuart dynasty. The Fates spun the web of life on occasion not on the battlefield or around the negotiating table but in makeshift hospitalisation, where armies crumbled upon the onset of cholera, typhus or dysentery.

*

In October 1644 the House of Commons ordered that no quarter should be given to any captured Irish Catholics, whom they described as idolatrous butchers. There was little to distinguish an Irish Catholic from an Irish Protestant (except his word), so merely being Irish was on occasion enough to warrant an immediate death sentence if captured. Shocked by the tone and substance of the Common's proclamation, Prince Rupert claimed the English nation was 'in danger of destroying itself and degenerating into such an animosity and cruelty, that all elements of charity, compassion, and brotherly affection shall be extinguished'. On one occasion, seventy Irish soldiers and two female camp followers bound for Bristol were thrown overboard when their ship was intercepted by the Parliamentarian navy; other killings followed. Savagery was not all one-sided; two of the earliest recorded massacres of the war were perpetrated by men from these so-called Irish regiments. At Batholomy, in Shropshire, Irish troops trapped twenty villagers in the church and then set fire to the pews to smoke them out before slitting the throats of twelve of them; Parliamentarian broadsheets claimed '1500 murthered'. The defenders of nearby Hopton Castle were stripped, tied back to back and had their throats slit by the Irish before being thrown into a ditch. In recompense for such acts, thirteen captured soldiers from Irish regiments were hanged by the Parliamentarians. Rupert then hanged thirteen captives in reprisal, sending the fourteenth man back with a warning that in future he would hang two rebels for every Irishman. The Earl of Essex, at the time commander-in-chief of Parliamentarian forces, enquired whether it was on the king's orders that Rupert had hanged the men. Rupert replied that it was by no other order than his own, adding that he had acted simply 'as a soldier, by soldier's law'. He also pointed out that English, Scottish, Irish, French, Dutch, Walloons, men of all religions and opinion had been captured by him in the past, but that he had always allowed quarter and equal exchange. Moreover, he insisted the Irish hanged by the English rebels had been 'His Majesty's good subjects'. It seems it needed a German prince to see beyond the inflamed passions of the time.

Atrocities also occurred in the heat of battle or its immediate aftermath. By and large, they fell within the accepted laws of war, but not always. When Prince Rupert's army arrived at Bolton in Lancashire in the spring of 1644, the town, a bastion of Protestantism described as 'the Geneva of the North', was defended by 2,000 soldiers and 1,500 armed civilians. When Rupert's first assault failed, the defenders strung up a captured Irish officer in full view of the Royalists. The enraged Catholic Earl of Derby, charging at the head of Sir Thomas Tyldesley's mainly Roman Catholic regiment, seconded by Colonel Robert Broughton's green-coated Irish battalion, led a second assault. In what might best be described as an accident waiting to happen, extreme English Protestants were pitted against extreme English Catholics, supported by justifiably enraged Irishmen. The Royalist cry was 'kill dead, kill dead'. Breaking through the town's defences, Bolton was said to have become 'the soldier's reward', a once sweet Godly place changed into 'a nest of owls and a den of dragons'. Tyldesley's Catholic regiment and the Irish green-coats were later blamed for much of what occurred. One of Tyldesley's officers openly boasted of being red up to the elbows with Protestant blood. Parliamentarian hacks claimed 1,500 murdered. The rebel commander, Alexander Rigby, admitted, however, to only 200. The rest, he said, ran away.

At the siege of Lyme in Dorset, conducted by Rupert's younger brother Maurice, the Parliamentarian defenders made it clear that no quarter would be given to any Irish or Cornish captured; the Irish and Cornish were despised in equal measure by the rough and ready townsfolk. When the siege was finally raised, a single, straggling Irish woman was taken prisoner by them. In an act of savagery consistent with the temper of the times, she was dragged through the streets of Lyme before being bludgeoned to death on the seashore. Little wonder the Irish troops in the pay of the king expected no quarter if they were captured. They fought on the basis of no quarter asked and none given. Even parliament's non-political and religiously moderate Lord General, Sir Thomas Fairfax, was obliged to enforce parliament's uncompromising policy toward captured Irishmen. After the decisive battle of the war, Naseby, fought in Leicestershire in the early summer of 1645, Fairfax mentioned in his official report his desire to proceed against captured Irishmen 'according to ordnance of parliament'. What that meant in practice is left unsaid, but among the more grisly relics of the battle are the knucklebones of unfortunate female Welsh camp followers, mistaken for Irish women, mutilated or slain by pursuing rebel troopers. Contemporary historian Elias Warburton described the Puritan horsemen as riding down these helpless women 'with all the fury of fanaticism'.

Another of the king's commanders, James Graham, Marquis of Montrose, relied on Irish troops from Ulster and the Western Isles to mount his campaigns in the Scottish Highlands against Scottish Presbyterian forces allied to the English parliament. Although typically smaller than those fought south of the border, battles fought in the Scottish Highlands were equally ferocious. At Tippermuir, in Perthshire, in September 1644, it was said that men might have walked upon dead corpses all the way to the town, so fierce was the fighting. At Aberdeen the same month, a witness claimed there to have been little slaughter in the fight, but horrible was the slaughter in the pursuit, mainly at the hands of Montrose's Irish. Patrick Gordon of Ruthven claimed the Irish slaughtered men and women with the same careless disregard as they would a hen.

By the end of 1644, Montrose planned to quarter for the winter in the lowlands, but his Irish commander Alasdair mac Colla insisted on campaigning in the Western Highlands. This led to the routing of the Campbells at Inverlochy, where Montrose's crack Irish troops won the day, described as firing by volley then dropping their muskets and falling on the opposing Campbells with broadsword and targe. Mac Colla also played a central role at the Battle of Auldearn, in May 1645. By leading a spoiling attack, he bought time for Montrose to launch a flanking movement that won the day; Scottish losses that day extended into four figures. Mac Colla's military tactics were rudimentary but effective. The Irishman was not with Montrose when the Highland army was later surprised and destroyed at Philiphaugh in the autumn of 1645, but 700 of his Irish troops died there, a massacre described as 'savage and inhumane ... outdoing the Turks and Scythians in rancour'. Even after Charles I's order to surrender and disband, mac Colla continued the fight in Argyll. For him there could be no ceasefire. Clan warfare stretched back through centuries of feuding with the Campbells and their allies and had become for him a way of life. As late as 1647, he was still holding out in the Western Highlands, albeit in increasingly desperate straits. Driven ever deeper into the wilds of Kintyre, he and some of his men found refuge on the Isle of Islay; others were massacred by their pursuers.

Whilst fighting raged in the Highlands, multiple armies with individual agendas criss-crossed Ireland doing untold damage. There were just a handful of battles. When they occurred the fortunes of the belligerents were mixed and rarely decisive. In the spring of 1643 Irish Royalists defeated a Catholic confederation army at Old Ross, co. Wexford. The ill-clad Irish infantry are said to have 'broken to pieces' when attacked, but Royalist troopers remained too intent on stripping the fallen to pursue, and the confederates were able to flee across the River Barrow to fight again another day. The war swung this way and that. A confederate army crushed the Scottish Covenanters at Benburb, in modern-day Tyrone, on 5 June 1646. The confederates' cry that day was 'Sancta Maria'. Volleys of musketry at point-blank range, followed by a charge delivered in the manner of mac Colla's Irish, decided the day. Between 2,000 and 3,000 Scotsmen were killed, set against 300 Irishmen. A separate Catholic confederate army was then worsted by Parliamentarian forces in the late summer of 1647, north-west of Maynooth at Dungan's Hill. Weak discipline and lack of cavalry made for random outcomes. English armies typically had the edge but confederate armies held up well when led by men of genius, as was the case with the war's most notable commander, Owen Roe O'Neill, the victor of Benburb.

Described as 'the Irishman who throughout the war had the clearest notion of what he wanted for his country and the Catholic Church', Owen Roe O'Neill was said to have been bred for war, having served in his teens in Ireland and then later in the Spanish Netherlands. On his return to Ulster he famously likened the province to 'a desert and a hell on earth'. With echoes of Calgacus prior to the Battle of Mons Graupius, he proclaimed himself to be 'up in arms', not against the English king but in defence and liberty of 'ourselves and the Irish natives of this kingdom'. When addressing his men, he stated, 'All Christendom knows your quarrel is good.' O'Neill's immediate enemy upon arrival in Ulster was the Scottish Covenanting army, led by fellow Thirty Years War veteran General Robert Monroe – a man considered to be O'Neill's equal tactically, a general who had notched up a string of successes when tying down Catholic forces in Ulster. Operating a scorched earth policy, Monroe plundered many northern towns, including Newry in the spring of 1642. Soon after this he raised the siege of Coleraine, but at Charlemont near Armagh the following year, he sought to surprise O'Neill and failed. Belfast then fell to him, by which time he had been promoted to command all the Protestant forces in the north of Ireland.

O'Neill's greatest victory against Monroe was at Benburb, mentioned in passing above, where he instructed his men 'in the name of the Father, Son and the Holy Ghost, to advance and not give fire till you are within pike-length of the enemy'. This important Irish victory demonstrated the effectiveness of well-drilled troops fighting in linear formation; also how, when well led, the Irish of the seventeenth century were a force to be reckoned with. After such a comprehensive victory, Ulster might have been won for the confederates, but their commanders immediately fell to infighting; 'divided councils', it was said, 'frittered away the advantages'.

Disheartened by the state of affairs in Ulster, having journeyed across the North Channel from Islay, Alasdair mac Colla might have travelled back to Scotland to renew his own personal war against the Campbells, but something prevented him. He remained in Ireland and served the Catholic confederate cause in Munster, gaining a lieutenant-generalship and the governorship of Clonmel. His immediate superior was Lord Taaffe, a man described by a contemporary as 'a brave, generous gamester and an exceedingly good partaker in any liquor you choose'. Prior to mac Colla's arrival, Taaffe had managed to avoid the attentions of the Earl of Ormond's Royalist ally, General Murrough O'Brien, Earl Inchiquin, who we last met at Liscarrol. O'Brien was a Protestant extremist known by the grim sobriquet 'Murrough of the Burnings', an allusion to his role in smoking out die-hard confederates. His most recent exploit in this regard had been at Cashel, where his troops had piled turfs of peat against the unyielding rocky bastion there to kill and at the same time cremate the confederate defenders and resident Catholic clergy.

On 12 November 1647, O'Brien mustered at Mallow, County Cork, and marched north-west to confront Taaffe's and mac Colla's army at a place called Knocknanuss, a wedge-shaped hill to the north of the small town of Kanturk, a strategic centre at the confluence of two rivers. A fortified house had been built there in 1601 as defence against the tide of English settlement. Taaffe's army faced east, occupying the length of the hill, with flanks and rear protected by the meandering River Awbeg, a tributary of the Blackwater, which flowed south to north. Mac Colla commanded the army's right wing. Numbers favoured the confederates, even if quality did not. Eight and a half thousand confederates faced just over half the number of Royalist troops. Taaffe's soldiers relied in the main on pikes. Opposing them, two-thirds of O'Brien's men were musketeers. The Royalists were also better provided with field artillery. O'Brien's account of the battle tells how he drew up two cannon, so that he might 'discompose' the formation of the enemy. He almost immediately succeeded: many of Taaffe's soldiers fled; those that did not rushed pell-mell down the hill toward the enemy, led on by mac Colla. Shock tactics that had worked so well in the Scottish Highlands proved once again effective. Mac Colla's men fired one or two volleys, then threw down their muskets and set upon the enemy with sword in hand, pursuing them a distance of 3 miles. O'Brien admitted to fifty common soldiers being killed in this action, whereas mac Colla and his men, though their losses were slight, found themselves cut off and isolated; no help was at hand when they were later set upon by O'Brien's cavalry. The exhausted redshanks fought on bravely.

> The horsemen gave a wheel [wheeled about] and came in [the] rear of the redshanks ... then began the mortality on both sides, the event doubtful ... never yielding, but rather gaining ground, [the redshanks] were all for the most part slaughtered.

Three thousand confederates lost their lives at Knocknanuss. O'Brien reckoned on a killing spree that lasted until darkness fell. Thirty-eight confederate colours were captured. Mac Colla was seized and shot by a junior officer, a man keen to gain the accolade of having made an end to such a prestigious adversary. While bards sang mac Colla's praises over fireside encampments, relieved enemies in Dublin, Edinburgh and London toasted his death. No tears should now be shed for him. He was a violent individual, even by seventeenth-century standards; a man who disdained the notion of quarter given, nor asked for it. Other than an unquenchable thirst for Campbell blood, he had few personal qualities, yet his death gave rise to many tales of courage and valour, gaining for him a stature more commensurate with his physical size than his achievements. More pertinent was that the twin set-backs of Dungan's Hill and Knocknanuss had brought confederate endeavours to nought.

14

THEY WENT NOT TOGETHER HAND IN HAND

When Charles I's final hopes of victory in England were dashed in August 1648 after a disastrous Royalist defeat at Preston in Lancashire, the Earl of Ormond sought to create an Irish grand coalition of Royalists, moderate confederates and disaffected Parliamentarians. This threat of further intervention into England from Ireland was recognised by the New Model Army commanders in England. Many of the king's private documents had been seized after the Battle of Naseby in 1645, and published in a pamphlet titled *The King's Cabinet opened*. Among them was a draft treaty with the Irish confederates, promising them public exercise of their religion plus sole possession of all churches in Ireland abandoned by Protestants. Charles was playing fast and loose with the Irish, willing to engage with them to gain short-term advantage, but in private admitting he would renege on any agreement made if other ways could be found of securing his throne. The papal nuncio, Rinuccini, realised this:

> I am alarmed by the general opinion of his Majesty's inconsistency and bad faith, which creates a doubt that whatever concessions he may make [to the Irish], he will never

ratify them unless it pleases him, or, not having appointed a Catholic viceroy, whether he might not be induced by his Protestant ministers to avenge himself on the noble heads in Ireland, and renew more fearfully than ever the terrors of heresy.

Even after the disaster at Preston, where thousands of Scots and Englishmen died in his name, Charles continued to hold out hopes of an invasion from Ireland. When secretly corresponding with Ormond, he promised to repudiate any terms agreed with his captors detrimental to the Irish if forces were raised to set him at liberty. The Irish remained undecided. Should they give the luckless Charles their unfettered support or abandon him? If the latter, they might instead work toward making Ireland impregnable to invasion from England and look abroad for allies.

When later incarcerated at Hurst Castle – a grim Solent fortress accessible only by a narrow spit of sand at low tide – the Royalist press raged that Lord General Fairfax sought to threaten the king's health with fogs and mists, 'as a more plausible way of murder than by pistol or poison'. Yet even while in extremis, Charles remained sanguine about the prospect of intervention from Ireland. It never came of course, nor, if it had, could it have prospered. Fairfax's army and fleet were among the most powerful in Europe. When the king was moved to Windsor, a strong guard was posted at his door night and day. None could see him without Fairfax's approval. Described as that 'Man of Blood', Charles was viewed as the fountainhead of past and present violence. Common Parliamentarian soldiers held him in outright hatred. Many had lived through two major conflagrations brought on by him. They blamed him for abandoning fellow Protestants in Ireland and of encouraging the Papist Irish to intervene in England. Their cry was 'Justice! Justice! Execution! Execution!' Charles stood condemned as a tyrant, traitor, murderer and a public enemy. Nevertheless, when a single blow from the axeman later struck off his head, a young bystander would later recall such a groan from the crowd as he had never heard before, 'and desired never to hear again'.

Command of the English Parliamentarian forces in Ireland devolved to Colonel Michael Jones. He arrived at Dublin at the head of 2,000 men in June 1647. A veteran of the final battles of the English Civil War, Jones' intervention placed the war in southern Ireland in the context of an English Parliamentarian confrontation against all the various local Royalists and rebels then in arms. Ormond attempted to hold Jones in check at Rathmines, near Dublin, with an army over 7,000 strong. Jones matched him in numbers, but had the advantage of loyal, seasoned troops, whereas Ormond's command was heavy with what were later described as recriminatory and demoralised soldiers. When fighting commenced, Jones quickly got the upper hand. After an unsuccessful cavalry charge launched by Ormond, an English officer commented that there was no fight worth relating left in the Irish. All took to their heels. In less than two hours Ormond's forces were driven from the environs of Dublin. Six hundred Irishmen lost their lives and a further 2,500 were taken prisoner. Lord Clarendon, the great historian of the wars, later wrote that there was nothing new or surprising about 'raw, new levied and unpractised men' under inexperienced officers being overcome by well-governed and disciplined soldiery.

Jones next marched on Royalist-held Drogheda, but was driven off by Ormond's reformed forces. The task of storming Drogheda was left to Oliver Cromwell, another of parliament's leading generals, now lingering at Bristol, awaiting £100,000 promised by parliament to make up the arrears in pay for his soldiers. Cromwell spoke of his army as Israelites setting out to 'extirpate the idolatrous inhabitants of Canaan'. Upon arriving at Dublin with a strong army in the late summer of 1649, he forbade his men from rapine and pillage; two men were hanged to help make the point. He also made sure to pay his troops promptly to deter looting. Cromwell hoped to gain the support of the civilian population of Ireland, and also to win over wavering English

Royalists. When news filtered through to Ormond's soldiers that Cromwell's army had received their pay, the English among them deserted to the Parliamentarian army in droves. Ormond is said to have remarked he feared Cromwell's 'money more than his face'.

Cromwell's troopers, infantrymen and gunners appeared outside Drogheda – 'the key to the north' – on 2 September. The army's guns were deployed south of the town, the eleven heavy siege guns taking some considerable time to be drawn up, unlimbered and sited to concentrate on a two-hundred-yard stretch of wall which ran on either side of the Duleek Gate. The army's passage from Dublin through the verdant green of August was remarked upon by one of its officers, who considered how bold a sight they made marching through an alien landscape, each soldier smartly apparelled in a Venetian red uniform. Lack of Royalist artillery along the town walls allowed Cromwell's sappers to entrench within musket shot. Experience of warfare in England yielded immediate results. Commanders like Cromwell and Prince Rupert did not hesitate to act with extreme violence when faced by intractable garrisons, especially so if reasonable terms were refused, thus putting at risk the lives of men who must of necessity attempt to take the place by storm. Drogheda would prove no exception. On 10 September, after terms of surrender had been refused by the garrison commander, the Parliamentarian batteries soon made themselves felt, bringing down the south-east corner tower and the steeple of St Mary's Church immediately behind the wall at the eastern end. Infantry burst through the gaps at five o'clock in the evening of the following day after a further period of cannonade had opening a great rupture in the wall beside the Duleek Gate. The Royalist foot soldiers put up a determined resistance, assisted by their cavalry, which launched counter-attacks in the confined space available to them. During the fighting the Parliamentarian assault commander, Colonel James Castle, was shot in the head and killed, one of several of Cromwell's officers and common soldiers to fall when scrambling to gain a foothold into the town. Cromwell himself led the final assault, his field artillery having swept the breach with grapeshot prior to the attack, driving the defenders back to the Mill Mount, a former

Norman motte-and-bailey castle built by Hugh de Lacy, located within 150 yards of the perimeter wall. Other Royalists made for the bridge across the Boyne, some taking refuge in St Peter's Church, or in St Sunday's steeple at the end of Magdalen Street, beside the northern section of wall. Many of those at St Peters were later incinerated when the Parliamentarian soldiers made a smoking pyre of the pews.

Cromwell ordered that no enemy bearing arms should be spared. His biographer, Antonia Fraser, considers he may have lost all self-control, and that he 'literally saw red' at Drogheda. She states that 'blood lust … swept across the Parliamentarian ranks', and that their commander did nothing to quell it. The Royalist garrison commander, Englishman Sir Arthur Aston, who had earlier boasted that any man who could take Drogheda could take Hell itself, was equally culpable, having allowed hubris to invite disaster. He paid the ultimate price, being battered to death with his own wooden leg. How many civilians were caught up in the violence is not known, but casualties that day may have exceeded total garrison numbers. Some civilians were doubtless targeted in the heat of the action; certainly this was the case with Catholic priests and friars, who were slaughtered wherever they were found, no matter if they cowered before their assailants, some clutching their crucifixes as if for protection. Parliamentarian losses were accounted at around 150 killed or wounded. Emulating the Roman practice of decimation, after the battle one in ten captives was shot. The rest were shipped off to the West Indies.

A second storming followed hard on the heels of the first. At Wexford, on 3 October 1649, Cromwell summoned the town and offered lenient surrender terms. His troopers had earlier crossed the swollen River Slaney at Enniscorthy and approached Wexford from the south. The Rosslare garrison further down the coast fled when Parliamentarian dragoons were first spotted. This allowed the Royal Navy unopposed access into Wexford Bay. Cromwell's heavy siege train was unloaded and batteries set up to concentrate their fire against Wexford Castle, key to the town's defence. Wexford's mayor and aldermen would have surrendered if they could, but the Royalists in the town urged them to stand fast and await an inevitable weakening of the Parliamentarians to disease and desertion. Negotiations dragged out for a week or so. During this time the garrison may have been reinforced by Ormond. Losing patience, Cromwell ordered his batteries to again commence fire. Crumbling defences persuaded the Royalists to parley, but their demands proved unacceptable. Not only did they demand freedom to march out with colours flying to the fortress at New Ross, they also demanded Catholic clergy should remain unmolested and that the Royalist ships in the harbour, mainly privateers, be afforded safe passage with full crews, ammunition and provisions. By this time two wide breaches had been made in the castle wall. Without further warning, Cromwell's troops stormed through. Royalists who made a stand in the town square were cut down. Civilians were shot or drowned when they sought to escape the mayhem by fleeing across the Slaney. Cromwell had not ordered a general massacre, his troops simply ran amok; but, as pointed out by Fraser, as at Drogheda he did little to restrain them. Much of the killing took place at the Market Cross; one observer claimed 200 women of the town, 'with charming eyes and melting tears', fell victim to the unrestrained carnage.

Contemporaries viewed the stormings of Drogheda and Wexford as extraordinarily severe. Ormond wrote of the horror felt by Royalists, saying, 'They are so stupefied that it is with great difficulty that I can persuade them to act anything like men towards their own preservation.' Cromwell, meanwhile, extolled the lustre and glory of English liberty. He promised that the Irish would be well used, so long as they never again took up arms. Ethnic contempt for the Irish was balanced by a keen appreciation of the value, commercially, of a compliant population and a return to normality. Cromwell's name has, mainly on the basis of these two events – Drogheda and Wexford – become abhorred by generations of Irish and still plagues the dreams of Finn McCool and the restless Fianna. His visitation on Ireland is still referred to today as 'the curse of Cromwell'. Yet Parliamentarian General Sir Charles Coote's massacre of Royalists at Coleraine in mid-September

1649 and his forcing of the Scottish inhabitants of Carrickfergus from their homes in the depth of winter, or Bishop MacMahon's massacre of Protestants at Dungiven, co. Londonderry, in May 1650, attract less attention, although arguably more cruel.

That Oliver Cromwell saw no need to excuse the excesses of his troops is understandable when the stormings are placed in the context of seventeenth-century European rules of warfare. Cromwell's main regret at Wexford, it appears, was not the loss of life but that the town was so badly damaged it could no longer provide winter quarters for the English army. Cromwell defended the killings at Drogheda and Wexford as a righteous judgement of God, telling parliament he hoped this bitterness would save much effusion of blood – words which would be echoed by the Duke of Wellington in the nineteenth century when he declared that 'the practice of refusing quarter to a garrison which stands an assault, is not a useless effusion of blood'. By acting harshly, lives might have been saved in the long run. This would prove true in Ireland; after Drogheda, garrisons at Carlingford, Newry, Trim, Dundalk, Arklow, Ferns and Enniscorthy quickly threw in the towel.

*

At least four major armies fought for control in Ireland during the so-called Eleven Years Civil War, with over 50,000 combatants among them. All these fighting men had to be supported by an already impoverished population and a resource base far less productive than that of England. Taxes to support the military raised revenues to levels seven times greater than in peacetime. The additional drain on communities caused by the quartering of troops and widespread looting added to common people's woes. When armies pulled out of areas they could no longer control, there was also the deliberate destruction of grain stocks and supplies. Famine resulted. Soldiers and civilians alike died for want of cats and dogs to eat. In Dublin by 1649 over 1,000 people were dying each week from malnutrition. Disease stalked hand in hand with hunger. Dysentery took hold of the Cromwellian army and never left it. If relatively rich Dublin was ravaged, what can conditions in other parts of Ireland have been like, where the apocalyptic four horsemen roamed free? An unknown Irish poet lamented the failure of his countrymen to combine against the Cromwellians and ward off these horrors:

> The Gael are being wasted, deeply wounded,
> Subjugate, slain, extirpated,
> By plague, by famine, by war, by persecution,
> It was God's justice not to free them,
> They went not together hand in hand.

Owen Roe O'Neill's position had already deteriorated before Cromwell's arrival. Out of favour with the Catholic confederate command, he agreed a temporary truce with the English. At the war's cessation, the Irishman may have been promised a pardon, but by then he was terminally ill. He died on 6 November 1649 at Cloughoughter Castle, a lonely fortress outpost located on a small island in Lough Oughter, co. Cavan. Some say he had been betrayed and that the castle had been a virtual prison. Why O'Neill ended his days there is debatable. Was he under house arrest, or did the castle provide sanctuary during his last days? The place is heralded today as a scenic attraction: a nineteenth-century newspaper article described it as standing on an island just sufficient to contain the castle and a small margin of rock around it. Deep water stretches away to distant shorelines. Now an evocative ruin, described as 'round and massive', the walls remain immensely thick, still able to constrain men, if not the spirit of the Fianna.

By the time of O'Neill's death the north of Ireland had become one huge battleground. In early December 1649, a month after O'Neill's death, the Parliamentarians defeated Monro and Lord Clandeboye at Lisnagarvey, twenty miles south of Carrickfergus. Over a thousand were killed. Many weapons and supplies were seized by the victors. Carrickfergus surrendered to Coote on 13 December, which left most of Ulster under Parliamentarian control. It seems O'Neill's death had left a gap in the Catholic confederate high command. When filled, it was by a cleric rather than a soldier, the fifty-year-old Heber MacMahon, Bishop of Clogher, a man described by papal nuncio Rinuccini as of great energy but with no military experience, 'a good bishop but a poor general ... and a man entirely swayed by political rules and motives'. MacMahon had been the moving force and principal architect of unity in Ireland in the face of English aggression, a champion in the Irish political tradition, if not of martial caste.

Coote was quick to take advantage of MacMahon's military inexperience, notching up a major victory against him at Scarriffhollis, co. Londonderry, on 21 June 1650, just a month after a massacre of Protestants by Royalist soldiers at Dungiven, mentioned earlier. MacMahon's army had crossed the River Swilly into Donegal a mile or so upstream of Letterkenny, his rearguard all the while under the bickering attention of Coote's outriders. The clergyman-general's encampment was described as 'a plain field among the rocks on the north bank'. The departure of the bishop's mounted foraging parties left him with just 3,000 infantrymen. This put his army roughly on a par with the Parliamentarians in numbers, if not in quality. Had MacMahon taken the advice of his officers and held his position, it seems likely Coote's army would have been thwarted. The confederate encampment was on high ground at Glendoon Hill, a feature inaccessible to horse or foot. Fired up by a Godly disrespect for danger, MacMahon railed at his commanders, accusing them of cowardice. A contemporary pamphlet claimed, 'MacMahon did so distemper the warlike deportment of those heroes ... that oblivious to all military advantage ... they put themselves in a distracted posture of battle.' The Irish recrossed the river to occupy a bog, where it was said no horse could fight. This at least negated Coote's advantage in cavalry, but could not prevent his brigades of foot striking the Irish frontally and in flank. Two and half thousand Irish fell for the loss of a hundred Parliamentarians. The losses represented the complete destruction of MacMahon's army and its rich officer cadre. Many men were trapped between bog and river, to be cut down where they stood. Those that were given quarter were later shot or hacked to pieces on Coote's orders. Owen Roe O'Neill's only son, Henry, was among them. Borrowing a script from Cromwell, the Parliamentarian commander boasted of that day's work being God's doing. MacMahon was among those later captured. His horse foundered and the bishop broke a number of bones in the fall. Coote had the bishop incarcerated until his thigh-bone had knit. He then made him limp to the gallows, where he was hung and quartered. His head graced Londonderry's main gate for a time; other body parts were interred at Devenish Island. Bards sang of him being a warlike lion, the most upright of the Gaels. His death at the hands of the Protestants placed him among ninety or more priests killed during the Eleven Years War. Their names would later be submitted to papal consideration for beatification in 1914 on the eve of the First World War.

When Cromwell fell seriously ill at New Ross in the winter of 1649 (he had probably contracted malaria), his son-in-law Henry Ireton, a man described by Clarendon as 'of melancholic, reserved and dark nature', deputised for him. Minded of mortality while on his sick-bed, possibly feverish, Cromwell cajoled the Irish, telling them that their supposed covenant with God was 'with death and Hell' and that he had come to take an account of the innocent blood they had shed. Meanwhile, Jones and Ireton were campaigning in modern-day county Kilkenny where they captured a number of confederate strongholds, including Ardfinnan on the River Suir, one of King John's old castles. Castles like Ardfinnan, Cahir, Cashel, Fethard and Clonmel formed an extensive and mutually supporting shield, guarding the rich agricultural heartlands of Munster.

The following year another of Cromwell's commanders, Roger Boyle, lord of Broghill, bloodlessly seized the city of Cork, after slyly persuading the English Royalist garrison to defect. Broghill had once ordered the execution of a number of confederate officers, in his words 'to affright these little castles from so peremptorily standing out'. This and word of what occurred at Drogheda and Wexford eased confederate decision making. A counter-stoke from Kerry designed to relieve beleaguered Clonmel, launched by the confederate commander David Roche, Viscount Fermoy, fell victim to Broghill's cavalry at Macroom, co. Cork, on 10 May 1650. Surprised and unable to set up a defensive cordon, 500 Irish soldiers of the 4,000 engaged lost their lives outside the town when charged by Broghill's cavalry. Eight company colours were taken and 1,000 muskets captured. The ornately castellated Macroom Castle had earlier been set ablaze by the confederates to deny it to Broghill's men. The following day, the Parliamentarians demanded the surrender of nearby Carrigadrohid Castle, on the north bank of the River Lee. They threatened the death of Boetius MacEgan, the confederate Bishop of Ross, captured at Macroom, should the defenders not comply. Having first ordered those manning Carrigadrohid's walls to stand to their posts, the brave bishop was hung by the reins of his own horse from a tree outside the castle walls, in plain view of the garrison. Shortly after this the castle garrison surrendered.

At Clonmel, co. Tipperary, the arrival of heavy siege guns and their siting on elevated ground to the north of the town at the appropriately named Gallows Hill might have predicated the town's fall, but, restricted to bombarding only the northern walls because of bogs to the west and east, the breach proved too stoutly defended for a breakthrough to be made. Moreover, confederate commander Hugh O'Neill's troops could concentrate fire at this point to repel all Parliamentarian attacks. A 'V'-shaped earth and timber bastion, constructed around this weak point by the confederates and lined with musketeers and cannon, proved more than enough to counter their attempts. Cut down by musketry and cannonade, up to 1,000 Parliamentarian infantry lost their lives before retreating beyond their siege-lines. Even the persuasive Cromwell, now recovered to better health, could not rally the runaways. Dismounted cavalrymen made a second attack, but this fared no better than the first. Officers were the first to fall. Those they led forward were quickly discouraged. Hundreds of Parliamentarians would lose their lives before the survivors were recalled by trumpeters, whose discordant blasts heralded a crushing defeat for the Parliamentarians, perhaps the most serious since the New Model Army's founding. The failure at Clonmel was also a personal blow to Cromwell's prestige. Writers have since posited that when faced by resolute opposition in Ireland Cromwell 'floundered'. Unlike the English, Irish commanders did not commit themselves to fighting set-piece battles or engage in dangerous marches en masse. There were to be no repeats of victories like Marston Moor, Naseby or Preston for Cromwell in Ireland. It was Cromwell's guns, described by the Irish as 'sons of Mars', which in the end would reduce Ireland, not the common English soldiery.

The lord general was now faced with the prospect of having to tie down his weakened army in a lengthy siege. His planned return to England had to be postponed until Hugh O'Neill capitulated. Meanwhile, within Clonmel, O'Neill also faced challenging decisions. Food in the town had run out and his remaining men were exhausted. In desperation, by taking advantage of Clonmel's boggy hinterland and unopposed southern perimeter, he managed to successfully extricate his soldiers under cover of darkness. Next day the mayor of Clonmel sought terms from Cromwell. Keen to end the siege, Cromwell promised a generous outcome. Although later infuriated when learning of O'Neill's escape, he kept to his word. None in the town were harmed, but Cromwell was described by a colleague as being 'as vexed as ever he was since he first put on a helmet against the king' by the outcome.

When Cromwell finally departed for England, Parliament ratified Henry Ireton's governorship. His instructions were to suppress idolatry, popery, superstition and profanity. This was to be achieved by widespread colonisation and ethnic cleansing. Irish peasantry in the south of Ireland were to be driven from their homes with the excuse that they had been instrumental in supporting the 1641 rising. Cashing in on this, Ireton invested heavily in dispossessed land, accumulating before his death almost 14,000 acres of farmland in counties Kilkenny and Tipperary. When plague broke out, Ireton naively sought to combat the pestilence by proclaiming eight days of fasting to be imposed on a population already faint with hunger. Typhus would not reach Ireland until 1708, but something like it, called the Irish Ague, existed in the sixteenth and seventeenth centuries, quite possibly malaria. Cromwell, as we have seen, became a victim. The governor of Waterford would later write that plague and famine swept away whole counties, so that a man might travel twenty or thirty miles and not see a single living creature, 'either man, beast or bird ... they being all dead or quit such desolate places'. A third of a million people may have died during the Eleven Years War and afterwards because of the collapse of the Irish economy. Rather than the headline massacres, malnutrition and disease were the main cause for this dramatic loss of life.

Ormond was by this time exiled. His replacement, the Royalist Ulick Burke, Marquis of Clanrickard, was at first reluctant to accept the post of king's deputy. Ailing from a complaint known as 'the bloody waters', probably gallstones, the marquis was only won over through unswerving loyalty to the Crown in the shape of the also exiled Charles II. Being cautious by nature, Burke made an indifferent soldier. He surrendered the last bastions holding out in Connaught to the Cromwellians in April 1652. Some claimed he betrayed the 'whole nation', one critic saying the 'dearest interests of rational creatures, religion, lives, and best fortunes had been lost'. The marquis would die five years later, in London. Oliver Cromwell toasted him as a man of honour, a plaudit also shared by exiled Royalists. Lord Clarendon remembered Burke as 'a person of unquestionable fidelity ... and of the most eminent constancy to the Catholic religion of any man in the three kingdoms'. He added that the peer had suffered 'unnatural fatigues and distresses' while in Ireland, which hastened his death.

With a substantial stakeholding in farmland to protect, Ireton proved amenable to the introduction of less draconian measures in Ireland. He argued that 'Irish lives, liberties and estates should be recognised, or the land would grow barren and further violence erupt'. Parliament rejected the advice. Their logic was that much of Ireland, including whole swathes of Connaught, Munster and Ulster, remained unpacified; the noose thrown around Ireland had yet to be tightened, and, at the very least, the rebellion's leaders should be punished by having their land confiscated to pay soldiers' arrears. Military campaigns were planned to make this happen, but attempts by Ireton to dislodge confederate garrisons holding out at Athlone were curtailed by the onset of winter.

The following year, Ireton marched on Limerick. He was a less decisive commander than his father-in-law; rather than launch an assault, Ireton chose to starve the town into submission. When civilians attempted to leave, he deterred them by threatening to hang them. (Some were in fact hanged to set an example.) Soldiers in his army faced execution if they did not obey such draconian orders; but it seems not every Englishmen agreed with the way the war was being prosecuted or how Ireland was being carved up. A strongly radical movement within the army, known as the Leveller movement, had at one time even supported the Irish rising of 1641, saying in their newsletter *The Moderate Intelligencer* that the rebellion was a reasonable response to tyranny. Their Leveller name came from a desire to set things straight and 'raise a parity and community in the kingdom'. Its adherents called for male suffrage, electoral reform, regular elections, religious tolerance and the closure of debtors' prisons. They also argued that the English army had no right to be in Ireland, that 'natural rights' of subjects had been abused. Unofficial spokesmen at a regimental level, known as agitators, produced a statement called *The Case for the Army truly stated*, wherein they laid out their demands of parliament to Fairfax. Debates held at Putney, near London, in the late autumn of 1647 discussed demands for greater social justice, some of which were later presented to parliament. Riots in London erupted the following year when it became clear the proposals would not be acted upon. Many from Ireton's own regiment mutinied in the summer of 1649. A junior officer named Thompson, the ringleader, was later blindfolded and shot against the wall of a church in Burford, Gloucestershire. Two others, both privates, were shot at Oxford. Many men who had supported the mutinies, having bought into the Leveller rhetoric, were now reluctantly fighting in Ireland.

Limerick proved a harder nut to crack than either Drogheda or Wexford. Its strong walls were buttressed by earthen bastions. Moreover a degree of sparring in the open, including a full-scale set-piece fight, famous as the last battle of the Eleven Years War, fought at Knocknaclashy (also referred to as Knockbreck) near Banteer, co. Cork, in July 1651, disrupted siege operations. At Knocknaclashy, when an Irish relief army attempted to resupply the city, better horsed and equipped Parliamentarians, under the command of Lord Broghill, scattered Viscount Muskerry's smaller force of cavalry at the first charge. Broghill's account of the battle speaks of the opposing sides pistoling into each other's faces before mingling in combat. Irish pikemen restored a degree of order to the army's position when advancing on the still rallying English horsemen, a rare event at any period of the civil wars in the British Isles. Broghill was wounded by a pike-thrust. The Irish were heard to cry out, 'Kill the fellow with the gold-laced coat!' but the general escaped to fight another day. A Major Willis had better fortune on the other flank that day by breaking through the ranks of more slowly advancing Irish pikemen, killing upwards of 250 of them. None captured were spared save those of quality. When stripping the dead, the English troopers found charms sewn into the young Irishmen's clothing, failed talismans to ward off death. Parliamentarian losses were twenty-six dead and 130 wounded. Broghill quipped that at Knocknaclashy there was never known 'better knocking' in Ireland.

Surviving Irish soldiers fell back on the fifteenth-century O'Donoghue castle at Ross, near Killarney. They later capitulated to the Parliamentarians in 1652, when the castle fell to a lakeside attack. A local legend prophesised that 'Ross may all assault disdain, until strange ships sail on Lough Laune'. Almost 1,000 men marched out from behind its walls. A further 3,000 from the surrounding region also surrendered. Mountainous and rugged Kerry was by this time the haunt of desperate men, and also wolves. Wolf packs roamed freely, not just in Kerry but elsewhere across Ireland, sometimes within settled areas. They had become of sufficient menace to attract bounty hunters, raising the price of wolf-hounds to a premium.

After the fall of Ross Castle, prominent Irish leaders were executed by being hanged for a time and then beheaded. Dispersed elements like those led by the famous rebel Richard Grace (a descendant of Raymond le Gros) were brought to battle near Loughrea and destroyed. Grace managed to escape. A reward of £300 was placed on his head. He survived the wars and would later, under a Jacobite administration, become Governor of Athlone. We will hear more of him.

By the time Limerick fell – an event celebrated by Ireton with a night of triumph, with volleys of shot and the sounding of drums – an estimated 5,000 Irish men women and children had lost their lives in the campaign, against 2,000 Englishmen, mainly to disease rather than the armed struggle. One of those to succumb was Ireton. He died a month after Limerick's capitulation, on 26 November. One of his last recorded statements was that Ireland was a conquered nation and 'the English might with justice assert their right of control'. His body was shipped back to London and later interred in Henry VII's chapel in Westminster Abbey. When Charles II later gained the throne in 1660 after Cromwell's death, Ireton's corpse was disinterred with Cromwell's and hung for several days at Tyburn, before being dismantled and buried beneath the gallows.

*

On 11 September 1652, a new Commander-in-Chief of what became known as the Army of the Commonwealth of England in Ireland named Charles Fleetwood arrived at Wexford. Thirty-four years of age when he arrived aboard the frigate *Revenge*, Fleetwood had risen through the ranks during the English Civil War in the wake of Cromwell's rapid ascent to power. He bolstered his career by marrying Cromwell's eldest daughter Biddy, who accompanied him to Ireland. It was her second trip there. Fleetwood had gained both wife and the control of Ireland from the late Henry Ireton. A month before his arrival, the English parliament (a mere remnant of its past size, representing only the army's narrow interest) passed the Act of Settlement on Ireland. The papist Irish were graded by 'guilt and wealth': the poor with less than £10 in goods were pardoned; all others were to be held accountable unless it could be proven otherwise and liable to forfeiture of lands and goods. In this way the Cromwellian administration sought to pay off its debts and reward the faithful at Ireland's expense. Follow-up legislation carved up the country geographically; only Clare and Connaught would remain under Irish control, becoming the focus for forced resettlements. All towns in Ireland would be administered from Dublin. In the case of Galway and Waterford, for instance, former burgesses would be evicted. The property of the Catholic Church would be seized and its ministry disestablished. With sinister undertones of the General Government of Poland under the Nazis, such was the legal and executive framework Fleetwood was to inherit.

Unlike Cromwell and Ireton, Fleetwood gets a guardedly positive press in Ireland, a man perhaps more inclined to parley than cross swords. The main pocket of rebel resistance continuing to threaten Dublin – comprising the Cavanaghs, O'Byrnes and O'Toole's – had been neutralised by the time he stepped onto the quay at Wexford. A newly fortified Pale had been established between the Barrow and the Boyne: anyone found in arms within its boundary was to be treated as a tory and shot. 'Tory' was the slang name for a Catholic rebel and the origin of the modern political term. Approximately 40,000 Irish men at arms were allowed to travel abroad rather than face an uncertain future in Ireland. These 'war-dogs', as they were called, joined the armies of Continental powers at amity with the Cromwellian Commonwealth. It was considered better that than they should join the tories. When the main leader of the 1641 rebellion, Sir Phelim O'Neill, was captured and brought to trial in the early spring of 1653, Fleetwood was said to have promised the knight a reprieve if he implicated the late Charles I in the rising. Sir Phelim had once produced a warrant saying as much, but it had proved to be a forgery, used at the time as a *ruse de guerre*. He resisted Fleetwood's appeal and was executed as a traitor.

There still existed the threat of a foreign invasion sponsored by the exiled Charles II's supporters. Diligence was therefore required. Meanwhile, discontent in the army over arrears in pay and religious affairs dogged Fleetwood's oversight of the armed forces. The impatience of businessmen who wished quickly to lay their hands on land confiscated from the Irish also acted as a source of friction. Fleetwood drew closer to radicals in the army and sometimes appeared to side with those threatened with dispossession of their lands and titles over the swarms of carpetbaggers, something which caused Cromwell sufficient concern for him to send his son Henry to Dublin to witness first hand what was occurring. The parallel to Henry II sending his son John to do much the same is unmissable, despite the changed circumstances. Edmund Ludlow wrote that Henry was sent to 'to feel the pulse of the officers there touching his coming over to command in that nation'.

The immediate result for Fleetwood was mild censure. By indulging the various partisan leaders in Ireland, it was claimed Fleetwood made a difficult situation worse. In London and at Dublin, investors were clamouring for the removal of the native Irish westward. Fortunes were at stake. 'Fat-rumped jeering men with shaven jaws and bragging accents' – as the freebooters were described by the Irish poet Daibh O' Bruadair – demanded results. The idea, as mentioned before, was for the dispossessed Irish to be transplanted west of the Shannon where the land was generally poor. Lt General Edmund Ludlow wrote that the objective of the transplantation was to encourage new settlers to colonise Ireland 'without disturbance [from the Irish]'. The fear was that intermarriage would weaken the colony. Other men, like Vincent Gookin, writing in 1655, feared that as a consequence of such ethnic cleansing Irish husbandry would be wrecked and that honest Irish workers would be made into brigands, the only alternative left to them other than to starve. When there was armed resistance, Gookin exclaimed, was it any wonder that many refused to be 'driven like geese by a hat upon a stick'.

Described as an 'ambitious but vindictive scheme', such racial purging was reluctantly approved by Fleetwood, even though he considered much that was proposed to be impractical. Resistance from armed tories, the need to retain Irish workers east of the Shannon, and the danger of creating an increasingly fractious frontier, all argued against mass transportation westward. One critic of the scheme pointed out that the Romans forged an empire through allowing retired soldiery to marry into the local populations, not by displacing the females, leaving none to breed with. Unsurprisingly, the pace and momentum of the transplantation slowed. In September 1655, Fleetwood was recalled to England. Henry Cromwell, who had arrived back in Ireland in the August of that year, replaced him. Fleetwood for a time maintained the lord governorship role, while the former commanded the army and oversaw administration. The arrangement has been described as one of Cromwell's least satisfactory compromises. The need for Henry to gain 'the grudging acquiescence' of Fleetwood slowed the execution of policy and soured relations between the two men. Not until 1657 did Henry Cromwell gain full authority to act as he pleased in Ireland, but this was almost on the eve of his father's death and the elevation of his elder brother Richard to the lord protectorship in November 1658. Henry was also promoted, becoming in effect the Lord Protector of Ireland. Henry admitted he had 'great strivings' before he could prevail with himself to accept the commission, a mark of the humility of the man. He continued to maintain a practical, secular stance when dealing with the many vying factions at Dublin. His rule was marked by moderation. He was not fanatically religious, yet possessed what has been termed 'a sincere personal faith'.

Like governors before him stretching back to medieval times, he suffered from lack of funding. Subsidies from England were progressively curtailed. Retaining a standing army sufficient for the task proved increasingly problematic. Sixteen thousand men was seen as the absolute minimum to keep the peace in Ireland, but was a number difficult to maintain. On the religious front, the Ulster Scots, described by Henry as 'a pack of knaves', were reluctantly given licence to minister their Presbyterianism to the victim Irish: one of their number even became the prelate of St Katherine's Church at Dublin. Henry more readily supported the work of Anglicans and Episcopalians in Munster, overseeing the establishment of churches in keeping with English norms, laying the foundation for a more widely practised Protestantism.

Henry remained suspicious of all Catholics and was concerned their leaders might look to Spain, then at war with England, for support. Round-ups of church leaders followed periods of unusual tension. Internment camps were built for them on the Aran Islands. Forces were despatched to a number of coastal areas to suppress agitators and guard against Spanish landings. For Henry, practical exigencies came to the fore when signing off a supply of young Irish boys and girls to the West Indies in the autumn of 1655. By the end of the decade many thousands of young persons were transported overseas to the West Indies or the Americas. This did not include the untold numbers driven into Connaught to face an uncertain fate. This enforced exodus of Irish men, women and children rates in infamy with any of the headline massacres. Well-meaning observers at Dublin were in no doubt about the morality of the case. One described 'the rapacious English' as inflicting greater suffering on the Irish than the Pharaoh upon the Israelites. Oliver Cromwell, on the other hand, viewed Ireland's fate as God's will.

15

NO SURRENDER!

The impetus for the restoration of the monarchy occurred in Ireland sometime in advance of England, when a group of Cromwellian officers declared for Charles II. General Monck's more famous intercession when leading an army across the Coldstream Brook from Scotland to England came later, in 1660. Ireland was by this time economically and politically ruined and beset by what can only be called religious apartheid: 75 per cent of the population were Catholic, but only Protestants, many of them non-conformist, held full citizenship rights; only Catholics who could prove they had played no part in the earlier insurrections were given leave to appeal against the seizure of their lands. As much in the wilderness politically as territorially, the Catholic majority during the reign of Charles II was further undermined by a reluctance on the part of the priesthood to acknowledge any guilt for the convulsions of the 1640s, which they claimed to have been a just, albeit lamented, war.

Charles II famously once told his ministers that 'he wished well to the Irish', but added, 'favour must be given to my Protestant subjects.' Entrenched positions on both sides made the task of moderates almost impossible. Politically, the Presbyterians were by far the dominant power in Ulster, and they had also made inroads elsewhere in Ireland. To buttress against them, incoming Royalists assisted in the re-establishment of the Protestant Church of Ireland. Men previously sidelined were brought back into positions of authority: one to the archbishopric of Armagh, another to the chancellorship of Dublin University. Rehabilitating Catholics could not be so easily achieved. Efforts to do so had to be made in the teeth of fierce opposition. Fear of loss of land rights matched religious bigotry. When a Roman Catholic priest named Peter Walsh sought to obtain freedom of religious practice he was checked by the all-Protestant Irish parliament, which feared a Jesuit revival and renewed violence. Walsh did at least secure the release of 120 imprisoned priests. These were the lucky ones – lucky not to have earlier been hanged or skewered by the Cromwellians.

The plight of the majority of Catholics in Ireland everywhere remained desperate. Richard Talbot, a prominent Irish Catholic soldier, a survivor of Drogheda and a close friend of the king's brother James, Duke of York, was nominated to raise the issue of land rights with Ormond. So heated did the subsequent exchanges become that Ormond, while attending on the king, asked if it was His Majesty's pleasure that he should put off his doublet to fight duels with Dick Talbot. When another Act of Settlement was passed in 1662, the Irish Protestants at Dublin attempted to amend the statute to ensure the dispossession of even more Catholic Irish. Talbot stood up to them and advertised himself as a recovery agent. Over the coming years he successfully managed the restoration of lost Catholic lands, making a fortune for himself in the process. When accused of false representation and of taking bribes, Talbot reacted angrily and was briefly placed under lock and key in the Tower of London.

The mid-1670s were years of famine in Ireland, a direct result of impoverishment and land seizures: as we have seen, a recurring theme throughout this narrative. The period between the years 1675 and 1685, however, witnessed a sustained recovery, attracting an influx of English planters from the north-west into the Laggan Valley, in Ulster. Even so, a resurgence of Catholicism was much feared. In London, the Whigs – Presbyterians who sought to limit if not altogether deny royal power and prevent any Catholic revival in England or Ireland – were appealed to by Charles II to remember that religion, liberty and property were all lost when the monarchy was shaken off. A feared return to popery became the number one issue; in part because Charles II's likely successor, his brother James, Duke of York, threatened a return to the old religion. Another contender for the throne, Charles' illegitimate son, James Scott, Duke of Monmouth, was a committed Protestant, the darling of the Whigs. Moreover, it was rumoured Monmouth had a marriage certificate in a black box that proved his father had been wedded to his mother secretly, so succession to the throne should be his by right. The Whig's rivals, the Tories, grew concerned that if Charles died the Duke of Monmouth would have made 'great troubles' in the land by either 'setting up for himself as king or for a [return to a] Commonwealth'.

A treasonous pamphlet entitled an *Appeal from the Country to the City* advocated Monmouth as the best person to succeed in the event of the king's untimely death, claiming, 'He who has the worst Title, ever makes the best King.' Cries of 'God bless our King Charles' and 'God bless the Protestant Duke' and 'No York and no bishops' would later become commonplace in London's streets. Parading Whig crowds openly chanted, 'No York, a Monmouth, a Monmouth'. Yet these noisy representations came to nought when Charles II died on 5 February 1685 and his brother James gained the throne unopposed. It was said that 'after grim apprehensions, James' accession came as something of an anti-climax'. The new king was greeted with joy by downtrodden Catholics on both sides of the Irish Sea, who forsaw a relaxation in the measures against them.

Fifty-six-year-old Richard Talbot remained the king's close friend. Whig hacks accused him of in the past procuring the services of whores and mistresses for James. Aged just twenty-three, Talbot had once travelled from Madrid to England in the hope of assassinating Cromwell. He and four others had been apprehended in the attempt. Cromwell had personally grilled Talbot to get to the bottom of the supposed plot and had threatened him with the rack, 'to spin the truth out of his bones'. Talbot replied, 'Spin me to a thread if you please, I have nothing to confess and can only invent lies.' Further establishing a reputation for ingenuity, Talbot contrived to escape from the Tower of London by rope, under Cromwell's nose. On another occasion, Talbot fought a duel with a Colonel Cormac MacCarthy; the latter wanted to promote a fellow Munsterman but Talbot had another man in mind. Ormond supported the colonel but such was Talbot's standing at court with James II, he got his own way.

In Ireland, Talbot, now ennobled as Earl of Tyrconnell, gained a commission placing him at the head of all armed forces in the country. He replaced English soldiers with Irishmen, many of them Catholics. By the autumn of 1686, 40 per cent of officers and almost 70 per cent of other ranks were Irish. James II was persuaded by Talbot that only Catholic troops would prove dependable in the long run. When challenged about this by a critic, Talbot denied saying this, gaining the dubious sobriquet 'lying Dick Talbot'. He sought to restore Catholics to previously confiscated lands and then to set up a Catholic dominated parliament at Dublin. Under pressure at Dublin, Talbot agreed a compromise whereby those who had gained during the Cromwellian settlement retained half their new land, while the other half was returned to Catholics. Talbot showed commendable foresight when looking to build a Catholic bastion against any colonising resurgence from Britain. He came closer than anyone had ever done before in placing Catholics in positions of control in Ireland.

When James II briefly threatened the dismantling of Protestantism in England, the Duke of Monmouth launched his famous invasion of England, landing at Lyme on the Dorset coast, from where he was rapidly hunted down. Among the hunters was the Irishman Patrick Sarsfield, who fell wounded in a skirmish with Monmouth's rebels at Keynsham. Later, on 15 July 1685, Sarsfield was left for dead at Sedgemoor, the site of James' decisive victory over his nephew. Monmouth was later executed on Tower Hill. (We will hear much more of Sarsfield.) Encouraged by the victory, James again looked to formulate plans for the re-establishment of Catholicism in England, but it soon transpired that his enemies in parliament had gained a march on him by promising to cede the crown to the king's son-in-law William of Orange. William was not unduly concerned with his father-in-law's religious leanings or with English political liberties: his focus was on prosecuting a coming war with France and gaining English military support. James had hoped to stand aloof from the looming conflict but now faced a battle for control closer to home.

When William's fleet was battered by storms and forced back to a Dutch harbour, a flustered but relieved James observed God's good grace in blowing the winds westerly that season. But then the wind began to blow from the east. The game was up. On 5 November 1688, William's forces under the command of the portly Marshall Schomberg landed at Torbay in Devon. Although William of Orange's invading army was smaller than that available to James, the Dutchman had been assured of a number of prearranged defections to him.

At the head of the king's Horse Guards, Irishman Patrick Sarsfield was perhaps the officer of greatest prominence who stood determined to halt the Williamite advance on London. While other officers deserted to William's camp, he fought one or more skirmishes with the Williamite vanguard, notably at Wincanton. Only the king's Irish troops, including 3,000 soldiers sent to England by Tyrconnell, in the end proved loyal. When wildly exaggerated rumours of the king's defeat reached London, the citizens there are said to have feared the arrival of the fleeing Irish and an inevitable sacking of the capital. Although an advance against the Williamite vanguard might have galvanised support for James, the king felt his army commanders would not stand by him; the later uncovering of plots implicating men of the stature of the future Duke of Marlborough to shoot James dead should he continue to press westward indicate James may have been right. Faced with such a possibility, James lost his nerve. He suffered a protracted nosebleed and ordered the army back to London. He told John Graham, Viscount Dundee, who, like Sarsfield, remained determinedly steadfast, 'There is but a small distance between the prisons and the graves of kings, therefore I go for France immediately.' Dundee is said to have wept in frustration when he learnt of the king's failure of resolve. James left Whitehall for the Continent on 18 December, having promised Dundee a commission to command his troops in Scotland. The two men were never to meet again.

Shortly after this, parliament passed a resolution saying the late king had endeavoured to subvert the constitution of the kingdom in league with Jesuits. By fleeing the country, James provided the Whig majority with what has been called the 'convenient constitutional fiction' that he had abdicated. William was crowned jointly with his wife Mary, James II's daughter, at Westminster Abbey, on 11 April 1689. Sarsfield joined James in exile. James Butler, since 1661 a duke in the Irish peerage, had died a year earlier. He had retired from public life in 1685 after loyally serving the Stuarts for over fifty tempestuous years, an astonishing achievement. It was perhaps a blessing he never knew the fate awaiting the dynasty he devoted his life to, nor of James' cowardice in failing to confront the Williamite threat.

The scene was set for a contest between rival kings on a grand scale, much of which would initially be played out in Scotland, where Jacobite sympathies were strongest in the Gaelic-speaking Highlands and along the lowland coastal strip between Aberdeen and Fife, a region of strongly entrenched Episcopalianism. In the spring of 1689, Dundee declared his intention of raising the Irish clans, saying that he sought to emulate his famous relative, James Graham, Marquis of Montrose, in exploiting the strong bond of loyalty among the Gaels to the House of Stuart. Legend has it that when asked by a colleague which way he would go, Dundee answered, 'Wherever the shade of Montrose directs me.'

Meanwhile, with civil war looming, the far-seeing Talbot, from now on referred to as Tyrconnell, looked to close down Ulster to any Williamite threat by replacing the Protestant garrison at Londonderry with a Catholic one. A fake letter, known as the Comber Letter, had threatened another massacre by Catholics of Protestants. Although a forgery, the letter created a widespread panic in Ulster. Protestant preachers and news-sheet purveyors whipped up propagandist hatred. One claimed, rather imaginatively, that planters' wives risked being prostituted to the lust of every savage bog-trotter, their daughters would be ravished by goatish monks and small children tossed upon pikes and torn limb from limb. Quoting the words of newspaper columnist Adam Lusher from the present day, we would perhaps recognise this as 'Islamophobic scaremongering'. In London, the Irish were mocked; balladeers mimicked the papist mobs, singing

> Now damn heretics all go down,
> Lillibulero Bullen a la,
> By Christ and St Patrick the nation's our own,
> Lillibulero Bullen a la.

Tyrconnell's orders for Londonderry to be vacated by the local Protestant garrison were quickly carried out, but, instead of a simultaneous handover to a replacement Catholic garrison, two weeks passed, by which time the gates of the city were firmly shut to any Catholics, Tyrconnell included. Londonderry's city elders had been in two minds whether or not to allow the Earl of Antrim's redshanks entry into the city, but local apprentice boys took matters into their own hands and shut the gates on them. Two companies of soldiers, all Catholics, about 120 men in all, were eventually allowed entry. Their commander was a man named Robert Lundy, of ill-fame.

In France, King Louis XIV, the 'the Sun King', pressed James II to travel to Ireland, arguing that without the Stuart king on hand his cause there would founder. Preparations were soon being made to send around 3,000 British Jacobites and a small French force to southern Ireland. Tyrconnell was also putting pressure on the king to travel with them. He pleaded with James to put behind him the seemingly endless round of dalliances in France and join his troops in Ireland; he even referenced the king's honour, or lack of it. To sweeten the pill, Tyrconnell promised unlimited hunting and an equally rollicking sex life in Ireland. James was a pliant king where his friend Dick Talbot was concerned. Left to his own devices he might have stayed in France and allowed the great crisis of his reign to pass him by.

Louis XIV's motives in urging James to depart for Ireland were more wide-ranging than Tyrconnell's. He sought to open up a second front in Ireland and the Scottish Highlands against William of Orange. The French and the Dutch were at war. Foreign Catholics and Protestants made for good proxies in the struggle for dominance between Europe's two opposing power brokers.

The new Williamite government in England continued to hope that Tyrconnell might be persuaded to back down in Ireland rather than risk another debilitating war. The man chosen to carry the terms for a settlement was Richard Hamilton, James II's major-general, captured after the Jacobite king's flight to France. Although Hamilton was a papist, he was also the late Duke of Ormond's nephew and a relative of Tyrconnell's. William of Orange considered him to be a man of honour who would respect his parole. Upon landing at Ringsend, near Dublin, in January 1689, Hamilton, however, headed straight for the nearest tavern, where he is said to have broken out into laughter, declaring proudly how he had 'shammed' the Prince of Orange. The Catholics in Dublin lit bonfires. Tyrconnell promoted Hamilton to lieutenant-general, boasting that alone he was worth ten thousand fighting men.

In March, Hamilton's army marched on Londonderry, scattering an opposing Protestant force at Dromore, co. Tyrone. They then occupied Coleraine and crossed the Bann on 7 April. At the so-called Battle of the Fords a week later, Hamilton helped drive the Protestant troops screening Londonderry back behind the city walls, but, despite the later arrival of James II in person outside Derry's gates, the city refused to surrender. A person or persons unknown even had the temerity to take pot-shots at the monarch, further souring the occasion. The cry from the ramparts was 'No Surrender!' Even so, Hamilton's energetic campaigning had almost completed the task of bringing Ireland under Jacobite control. Only Londonderry, under Robert Lundy's command, and the town of Enniskillen still held out for 'King Billy', as the Protestant Irish called William of Orange. The Ulster colonists' fate depended directly on them holding out.

*

James II's champion in the Scottish Highlands, Viscount Dundee, was meanwhile faced by forces much larger and better equipped than his own. He also impatiently awaited promised reinforcements from Ulster, now tied down outside the gates of Derry. The Williamite army in Scotland comprised crack regiments like the Scots Brigade, veterans of William of Orange's Dutch wars. Eleven hundred strong, the brigade joined up with the newly raised Earl of Leven's infantry regiment and a small body of cavalry. Despite the disparity in quality between troop types, on 11 May, exactly a month after William III's crowning at Westminster, Dundee had the temerity to attack and surprise a small Williamite garrison at Perth, turning several officers out of their beds. There was minimal violence and private property was respected. From Perth he rode on to Dundee, but found the town barred to him by government forces. His proximity nevertheless created a shock wave of anxiety in Edinburgh. The authorities hurriedly ordered the capital to be reinforced with additional soldiers and for a further 600 men to be made available for the field army, under the command of General Hugh Mackay. The plan was for them to link up with the main body of troops, stationed at Badenoch, on the road between Inverness and Perth. These reinforcements had set out from Perth on 22 May, but had not got far. After three days of marching through hostile country it seems their resolution failed them. Rumours that the Irish were out in force so unnerved them that they returned to Perth. Comparison with Strongbow's forces when marching through the uncharted wilderness of Ossory in the twelfth century, and of Agricola's Spanish legions in the Highlands, come to mind. Four days later, army commander Hugh Mackay set out for the rendezvous at Badenoch, unaware that the troops promised were already retracing their steps. Heralds alerted him of the disquieting news of Jacobite movements. Dundee's forces were close by. On a more positive note for the Williamites, a prisoner taken by Mackay reported Dundee to be 'sick of a flux'. A propagandist newsletter dated 22 June claimed the viscount's 'unsuccessful rebellious campaign hath reduced his body to a low and wretched state'. Dundee's poor state of health may help explain the increased occurrence of ill-discipline in the Jacobite army. Disorderly at the best of times, the Gaels fell to plundering indiscriminately. Worse, only 300 promised reinforcements arrived from Ulster. Described as 'new-raised, naked and undisciplined', they were a disappointingly far cry from the 5,000 soldiers originally promised by Tyrconnell, many of whom were now tied up at the siege of Londonderry.

On 26 July, while at Blair Castle, Dundee learned that Mackay's army was less than a day's march away at Dunkeld. By noon the next day, the enemy were at the Pass of Killiecrankie, a few miles south of Blair. Described in the nineteenth century as 'a dark and profound abyss', the Pass could barely be traversed by three men abreast. Mackay's long column, which included 1,200 baggage horses, was ripe for ambush, but, surprisingly – astonishingly in fact, if we are to believe the reason given – none was attempted. According to tradition, Dundee vetoed the idea because of a time-honoured Highland maxim never to attack someone who could not defend himself on equal terms.

Upon debouching from the Pass into an extensive cornfield near the village of Killiecrankie, Mackay sent out scouts to reconnoitre toward Blair. They returned with disturbing news that parties of kilted Irish were approaching from the north. The general rode forward to see for himself and soon discovered the main body of the enemy a mere quarter of a mile away. Mackay caustically observed that the position chosen by Dundee was consistent with Highlander tactics, saying kilted Gaels never fought against regular forces 'without a sure retreat at their back'.

The ordering of the armies, which included some inconsequential skirmishing, was typical of the period and was time consuming. It was late afternoon before Mackay's three light cannon briefly came into action, doing little harm other than to infuriate Dundee's men. The afternoon wore on. Mackay became ever more anxious, knowing that twilight would add to the terrors of the wild Irish charge. His fears would be more than justified. Dundee waited to give the order to attack until the sun began to set behind the mountains. He had earlier exchanged his scarlet coat for another of a darker hue to conceal his rank. His battle cry was 'King James and the Church of Scotland'. An eyewitness related how, 'The sun going down caused the highlanders to advance on us like madmen, without shoe or stocking: covering themselves from our fire with their shields, at last they cast away their muskets, drew their broadswords, and advanced furiously upon us.' Careering down the slope, coming under fire at about 100 paces, many McDonnells and Macleans fell in this first exchange, but before three volleys could be aimed at them, the Gaels had crashed into Mackay's regiment and the centremost division of another. With no time to fix their bayonets, and assailed by men wielding axes and broadswords, the government troops buckled and broke. Mackay later claimed many of his men behaved 'like the vilest cowards in nature'. In a bold attempt to save the day he ordered his cavalry forward against the exposed inner flank of the enemy, only to find that just a handful of troopers would follow him; the rest ran away.

Mackay was able to extricate himself and just over 400 men from unbroken remnants of his regiments. Falling back in good order, fording the river they eventually reached safety. He left behind him 2,000 dead or captured. Dundee was killed by a random musket shot at the very commencement of the battle. His body was taken back to Blair Castle and later interred in a vault at nearby St Bride's Kirk. Mackay was at Blair the following September. He viewed the corpse while it still lay open to view. He stated the musket ball that killed Dundee entered his brain through his left eye. He must have been dead before his body hit the ground.

Two months earlier than Killiecrankie, the first major battle of the Jacobite wars in Ireland had taken place at sea on 1 May

1689, when a French fleet of twenty-eight ships clashed with the Royal Navy off Bantry Bay, co. Cork. The twenty-two English ships – eighteen ships of the line, a fifth-rater and three fireships – were commanded by the experienced Admiral Herbert, Earl of Torrington, a man described by the diarist Pepys as something of a martinet. Pepys tells of Herbert forcing his officers to submit themselves to him 'in the meanest degree of servility', acting the part of a king at sea, and while ashore being attended upon by a stream of mistresses. Herbert's opponents off Bantry were the Comte de Châteaurenault and Louis Francois de Rousselet, men who on the day proved the Englishman's equal, avoiding a general action and managing to disgorge their cargo of troops and military supplies without undue loss. Both sides claimed victory, but English casualties were higher, 365 men killed or wounded against 133 Frenchmen. Jacobites at Dublin peppered the sky with fireworks when news of the French success reached them.

Herbert's own account of the action stressed his aggressive spirit, contrasting his conduct with the caution and lack of resolve of the French, who had for the most part kept their distance. His report described how the enemy concentrated their cannon fire on the masts and rigging of the English ships, rather than seeking to close the range. Other accounts, however, speak of the opposing fleets sometimes being within pistol shot of one another, and of French marksmen forcing the closure of the English gun ports.

At Portsmouth, William III congratulated Herbert and his commanders for keeping the English fleet intact – and, perhaps with Richard Hamilton in mind, for remaining loyal to him. The House of Commons passed a vote of thanks to Herbert for his resolve and gallantry. Being the man of the hour, he pressed the case for the establishment of a home for wounded sailors, 'for support of such as are maimed in the service and defence of their country'. In doing so, he was anticipating the establishment of Greenwich Hospital five years later, one of the few good things to come from a conflict which would otherwise prove uncompromisingly brutal and divisive.

Patrick Sarsfield had earlier accompanied James back from France to Ireland and had been tasked on arrival with organising the newly raised and poorly equipped Jacobite army. In April 1689 he took 2,000 men to secure Sligo from a threatened attack by Williamite forces based at Enniskillen, co. Fermanagh. The latter posed an ongoing problem to Jacobite communications between Londonderry and Dublin. The fifteenth-century castle at Enniskillen was built on an island between the upper and lower reaches of Lough Erne. The whole Erne Valley had become an armed base for Protestant guerrilla groups, who launched destructive raids against the frontiers of the Pale. Having occupied Sligo, Sarsfield laid siege to Ballyshannon in early May, but was forced to withdraw when his scurriers and supporting foot were scattered in a fight later known as the Break of Belleek. The fighting took place in a narrow pass, flanked by lake and bog. It was a skirmish more typical of earlier warfare in Ireland, but betokened worse to come. The Jacobite cavalry fled at the first onslaught, without firing a shot. Two hundred casualties were inflicted on them by the victorious Williamites. Surviving Jacobite foot soldiers scattered and made good their escape across the bogs to Sligo.

Sarsfield raised the siege of Ballyshannon and fell back on Manorhamilton, where he successfully held the enemy at bay for the next three months. In doing so, he prevented the Enniskillen Protestants from attempting a relief of Londonderry, thus extending the city's plight. From his camp, Sarsfield boasted, 'I am so well posted that I do not fear the enemy were they double the number.' Only the defeat of his colleague, Justin MacCarthy, Viscount Mountcashel, at the Battle of Newton Butler, co. Fermanagh, on 31 July, a few days after Killiecrankie, prevented the two men from combining forces and mounting an attack on Enniskillen. MacCarthy that day had taken up a favourable position on rising land fronted by a bog and artillery. The Williamites bravely advanced across the bog, which turned out to be drier than the Jacobites had supposed, killing the gunners before bringing up mounted support. The Jacobite horse bolted. After putting up a spirited fight, MacCarthy's infantry surrendered almost en masse. Those who attempted flight, being unfamiliar with the terrain, drowned trying to cross Lough Erne. James II later wrote, 'Though the foot fought with great obstinacy, and the general did all that could be expected, when the king's horse gave way the rest were totally routed.' Mountcashel was not among them: after the first panic had subsided he rode forward and sought to win back his guns now in enemy hands. When captured and led away, he is alleged to have to have told his captor he would rather not have outlived such a day. Protestant commentators gloated that the reverse at Newton Butler was 'the greatest blow to the Irish that they ever had'. The result was the immediate loss to the Jacobites of Sligo. Now isolated, Sarsfield was forced to abandon the town, in part through believing he faced a greater threat than eventually materialised; he also abandoned plans he and Mountcashel had prepared for an assault on Enniskillen. The Shannon barrier in north-east Connaught, which the Jacobite Irish high command had hoped to retain intact, was in this way breached.

Occupying an oval hill surrounded on three sides by the River Foyle, Londonderry was well adapted for defence. A mile-long stretch of high stone wall, still extant, protected by eight gun bastions, made it almost impregnable to assault. But by the summer of 1689 the garrison and townsfolk had become reduced to living on 'salt hides, tallow pancakes and dogs fattened on corpses'. Potatoes had by this time become the staple diet of the Irish, but few were to be found within Londonderry's walls. Lieutenant-Colonel Robert Lundy, earlier applauded for his 'zeal and encouragement' in preparing the city for defence, had lost much of his popularity, and would later be vilified by the besieged. Orders for his troopers to ravage the surrounding countryside for 'oats and hay' had already angered local landowners, who claimed Lundy was acting worse than any plundering papist. In Londonderry itself, Lundy had encouraged those who could do so to flee the city, saying the place would become untenable otherwise. Addressing his officers, he told them that 'due to great numbers present they must [otherwise] perish by starvation'.

Pressed to do more to relieve the situation, he put together a plan to sally out and meet the enemy head on. At the resulting Battle of the Fords – briefly mentioned earlier in the narrative – fought to the west of the Rivers Bann and Finn on 13 April, Jacobite heavy cavalry led by Hamilton had broken through the Protestant cordon on the west bank and forced Lundy's infantrymen back on Londonderry. For some it was a precipitate fight, but for others the retreat was made with colours flying and in good order. Jacobite Dominic Sheldon later wrote how he and his men charged the enemy rearguard three times, but were each time put into disorder by musketry and the firmness of supporting pikemen. He applauded the Williamite commander, saying, 'Whoever he is, he has not his trade to learn.'

This Williamite reverse encouraged naysayers within the city to question Lundy's military competence; some even questioned his loyalty. Accusations of treachery reached fever pitch when reinforcements promised by sea were rejected by Lundy on the basis the city could not support them. Many considered such defeatism impossible to countenance. Yet Lundy's stance had merit. By this time the defenders were so weak they could 'scarce creep to the walls'; some were dying at their posts every night. Rumours that Lundy was intent on surrendering the city spread. A mob gathered. Fearing being lynched, Lundy dressed himself in the guise of a common soldier and somehow fled the city. With four others, he then made a getaway by boat to Islay. He was later tried, and for a time imprisoned in the Tower. He died sometime before 1717. Now each year his effigy is burned in Londonderry; a scapegoat singled out, perhaps unfairly, from these dangerous times.

Had the besieged but known, the Jacobites outside the city were faring hardly any better. Armed more often than not with pitchforks and scythes, they were on occasion outnumbered and outgunned by the defenders and existed on short rations. The Jacobite siege train was not really fit for purpose, consisting of just one twenty-four pounder gun, one eighteen-pounder, and two mortars – one of which was cracked. Ineffective against the walls, the battery nevertheless managed to pummel the 16-gun Williamite warship *Greyhound*, preventing it from gaining a mooring and resupplying the city with victuals. The mortars were sited to lob shells and anything else that might prove to be to the defender's disadvantage over the city walls, causing numerous deaths and significant damage to property.

A larger squadron of ships, under the command of Major-General Percy Kirke, arrived at Lough Foyle sometime between 13 and 15 June. Bad weather had delayed its arrival. A month later, Kirke sent a message to the Londonderry leaders, advising them to be 'good husbands to your victuals and by God's help we shall overcome these barbarous people'. On Sunday 28 July, a day after Dundee's victory at Killiecrankie and three days before the dramatic Jacobite reverse at Newton Butler, a gale blew up from the north-west. This was the opportunity Kirke had awaited: wind and tide combined to allow three of his ships – the *Dartmouth*, *Phoenix* and *Mountjoy* – to navigate the five-mile river passage to the city. While the *Dartmouth* engaged the Jacobite fort at Culmore Point, the two other ships headed downriver to break a boom erected by the Jacobites north of Foyle Bridge. For a time the *Mountjoy* became becalmed and partly grounded. There was nothing for it but to manhandle the ship down the final stretch, something successfully achieved with the help of the rising tide and plenty of muscle. All three ships finally reached Derry Quay at about ten o'clock in the evening. Their precious cargoes of meal, dried peas, salt beef and biscuit proved to be the city's salvation. Kirke entered the city as a deliverer. He and his captains and crews were feted and fussed over.

Percy Kirke was a vastly experienced soldier who knew what he was about, but, like many others of his generation, would fall victim to Pepys' diaries, where he was described as 'violent, high-handed, anti-Semitic, bawdy, sexually driven, profane and intimidating, a very brute'; also, according to Pepys, he kept a mistress ever ready in his bath-house, where he allowed his tyranny and vice full rein. The Londonderry citizenry were soon to see Kirke's 'dark side'. Gallows erected by him threatened any who crossed him. All leaving the city were first disarmed and some prevented from doing so. He also stripped the garrison of fighting men, leaving just a skeleton command, much to the resentment of those who feared a Catholic backlash. Great armies were known to be massing elsewhere in Ireland. Sir James Caldwell, a contemporary, wondered whether Kirke's professed atheism and debauchery were in themselves 'fit weapons to beat down popery'. Kirke would prove him wrong: from Londonderry, he marched on Coleraine, which was hurriedly abandoned by the Catholics. He then joined the main Williamite army at Dundalk in early September.

16

BY MANY PATHS AND SECRET SHALLOWS

The deliverance of Londonderry, the loss of Sligo, and the defeat at Newton Butler confirmed the brittleness of Jacobite morale when indifferently led. On 21 August, an Irish commander named Alexander Cannon, Dundee's successor, was defeated by a Presbyterian force at Dunkeld, Perth. When attacking prepared positions under cover of the town and cathedral, the victors of Killiecrankie were driven off with heavy loss. The battle is said to have raged for sixteen hours. Many Scots perished in burning buildings, but somehow managed to prevent the town from falling into Jacobite hands. The failure of the Jacobite rising in Scotland owes much to James II's inability to ship trained soldiers in any number to the Scottish Highlands from Ireland because of the continued 'No Surrender' policy of besieged Protestants in Ulster. The few Irish reinforcements Dundee received proved wholly inadequate.

Sarsfield arrived back in Dublin in mid-August. An attempt to retake Sligo was launched by him soon thereafter. Roscommon fell on 12 October and he then chased Irish Williamite troops from Sligo. Six hundred French Protestant troops remained holding out against him in the town's stone fort but capitulated when Sarsfield threatened to storm the place – this after erecting the last ever mobile siege tower to be used in the British Isles. His lightning campaign plugged the breach in the Shannon line and prevented a proposed south-westerly incursion by the Williamites, designed to seize Athlone and threaten the Jacobite flank and rear. Sarsfield had by this time become the most celebrated and feared general in Ireland. The French ambassador at the court of King James II described him as 'greater than that of any man I know ... brave but above all he has a sense of honour and integrity in all that he does'. James on the other hand called him a blockhead, but nonetheless valued him militarily. When asked to release Sarsfield for service in France, James fell into a temper, posting him to the frontline at Cavan to prevent any underhand deals being struck. Sarsfield only rejoined the main Jacobite army when it later massed south of the Boyne.

Now a Jacobite duke, Tyrconnell is said by 1689 to have grown heavy, of a size to fill a porch; in fact he become an old and infirm man, and for a time was bedridden. When he rose and dusted himself down, the Battle of Newton Butler had been fought and a large Williamite army, comprising English, Dutch and Danish troops, had landed at Bangor, on the Down coast. Belfast and Carrickfergus were occupied by them unopposed. This concentration in the north would later persuade James and his commanders to consolidate the Jacobite army, reinforced by a strong French contingent, in and around Meath to block any enemy advance on Dublin. The ailing Tyrconnell advised James against offering battle. He saw the loss of Dublin as a small price to pay for maintaining the army intact. He advised James to avoid a general action, saying that then you will have 'a hundred chances of success'; in doing so he was referencing the unstable political situation in Europe and the possibility that William would tire of campaigning in Ireland and depart. What is more, all the while a relative stalemate existed – with the Williamite army concentrated in the rugged north and the Irish better provided for in winter quarters in the Pale, there was a chance that disease and desertion would undermine the former to a greater extent than the latter.

This did in fact occur. While encamped south of the Moyry Pass, approximately 7,000 Williamite soldiers perished of disease.

A third of the allied army was lost before a shot was ever fired. James II wrote, 'The enemy's army was grievously afflicted with the country's disease [dysentery] and so overrun with lice that vast numbers of them died, especially the English.' The latter comment may have been a barb pointing out his countrymen's ill-usage at the hands of their Continental masters. As the weather worsened, conditions for the Williamites became so bad that they were forced to fall back on Dundalk, north of the Moyry Pass. Many of them, suffering from 'a burning fever', never made it back. James wrote that 'all the roads from Dundalk to Newry and Carlingford were next day full of nothing but dead men, who, even as the wagons jolted … died and were thrown off as fast.'

Much of the blame for this state of affairs in the Williamite camp has been cast on the seventy-four-year-old Marshall Schomberg, commander of the Williamite forces in Ireland, but the real blame lay at Westminster, where politicians failed to provide him with sufficient resources for campaigning in Ireland. Schomberg's forces were raw and undisciplined and now afflicted by pestilence. What is more, until mid-May lack of grass meant neither side was able to maintain large numbers of horses. Tyrconnell wrote to the queen in France, 'We are impatient until the grass be of such a growth as that our horses may be able to feed on it … [and the enemy, unless supplied from England] must lie idle as well as we until then.'

The war in Ireland was always something of a sideshow for men like William of Orange and Louis XIV, in much the same way as it had been for Henry II when Strongbow seized control at Dublin. Louis XIV's invasion of the Rhineland in the autumn of 1688 and his opening of hostilities against the United Provinces of the Netherlands threatened an eastward expansion and the imperial annexation of William's lands. It was feared the French king aspired to nothing short of 'a universal monarchy of Europe'. Louis therefore posed a much bigger threat to William of Orange than Jacobite Ireland ever did.

The war in Europe, of which the war in Ireland had now become a part, was not simply a religious struggle, though it has often been presented as such. It was a power struggle for the control of Europe.

Containing the French remained William's number one priority, not the subjugation of Catholic Ireland. Moreover, concentrating an army in the north of Ireland increased the threat of a French invasion of England. William admitted as much when he wrote to the Duke of Bavaria to say, 'I am terribly embarrassed to be obliged to go to Ireland, where I shall be ... beyond all knowledge of the world. If I can reduce that kingdom quickly, I shall then have my hands free to act with so much more vigour against the common enemy [the French].'

Tyrconnell understood the political dynamics, but underestimated the Protestant king's resolve. It appears William eventually came to the conclusion that to successfully prosecute a war against France he must also take action in Ireland, since the island might otherwise become a launch pad for a combined French/Jacobite assault on England. Ireland being occupied by French forces and Jacobite surrogates had become 'a danger grown too great'. Schomberg's army could never of itself make inroads against the main Jacobite army. This had become clear. A larger, better equipped and officered force was needed, led by William of Orange in person.

The Dutch king's fleet berthed in Belfast Lough on 16 June 1690, disembarking an army worthy of any major European conflict. An observer remarked: 'The great numbers of coaches, waggons, baggage horses and the like is almost incredible to be supplied from England, or any of the biggest nations in Europe ... I cannot think that any army of Christendom hath the like.' William himself had earlier stepped ashore at Carrickfergus on 14 June 1690, telling those who waited on him that he had come to ensure the people of Ireland would be 'settled in a lasting peace'. His faltering English and asthmatic delivery cannot have encouraged onlookers, yet he would prove to be resolute in his endeavour. After ten months of campaigning alone, Schomberg was at last reinforced. In the face of this sudden and potentially disastrous Williamite build-up in the north, the options open to James were now fourfold:

1 Fall back on Dublin and attempt to hold out under siege.
2 Hold the Moyry Pass and prevent the Williamites from breaking out into the plain of Meath.

3 Hold the river line of the Boyne beside Drogheda and accept battle.

4 Hold a line behind the Shannon at Athlone and sacrifice Dublin.

The third option was chosen, but military historians have since concluded that either of the first two might have been preferable. From armchairs, arguments still rage. Critics of the Jacobite command cite Frederick the Great's maxim never to base a defence on rivers, advice reiterated by the great military strategist Clausewitz, who pointed out that defending a river line risked an envelopment from upstream should the enemy be allowed to cross. The fourth option, to fall back behind the Shannon barrier, was rejected by James because of problems of supply: Connaught was the most underdeveloped province in Ireland. What was more, bottling the army up in garrisons there and in Munster smacked of defeatism. James sought a decisive battle, declaring he did not want to lose all 'without a stroke'.

When the Williamite army penetrated and broke through the indifferently defended Moyry Pass they had around 37,500 effectives, including officers, artillerymen and commissaries, of which approximately 7,500 were made up of cavalry and dragoons. Facing them across the broad River Boyne was James II's smaller army, made up of approximately 5,000 cavalry and dragoons and 20,000 infantrymen. Such very large numbers, when added together, had never previously been seen in Britain or Ireland. Opposing armies at Worcester in 1651 (46,000), Marston Moor in 1644 (45,000), Pinkie in 1547 (43,000) and Flodden in 1513 (46,000) were comfortably surpassed by the numbers massing on the Boyne.

Arguably, the Jacobites had already missed their best chance of holding the Williamite army at bay. When the latter created a bridgehead south of the Moyry Pass, a Williamite commander claimed that had the enemy had any spirit they might 'have stopped us for some time'. Schomberg had also expected to have to fight his way through. (If only the comb-wielding Morrighan had been on the banks of the Boyne, to warn James of impending doom, as she had done on the eve of the Battle of Dysert O'Dea, much of what followed might have been avoided.)

William of Orange's best troops were the three regiments of horse and eight battalions of foot he brought across from Denmark, described as 'stout fine men ... the best equipped and disciplined of any that was ever seen'. Other crack units in the Williamite army hailed from the Low Countries: nine Dutch cavalry regiments, one dragoon unit and six infantry battalions. Two troops of English Life Guards, the Royal Regiment of Horse Guards and six regular English battalions were also by any definition elite units.

By the 1690s, infantry tactics had changed considerably from Oliver Cromwell's day. Because of the introduction of the bayonet, pikemen had become all but obsolete in the Williamite army. Foot regiments comprised in the main musketeers and grenadiers. Just one in five of the Williamite foot soldiers trailed a pike by the summer of 1690, compared to one in two in earlier wars: the musket was now the dominant arm. Late seventeenth-century smooth-bore muskets had a flintlock mechanism, which replaced the cumbersome and unreliable matchlock system previously employed. Ranges for these muzzle-loaded weapons extended to 200 yards and they could be fired twice every minute instead of just once, making firepower more decisive than hitherto. Formations six to ten ranks deep were thinned to a three-deep line to maximise fire impact. Drill books enabled sergeant-majors to shift columnar formations into line or square without becoming disordered – important when manoeuvring in the face of the enemy. Under cannonade or small-arms fire, undrilled troops were liable to break in panic. When faced with native soldiery determined to close and engage hand to hand, as in the Highlands of Scotland, it was important a firing-line did not falter. The need for a continuous roll of musketry was essential. During the Williamite wars in Ireland, English troops made sure to adopt the Dutch practice of firing by platoons. This ensured a rolling-fire and also ensured a proportion of soldiery was always ready to give fire. This was perhaps the main lesson of Killiecrankie.

Cavalry remained the main offensive arm on the battlefield and was available in higher numbers than in the Scottish Highlands. Dragoons no longer dismounted to fight as they had during the civil wars. Instead, they formed up with the regiments of horse to make up a general purpose mounted arm. A horseman's sabre and a dragoon's carbine allowed either a rapid charge, relying on shock and awe, or a slower caracole, with a measured discharge of firearms at point-blank range.

On a less positive note, the Williamite artillery had no formal organisation until the formation of the Royal Regiment of Artillery in 1716 and remained very much an auxiliary arm, unlikely to disrupt a determined attack or break down a resolute defence. Only the death of a leader to a cannon-ball's strike would prove a decisive intervention on the battlefield.

In the Jacobite army, trained officers and men were at a premium. Tyrconnell's earlier purge of Protestant officers and common soldiers had affected both the officer corps and rank and file in equal measure. Summer drill camps held in 1686 and 1687 at the Curragh of Kildare helped the regimentation of volunteers, but by the eve of the Boyne many soldiers remained ill-trained and lacked experience under fire; this despite great efforts made by James II's French allies to assist in the training. The army remained by and large a volunteer force. Muskets sent across from France were often obsolete models. Manoeuvring on the battlefield was not advisable for troops such as these; fighting behind fixed defences was to be preferred. Only the Jacobite cavalry had the wherewithal for aggressive action. Led by men of the calibre of Patrick Sarsfield, the Jacobite horsemen would rival Jeb Stuart's rebel troopers during the American Civil War, but mainly through raiding, not in open battle. One positive development for the Jacobites was the arrival of the suspiciously precise reported number of 6,666 well-trained and highly disciplined French troops, under Brigadier-General Comte de Lauzon, but this gain was offset to some extent by the despatch of a similarly sized brigade of Irishmen to France.

The coming battle would be untypical of prior encounters in Ireland in size, scope and make-up of the armies. Neither of the two competing kings, nor their sponsors, cared a jot for Ireland, only their own dynastic ambitions. From the hilltop at Tara, shades of kings of old apprehensively awaited the fateful outcome.

In the face of the Williamite advance on Dublin, downstream bridges closer to Drogheda were destroyed by the Jacobites. Their army concentrated further upstream, on the south bank, near Oldbridge. Opposite this, the newly arrived Williamite army rested its left flank on the main road leading south to Drogheda. Its right wing was secured by an area of deep, broken ground, now known as King William's Glen. William rode forward to get a better view of the ground across the river, much to the horror of his aides. On the southern bank, Jacobite gunners could hardly believe their luck. They hurriedly unlimbered two small field pieces and opened fire as the king's party fell back from the riverbank, killing a single Williamite and two horses. A second cannonball grazed the ground and then rose to strike the king's shoulder, tearing into both coat and flesh before travelling on to smash the head of a gentleman volunteer's pistol. The battle might have been won for the Jacobites at that instant but for a centimetre or two. The Dutch king was wearing a thick coat. Even so, the ball's impact unhorsed him and drew blood. He bravely remounted, ordered a cloak to be found to cover his wound and then rode forward with Marshall Schomberg at his side, to the cheers of his troops. William III, though slight and of indifferent health, was cast in an altogether firmer mould than James II. Ghostly onlookers on the Hill of Tara would not have missed such a distinction. The Dutchman also enjoyed better fortune than his English rival. Poor reconnaissance on both sides would work in William's favour, not James'.

Overnight at Mellifont Abbey, a roofless ruin that served as William's HQ, the Williamite high command concocted a plan to shift the army to the right and launch an attack further upstream to encompass the Jacobite left. This would, it was hoped, be followed by a decisive breakthrough at Oldbridge with the main body of the army. Marshal Schomberg in fact wanted the bulk of the Williamite army to cross upstream while a small force pinned the Jacobite army down. William, however, wanted a more direct attack to be made, and would only sanction a third of the army to make the flanking movement. Because the Boyne is a tidal river, there was just a short two-hour window to make the crossings. The planning had to be meticulous and orders clear. Every man was to wear a green bough in his hat to distinguish friend from foe. Flanking columns were to set off at first light, when mist from the river would hamper Jacobite onlookers on the south bank.

News of the turning movement reaching the Jacobite command tent appears to have generated an over-reaction. James' generals committed in excess of half their army, including Sarsfield and his brigade, to confront it. They also pulled back their guns from the main position at Oldbridge, not anticipating a massed attack in this sector. This proved a fatal error. Broken ground, known as Roughgrange, in Abby Parish, made their left flank virtually impassable, the ground there comprising a long ravine intersected by double ditches. A small covering force would have been sufficient to secure it. Facing the remainder of the Jacobite army across the Boyne at Oldbridge was now a Williamite force more than twice its size. The commander on the spot, General Richard Hamilton, risked defeat in detail.

When the Williamite attack came, William of Orange charged across the ford at its head, dicing with death and providing a moral edge that James could not emulate. Patrick Sarsfield would later quip, 'Let us switch kings and we will be happy to fight you again.' One Jacobite account speaks of the Williamites crossing at different points, by 'many paths and secret shallows'. The elderly Williamite Marshall Schomberg also displayed reckless courage, but in his case it proved fatal. Surrounded in mid-stream, he suffered sabre cuts and the discharge of a carbine into the back of his head. William was at one point grounded when his horse foundered in the mud. A quick thinking man, he pressed a battalion of Enniskillen troops to protect him. An army chaplain described the Enniskillen contingent as 'half-naked with sabres and pistols hanging from their belts, like a horde of Tartars'. According to another onlooker, 'Nothing was to be seen but smoke and dust, nor anything to be heard but one continued fire for nigh on half an hour.' In the midst of this, when William cried out, 'You shall be my guards, let me see something of you,' the men gave out a loud cheer. Despite suffering casualties to the Jacobite cavalry, they rallied round their king and remained with him throughout the battle. James II's own account perhaps touches on this episode:

> The [Irish] horse did their duty with great bravery and though they did not break the enemy's foot it was more by reason of the ground's not being favourable than for want of vigour, for after they had been repulsed by the [Williamite] foot they rallied again and charged the enemy's horse [the Enniskillen horse] and beat them every charge ... Lieut. General Hamilton being wounded and taken prisoner at the last charge, and the Duke of Berwick having his horse shot under him was some time amongst the enemy, he was ridden over and ill-bruised; however by the help of a trooper got off again. Sheldon who had commanded the horse had two [horses] killed under him.

Despite valiant efforts on the part of Hamilton and his men – especially, as we have seen, the cavalry, whom the general led forward in three desperate charges – the danger of being trapped in the pocket created by the looping river turned Jacobite resistance into a fighting retreat. Tall, yellow-coated Dutch reserves sporting green sprigs of foliage in their hats could now be seen wading chest deep across the river, holding their muskets and cartridge cases as well as their officers above their heads. For some facing them it was all too much. Captain John Steven's account of the battle speaks of elements of the Irish cavalry bolting and a general panic setting in. Foot soldiers disordered by their own cavalry threw away their weapons to disencumber themselves for flight; others even discarded their coats and shoes to run the lighter. Men would later quip that the Dutchmen's crossing of the Boyne was the precise moment 'the one hope of Mother Ireland died'. Only thanks to the discipline of James' French troops did the withdrawal never become a rout. The French brigade are said by Stevens to have made 'a most honourable retreat', retiring in good order, facing the enemy all the while. The captain went on to give the credit to the valorous conduct of M. Zurlauben, Colonel of the Blue Regiment, who with unparalleled bravery headed and brought off his men. The Williamite cavalry was several times repulsed by them and did not dare pursue far. The battle was over.

James II lost approximately 1,000 men at the Boyne, William of Orange half that amount. Among the Jacobite prisoners was Hamilton, who had earlier betrayed William when absconding under parole. Brought before the Dutchman, he was quizzed as to whether he thought the Irish would continue to fight. 'Yes,' said he with a glint is his eye, 'if it please Your Majesty, upon my honour, I believe they will.' William looked somewhat askance at Hamilton, repeating the word 'honour' several times, as if weighing up whether the Irishman might be allowed to boast of having any. Hamilton would be imprisoned, but was later exchanged. Fuming at the supposed cowardice of the Irish, and exclaiming he would never again trust them, James II meanwhile rode hard for Waterford where he almost immediately took ship for France, living out the rest of his life an exile, becoming something of a recluse. Realising James to be a lame duck, the French king would be loath to ever back him again. Later entreaties to do so by trusted men like Tyrconnell were put aside by the monarch. The monastery of La Trappe in Normandy became James' place of retreat. Much of the remainder of his life was spent ruminating over his failings and seeking God's solace. The probable truth is that James' nerve at the Boyne had once again failed him, as it had done after Wincanton. While in retreat he is said to have been always a wretched figure, convinced he was being hotly pursued. This was in fact not the case. William of Orange would have been too embarrassed to have captured his own father-in-law and was happy to allow James to distance himself. Recurring thoughts of his father's cruel fate on the block at Whitehall and of his own precipitous flight when confronted by the Williamite invasion in 1688 made grim flashbacks for James. At Dublin, he is said to have opined, 'The Irish had run well.' 'You, Sir, seem to have beaten them,' replied the wife of Tyrconnell.

Did both king and countess truly realise the gravity of the situation? At Kinsale, the old Gaelic order in Ireland had been toppled, but was it clear to either that after the Boyne the last great Irish loyalist lordships would soon be eclipsed and that the Irish language would become the language of the downtrodden? Would they even have cared? Probably not, but the reek of defeat in James' presence was palpable nonetheless. More sanguine men like Sarsfield, a true Irish patriot, remained minded to continue the fight; the Jacobite army, though headless now that James had bolted, remained intact; and another Irish winter beckoned.

17

EACHDHROIM AN ÁIR

Limerick and Athlone became the next targets for the Williamite high command. The Jacobite army, much of which as we have seen had remained unengaged at the Boyne, reformed on the road back to Limerick. It soon became clear that Tyrconnell would seek an armistice at the first opportunity, and this led to a breakdown in relations between him and Sarsfield. Tyrconnell argued that Limerick would not be able to hold out against the might of the Williamites. Supported by the weight of military argument, this nevertheless came across as defeatist. The duke argued that an accommodation with William III would best be accomplished from a position of strength while a credible Jacobite army still existed. Faced with a stony silence and angry looks from those who supported a continuation of the struggle, he backtracked. Rather than remain behind in beleaguered Limerick to face the horrors of a protracted siege he travelled on to Galway for his better safety, later issuing his orders to the Limerick garrison from there.

Meanwhile, Sarsfield led a relief force to Athlone, designed to break through the Williamite cordon that threatened to tighten around the town. Rumour of his approach proved enough of a threat to see tents hurriedly packed away and a rapid retreat eastward on the part of the would-be besiegers. Sarsfield's return to Limerick, on 8 August, coincided with the arrival of the main Williamite army, led by William of Orange in person. No other English king had ever before ventured so far westward into Ireland's interior. Sarsfield led 600 troopers in a daring raid against the Williamite supply lines, an act reminiscent of great cavalry commanders of the past like Prince Rupert and the future Jeb Stuart. At Ballyneety, near Cullen, co. Tipperary, just twelve miles from Limerick, the general penetrated deep behind enemy lines and attacked the Williamite siege train. When challenged by pickets to give the password, he is reputed to have answered, 'Sarsfield is the name, and Sarsfield is the man!' At such moments legends are born. Wagons were burned by his men, artillery pieces destroyed and two of William's eight siege guns disabled. More important was Sarsfield's destruction of ammunition stocks and supply caches; the shortages these created would delay William's plans, allowing the defenders at Limerick to strengthen their defences.

When attacks resumed, the Williamites struck hard at a section of breached wall, which proved too narrow to break through. During heavy fighting, carried out in atrocious weather conditions, the attackers suffered over 2,000 casualties. The lack of success owed much to want of ammunition, the result of Sarsfield's celebrated raid. The final Williamite attack saw the king's Brandenburghers repulsed by Irishmen throwing stones, and two crack English regiments driven off by a handful of Irish horsemen at one of the city's gates. William weighed the costs and fell into a deep depression. One of his regiments had just six officers left fit to serve. Other regiments had fared equally badly. His Danish brigade had suffered forty-five junior officers killed or wounded. William's chaplain, Reverend Story, spoke of one half hour period that day when the sound of gunfire had been continuous and smoke had created a cloud which reached up to the top of a mountain six miles distant. To make matters worse, requests for a temporary truce to bury the dead were refused by the Irish. Within weeks, bad weather had made the trenchlines untenable. Men who could afford it burnt bowls of spirits to make inroads against the damp. Conditions outside the city were worse than within.

William had had enough. He raised the siege and left Ireland to his commanders to subdue. Cork and Kinsale had already by this time fallen to the Royal Navy. A full chapter could be written as to how this was achieved. Suffice to say, the campaign's architect was John Churchill, the future Duke of Marlborough, arguably England's finest ever general. These harbours falling to the Williamites denied the French a port in southern Ireland to land men and supplies, whereas supplies from England could be transported from West Country ports to the Williamite army in Munster quickly and safely.

Tyrconnell also left Ireland, rejoining James in France. He was no longer trusted. Rumours that the duke was in receipt of French gold in exchange for fighting men shipped to France had undermined his position. Forty thousand gold coins sent to Tyrconnell's wife and daughter in France appeared to prove such claims. Among Tyrconnell's accusers was Sarsfield, who, pumped up after his famous Ballyneety raid, now considered himself the greatest of generals. He exclaimed:

> There are two factions here, Lord Tyrconnell's and mine: he can do whatever he wants, I do not care. I will always be stronger than him … he is very jealous and he despairs of the influence I have over the army. This perfidious and ungrateful man knows full well that during the siege of Limerick he would have been massacred without me, and he is not ignorant of the fact that I prevented and resisted the pressing entreaties of the whole army who adamantly wanted to remove him and proclaim me general in his place.

Writing to James II, Sarsfield explained the reasons for his concerns over the duke's fitness to lead, saying:

> My Lord Tyrconnell [is] not qualified for such a charge as he has hitherto exercised; that his age and infirmity made him require more sleep than was consistent with so much business; that his want of experience in military affairs rendered him

exceedingly slow in his resolves and incapable of laying projects, which no depending General officers would do for him, first by taking a great deal of pains to make him conceive it; and then either have it rejected, or he to have the honour of it, if successful.

On Tyrconnell's departure a deputising council of twelve men was formed to govern Ireland. Sarsfield became governor of Connaught and Galway Town. Galway was by now the only major Jacobite outlet for communications to the Continent. Williamite attempts to gain a foothold in Connaught were frustrated by swarms of Sarsfield's irregulars; these were men known as 'rapparees', men who offered no quarter and were therefore much feared by the Williamite raiding parties. In Galway town the French army massed, awaiting departure back to France. To a man they were sick of Ireland. Its damp climate had sapped their health and it offered few amenities for recreation.

Sarsfield's attempts to discredit Tyrconnell were dashed when the duke arrived back in Limerick on 14 January 1691. But the duke was nearing the end of his life and was soon bedridden with a swollen foot. Ill-health dogged him from then on. Attempts on his part to mend relations with Sarsfield fell on stony ground. The general failed to present himself at Limerick until the end of February. When he did at last make the effort, he remained churlish. Tyrconnell's charm was wasted on him. Nor was Sarsfield of a mind to tolerate interference in military matters. Hopes he had of exerting unfettered control over the Irish army were dashed however when in May 1691 a new commander-in-chief arrived at Limerick from the Continent, accompanied by artillery officers and cloth to make 20,000 uniforms. This was the French Marquis de St Ruth, known as 'the hammer of the Huguenots', described unkindly by a contemporary as 'tall and well-built but exceptionally ugly ... a gallant soldier but notorious for domestic cruelty'. St Ruth's treatment of his wife had become so vicious she had asked the French king to intervene. Louis ordered her husband to desist, but when the ill-treatment continued he ordered the marquis to Ireland. His wife remained at the French court.

It remains unknown if Sarsfield submitted gracefully to this new hand at the tiller. More certainly Tyrconnell became sidelined. At Athlone, St Ruth ignored Tyrconnell's advice to tear down the town's western walls to ease the town's supply problems. The duke also pointed out to the Frenchman that if the town fell to the enemy they would not long be able to retain it without considerable rebuilding work being undertaken. By leaving the walls intact the Frenchman relied instead on a strict rota of front-line troops manning the town's walls. At all times there were to be at least three regiments within Athlone, with others in reserve to regularly relieve them. The Williamites were encamped on the east bank of the Shannon. Preventing them from crossing the river was key for the Jacobites. Williamite work parties risked their lives in an attempt to make the single bridge crossable. The structure had been slighted on the orders of Athlone's Jacobite governor, Richard Grace (Raymond le Gros's ancestor), who we last came across when fleeing after the defeat of his forces at Loughrea in 1652. Williamite pioneers sought to achieve this by throwing planks across the gaps while under musket fire. The Irish attacked them with axes. All save two of the twenty-two Irishmen attempting this were in turn killed by incoming fire from the eastern bank. Here 20,000 Williamites were now massing. With them was a large artillery train, comprising thirty-two guns of various calibres, plus 1,000 cannonballs for each piece.

A second attempt on the part of the Williamites to repair the bridge fared no better than the first. The Irish counter-attacked and set the planks alight. Only by sending a large assault party of tall grenadiers across the river at a shallow point – 1,500 of them in the first wave, their fuses and bags of grenades held above their heads – did the Williamites eventually gain control of the west bank. An artillery barrage kept Irish heads down while the crossing was carried out. When heads were raised their owners spied to their horror a riverbank teeming with the enemy. Williamite work parties were already making good the bridge over which cavalry would soon be crossing. Irish defenders of Athlone were seen to be 'running like conies from one hole to another', their supports driven back by cannonade and the flight of their panicked colleagues. Control of the west bank was lost in minutes. Cannons salvaged by the Irish were later abandoned in the bogs further to the west. Williamite Lieutenant-General Godard van Reede wrote of the Jacobites leaving around 2,000 dead in Athlone. According to another eyewitness, the figure was more realistically half this number. Among the dead was Richard Grace. When called upon by the Williamites to surrender the town, he had fired a pistol over the herald's head, declaring, 'These are my terms; these only will I give or receive; and when my provisions are consumed, I will defend until I eat my old boots.' His body (sans boots?) was later discovered in the town ruins.

The loss of Athlone left the Jacobite command with two options: to fall back on Galway and Limerick, or to take up a suitable defensive position and give battle. St Ruth again refused the advice of others when he opted for the latter, choosing to make his stand on an entrenched ridgeline known as Kilcommodan Hill beside the small village of Aughrim, co. Galway, five miles south-west of Ballinasloe. Sarsfield advised holding out in Galway and Limerick, sapping Williamite strength by launching sorties against their supply lines, but was overruled.

Where the Boyne was described as akin to a skirmish, and where casualties on both sides were low, the resulting Battle of Aughrim would prove to be a much more hard-fought affair, pitting 20,000 Williamites against a similar number of less well-equipped and previously defeated Jacobites. The latter did, however, benefit from prepared defences and a boggy frontage, across which only two narrow causeways allowed access. St Ruth was a modern commander who knew the value of well-located skirmish screens, which served to funnel enemy attacks toward defended ridgelines and strongpoints. The Williamite commander, Lieutenant-General Godard van Reede van Ginkel, a veteran of the Boyne now entrusted by William of Orange with the conduct of the war in Ireland, positioned his army opposite on Urrachree Hill. In Gaelic this means *O Mo Chroi* – translated as 'my heart is broken' – allegedly after the cries of the wives of dead Williamite soldiers.

Part of Ginkel's front line comprised seven English battalions under the command of General Hugh Mackay, the Scottish commander defeated by Dundee's highlanders at Killiecrankie two years before. The experience of Killiecrankie had led to the replacement of the old plug bayonet with a bayonet of Mackay's own design, fixed by two rings alongside the barrel rather than in the muzzle. In Mackay's own words, 'The soldiers may safely keep their fire till they pour it into [the enemy's] breasts, and then have no other motion to make but to push, as with a pike.' The importance of this in relation to the defeat at Killiecrankie has in the past been overstated, but it was nevertheless an important innovation that no doubt saved lives.

When battle commenced, determined Williamite attacks resulted in equally fierce counter-attacks on the part of the defenders. Many Williamite troops (Scots, Danes, Dutch, French Huguenots and Irish Protestants) fell back, some planting sharpened stakes to their front to guard against Jacobite cavalry. Others were driven back into the bogs, where some are said to have drowned. Mackay's brigade was an exception. An onlooker referenced this when he wrote, 'The English marched boldly up to their old ground again from whence they had been lately beat; which is only natural to Englishmen, for it is commonly observable that they are commonly fiercer and bolder after being repulsed than before.' The brigade forced a passage over the causeway beside Aughrim Castle, then dug in to face a Jacobite counter-attack. Elsewhere, the momentum of the pursuing Irish was such that a battery of Williamite guns was overrun and the cannon spiked. Had not a shortage of ammunition of the correct calibre allowed the encroachment planned by Ginkel on the Jacobite right flank, where the causeway allowed ingress free from the cloying bog, and had not St Ruth been decapitated by chain-shot at the height of the action, the Jacobites might have prevailed. Instead, they failed to hold their ground.

Final Jacobite hopes lay with General Dominick Sheldon's men on the left wing, fronted by Colonel Henry Luttrell's dragoons.

Sensing defeat and facing Mackay's still intact brigade, the shaken commanders ordered a general retreat. Their escape route is known to this day as Luttrell's Pass, a topographic feature which will forever reflect upon Luttrell's alleged faint-heartedness. Sarsfield commanded the Jacobite right wing on Kilcommodan Hill, blocking the Galway road. He was not as far as is known engaged during the main battle. His fresh cavalry were now available to cover the retreat of the broken army, but failed to prevent a wholesale slaughter of native Irish. At least 4,000 Irishmen and hundreds of officers probably lost their lives at Aughrim, with many more listed as missing or captured; some authors put the Jacobite death toll as high as 7,000 men. Additionally, up to 3,000 Williamites may have fallen dead or wounded; diarist John Evelyn assessed the Williamite outright dead as close to 1,000. It was by far the bloodiest battle ever fought for control of Ireland. The event is known in Ireland to this day as 'Aughrim of the slaughter' (*Eachdhroim an áir*). For some considerable time, passers-by noted the large flocks of sheep on Kilcommodan Hill, only to be told by locals that what they took for sheep was in fact a mass of human bone. Monks from nearby Kilconnell and Clontuskert later interred the remains in a series of mass graves. General Ginkel's report to William III gives an early and (typically, after a great battle) sketchy précis of events:

> The fight lasted four hours and was very obstinate. The enemy's force was much superior to ours and their position more advantageous. Yet your troops attacked them with the greatest determination and bravery, totally defeating them. Prisoners include Maj. Gen. Hamilton, Dorrington & other officers. It is said St Ruth is killed but I have not been able to make sure of it … nearly 4,000 lie dead on the battlefield.

A more general collapse of Catholic Irish arms followed: Galway fell six days after the battle. A renewed siege of Limerick commenced a month later, on 25 August. Tyrconnell was by this time dead, having suffered a stroke. He died on 14 August and was buried two days later at Limerick Cathedral. Suspected of collusion with the enemy, Sarsfield had Henry Luttrell arrested. Luttrell's breach with Sarsfield followed the former's failure to stand his ground at Aughrim, but the accused was subsequently cleared by a court martial of cowardice. After the eventual fall of Limerick and the signing of a treaty of the same name, the enmity generated was enough to drive Luttrell to make his peace with the Williamites, taking with him a substantial following estimated at 8,000 men. The surrender terms of the treaty of Limerick provided the Irish troops with the choice of either service abroad in the pay of King William or of joining the deposed James II in France. The only caveat was that they were not allowed to travel via Scotland or England if they opted for France as their destination. Twelve thousand men would later travel to the Continent. Clauses were incorporated into the settlement to preserve the rights to property of Irish who submitted to William. This made submission a preferred choice for many. Transports nevertheless proved insufficient to take away all those who opted to leave Ireland. Loud cries and lamentations of wives and children left behind to face an uncertain fate made for a heartrending and tragic finale. Reports speak of distraught women dashing into the water and perishing, of others clinging to the departing boats as they made away from shore.

18

LEST FINN AWAKEN

Sarsfield's capitulation at Galway on 23 September came as a surprise at the time, but with hindsight, given the failure of the French fleet to supply the city before the onset of winter, it was inevitable. It was at around this time that the general made his rueful quip about exchanging kings and starting the fight all over again. He would go on to serve the French, before being mortally wounded in action at the Battle of Landen, in present-day Belgium, in the summer of 1693. His fame in Ireland by then was such that generations of male Patricks swamped the records of parish registers – the slang 'Paddy' now being synonymous with Irishman. General Hugh Mackay died a year before Sarsfield in the same theatre of war at the Battle of Steenkirke. When ordered to defend an indefensible position he said only that 'the will of the Lord be done' before being killed. William of Orange succumbed after his horse tripped over a mole-hill; the king fell, breaking a collar-bone, the shock of which may have brought on a pulmonary inflammation. He died on 8 March 1702. The English had never really taken to him. William's agenda was modern for its time. He was a courageous man who sought religious toleration and 'peaceful politics'. His latter-day legacy in Northern Ireland would have appalled him.

Up until the year 1745 Catholic Irish gentry would continue to supply the French with soldiers. In part this was to rid Ireland of a potentially disruptive generation of youthful malcontents, but, when the French supported the invasion of Scotland by Bonny Prince Charlie with Irish troops, the dangers of such a policy became immediately apparent. Irish Jacobitism had become by this time 'a badge of loyalty', attracting highlanders in great numbers. The '45 campaign lies outside the scope of this book, but it should be noted that Catholics in the west of Ireland sported Highland plaid in honour of their kinsmen across the North Channel when news of the Jacobite victory at Prestonpans on 21 September 1745 reached them. Gaels looked to Prince Charles to 'end the tyranny' of the 'swarthy Johns' and prayed for further victories. Fear of local Jacobite risings in Ireland and a possible French invasion led to Protestant irregulars in Ireland being recruited to quell any trouble that might arise. The most likely regions where they might flare were considered to be Cork and Galway. The English viceroy in Ireland, Philip Dormer Stanhope, Lord Chesterfield, refused to be phased. When told by an excited Protestant that the Catholics were rising, he quipped, 'No doubt, it is almost nine o'clock.'

*

Gaelic Ireland would continue to pose an ongoing concern for politicians at Westminster and Dublin throughout the eighteenth century. The country remained the most likely conduit for foreign invasion yet was at the same time an important source of manpower for Britain's armies. Ireland has been described as England's first colony, but it lay in too close proximity to be treated as a foreign possession. With its undigested mix of planters and natives, it nevertheless remained sufficiently different to prevent absorption into what might be termed 'the metropolitan centre'. The outbreak of war in the American colonies in 1776 provided Irish patriots with a practical ideological platform for protest, especially when Britain imposed an embargo on Irish exports to America, undermining Irish trade at a time of great economic hardship. Those in Ireland who acquiesced to the restrictions were referred to by one nationalist politician as 'giving in to a tyrant's plea'. The victorious American colonists who won their freedom from British colonial oversight would become a potent example of what might be achieved through focussed armed struggle, and the 'spirit of 1776' inspired what has been termed 'worldwide resonance', particularly in Ireland and pre-revolutionary France. The first signatory of the American Declaration of Independence, Hugh Wallace, was an Irish émigré, and other Irishmen rose as leaders in America, like Commodore John Barry, 'the father of the American Navy'. Born in County Wexford, his surname links him to one of the original Anglo-Norman invaders of Ireland from the twelfth century.

The emergency in the American colonies also witnessed a spontaneous sign-up of Protestant volunteers to guard against foreign invasion while British troops were deployed from Ireland to fight there. This was not the first time the Protestant Irish had rallied to the defence of the status quo: in 1745, during the Jacobite rising in Scotland, 100 volunteers had registered at Cork, becoming known as the 'True Blues'. The same happened during the Seven Years War (1754–1763) with France. A muster of volunteers in 1760 was organised in response to fears that the French might attempt an invasion of Ireland by first seizing Carrickfergus in Belfast Lough. They became known as 'the Ulster Volunteers'. Other named volunteer units included 'the Irish Volunteers', 'the United Independent Volunteers', 'the Wicklow Volunteers', 'the Kilkenny Rangers', and 'the Offerlane Blues', to name but five. These units operated independently of government and by 1778 they had a political voice in the form of Henry Flood, a noted parliamentarian debater and radical, described as 'one of the most powerful voices of eighteenth-century Irish Protestant patriotism'. The Lord Lieutenant of the day, John Hobart, 2nd Earl of Buckinghamshire, attempted to gain a modicum of control over the volunteers by granting temporary commissions to their officers, but failed. Reluctance on the part of the British to address constitutional grievances led the volunteers to flex their muscles. On 4 November 1779, 1,000 strong, they protested in grand manner on the College Green, Dublin. By the spring of 1782 they numbered 60,000, forcing the British Prime Minister, Lord North, to yield to a number of their demands concerning trading rights. North was not unsympathetic to Irish grievances and made concessions which another man at the helm might have quibbled over.

Two Irelands had evolved since the Cromwellian and Williamite Wars: a marginalised Gaelic Ireland and a more prosperous minority Protestant Ireland, the domain of an ascendant gentry class who lived well on both sides of the Irish Sea from incomes gleaned from confiscated Irish land, often supervised by unscrupulous land agents. Religious differences remained a barrier to assimilation, language perhaps less so, since many Gaelic Irish picked up a smattering of English, making the country largely bilingual. Men like Jonathan Swift (d. 1745), author of *Gulliver's Travels*, famously detested both Catholics and Presbyterians in equal measure, seeing Irish Episcopalians (the equivalent of English 'low church') as the natural rulers of the country. This did not mean he was immune to the suffering he witnessed at first hand; Swift's biographer has noted in his subject an 'anti-colonial humanitarianism'. In particular, Swift attacked the punitive trade laws which favoured England at the expense of Ireland; he also targeted the 'ascendant' landlord classes for their bullying methods.

There was much poverty among the native Catholic Irish right throughout the eighteenth century, and also a great deal of oppression against them. An English traveller named Arthur Young wrote in 1776 that landlords were so feared that an Irishman dare not openly cross them. Disrespect shown might be punished with a horse-whip or worse. A man who attempted to defend himself would put his life in danger. Cottagers informed Young that their wives and daughters were often obliged to warm a landlord's bed at night. Many peasant homes were wretched hovels, a situation most pronounced in Connaught, where one room might serve a family and where the front door was the only outlet for smoke from the ubiquitous Irish turf fire. Such dwellings contrasted to an absurd extent with the homes of the great estates of the landed classes.

By 1782 relaxation of the 'penal laws' against Catholics had risen high on the political agenda. Moderates at Dublin Castle spoke of being willing to embrace a more inclusive concept of the Irish nation. Given the uncertain international climate, the British Crown had little hesitation in giving the nod to this new approach, allowing the Dublin parliament to pass a number of laws free from Westminster's sign-off or interference. Legislative reforms similar in scope to those turned down by the American Congress on the eve of the Revolutionary War were agreed and enacted in Ireland. Nationalists claimed that through these reforms the Irish had proceeded from 'injuries to arms, and from arms to liberty', but, when further moderate reforms were drafted and ratified by twenty-two of the counties of Ireland and eleven of its major towns, an attempt to bring forward the bill in March 1784 was rejected at Dublin. Patriots railed that parliament had once more fallen victim to 'tyranny, rapacity and malice'.

Young's sojourn in Ireland, mentioned above, pre-dated the era of the Corn Laws (1784–1846), a period during which Irish farmers, often working smallholdings of less than ten acres, were required to supply wheat to Britain while they and their families subsisted on a diet of potatoes. Increased agricultural output, dateable from the 1740s, extended into the nineteenth century. There was also a burgeoning Catholic middle class, grown rich through manufacturing, in particular textiles. How much of this new-found wealth percolated down to the peasantry is an open question, one that is still debated today. There was certainly a growth in infrastructure: the era saw the start of canal building and the expansion of urban centres, the latter inevitable with a rapidly growing mercantile population. Yet according to historian Peter Berresford Ellis (writing for the *Irish Democrat* in 2004), between 1728 and 1845 the colonial landlord system produced twenty-eight 'artificial' famines in which millions of Irish men, women and children died. In June 1822, in Cork alone more than 120,000 men, women and children were on the verge of starvation or existed on charity. Economic expansion therefore came at a cost, creating, even earlier than the great famine, a series of now seldom discussed humanitarian emergencies. (So much for that slippery term 'trickle-down economics'.) Nevertheless, men like Francis Moylan, the Catholic Bishop of Cork, went to great lengths during the 1790s to stem what he termed the 'French disease', the impulse, along with ever-present sectarian animosities and economic burdens afflicting Catholics, toward revolutionary republicanism.

Britain was at odds with itself. The power of the Crown had for some time been in decline, the result of a shift in patronage from monarch to government committee. The eighteenth century also saw the rise of an increasingly literate and engaged public, well served by newspapers, lobbies and appeals. By the second half of the eighteenth century, the provisions of the monarchy lacked clarity. Better defined were its proscriptions: a king or queen could not be a Catholic or marry a Catholic; nor could a monarch raise an army in peacetime or dismiss judges. Under such an interdict there could be no return to the sort of autocratic rule enjoyed by the Tudors or the Stuarts. Although the Crown might choose its ministers, they came from a shallow pool of increasingly partisan politicians. There were no elections. Men chosen by the king enacted policy, often without too many effective checks and balances. The development of a formal opposition has been described as 'a plant of slow growth' in the eighteenth century. Political dissent remained too closely linked to Jacobitism to flourish. Nevertheless, British imperialism was transforming from an essentially commercial endeavour into a more libéral, humanitarian aspiration. Historians speak of the 'spirit of 1783', the year when Britain lost her thirteen troublesome American colonies and was forced to reset her worldwide objectives.

George III was a man of moderate intellect, described when young as backward, probably because of shyness rather than stupidity, a trait he carried forward into adulthood, remaining uncomfortable in formal society. To some he appeared sullen and uncommunicative, to others censorious, perhaps overly aware of society's pitfalls and failings. Today he is remembered for his verbal tics and exclamations – 'what, what!' – and succumbing to a bout of mental illness in later life. But despite his flaws he was astute enough to realise there was a need for Irish Catholics to be brought back into the mainstream of politics. In 1793 he backed concessions that gave Catholics the vote and allowed them entry to Trinity College. Importantly however, the right to sit in parliament and to legislate was denied them, and only certain public posts were deemed suitable. Because the Irish parliament was by this time independent of Westminster, William Pitt's government was not required to ratify these changes, but his cabinet supported them nonetheless.

Historians have since seen these dispensations as raising the expectation among the Catholic majority in Ireland of further emancipation and therefore of building up a tide of expectancy which in the end was dammed. George III came to harbour reservations about further concessions to the Catholics, on one occasion protesting his astonishment that the Protestant supremacy in Ireland might be put in jeopardy, saying his family's (the Hanoverian's) first objective since the abdication of James II had been to ensure no return of popery to Britain. These words may have been put into the monarch's head by one of his peers, Lord FitzGibbon, who counselled that by consenting to the Catholic Relief Bill he would be infringing his coronation oath. The new deputy-lieutenant at Dublin, the forty-three-year-old William Wentworth, Earl FitzWilliam, was the unwitting initiator of this outburst. Of a mind to support further Catholic emancipation, he had carelessly pushed ahead with it without gaining formal backing. In January 1795 he wrote that 'not to grant cheerfully on the part of government all the Catholics wish will not only be exceedingly impolitic, but perhaps [in the context of the French threat] dangerous'.

Meanwhile the society of United Irishmen had made inroads across the Irish political spectrum. Begun as a liberal movement led by men like politician Henry Grattan, who sought reform through parliamentary debate rather than at the point of a gun, the society had by the late 1780s become heavily radicalised. The American Revolution was a factor in this, and so too of course the French

Revolution, which had begun in earnest in the summer of 1789: both were upheavals portending an age of fervent republicanism, a system at odds with the British model of liberal, constitutional monarchy. A number of splinter and opposition movements came into being; one of these, the Defenders, developed a political ideology aping revolutionary American and French influences while at the same time drawing on more archaic Gaelic traditions, harking back to the days of Finn McCool and the legendary Fianna, a vanguard for Finn's awakening. Opposition to them came from equally colourfully named factions like the Oakboys, the Peep O'Day Boys and the Orange Boys.

In 1795 a battle fought near Loughgall, co. Armagh, between opposing gangs, known as the Battle of the Diamond, left thirty, mainly Catholic Defenders, dead, perhaps 10 per cent of those who had massed to confront the Protestant Peep O'Day Boys, described by a contemporary as a 'low set of fellows', armed with guns and bayonets and reinforced by members of another gang known as the Bleary Boys. The fight was not a brawl decided by fisticuffs and rudimentary weaponry, but a shooting match fought out by opposing marksmen. The outcome, known as the 'Armagh Outrages', saw a Protestant mob egged on by fanatics drive several thousand Catholics from their homes. Victory at the Diamond became, it was said, a sanction for 'the Godly to despoil the homes of the Philistines'. Even earlier than this there had been unrest in Armagh. Victimisation of Catholics worsened. Local Orangemen threatened forced evictions and erected notices warning Catholics that unless they left Armagh they would 'have their souls blown to the low hills of Hell'. Other notices threatened 'Hell or Connaught', a sinister playback of abuses suffered by the Catholic Irish in Cromwellian times. Much of the destruction wrought targeted Catholic means of livelihood, weaving looms and the like. Tensions over competition in manufacturing between the two communities appear to have lain at the heart of the violence. County Armagh was the most heavily populated county in Ireland, split almost equally between Protestants and Catholics. Pressure on land and Catholic penetration of the linen industry occurred at a time when mechanisation was putting downward pressure on wages, stoking sectarian tensions. In 1797, William Richardson wrote, 'Much offence has lately been taken because the Catholics in the general increase in wealth have raised the price of land by bidding high when it became vacant.'

The Diamond has been linked with the first formation of a secret society known as the Orange Order. The Order's objectives were described as defensive; their creed was 'to defend the King and his heirs so long as he or they supported the Protestant Ascendancy'. The year 1795 also saw the United Irishmen reorganised from a political party into 'a secret revolutionary society' – its aim, with French assistance, to overthrow British rule and declare Ireland a republic. With some justification, 1795 might be seen as the year when the troubles in Ireland first cloaked themselves in a discernibly modern form.

Ironically, the man most closely identified with the United Irish movement, Theobald Wolfe Tone, was descended from a Cromwellian planter. A Presbyterian barrister, Tone was described as slight, handsome and genteel, with lank, straight hair, a sallow, pockmarked face and small, bright, lively eyes. His avant-garde outlook predisposed him to a revolutionary career, his main achievement in this respect being to unite dissident Protestants and Catholics under a common banner which asserted the 'rights of man', separatism from Britain and Catholic emancipation. He and the poet Thomas Russell, along with others like Henry Joy McCracken, Samuel Neilson, and the Simms brothers, famously made a solemn oath never to desist in their subversive efforts until they had overthrown the authority of the English in Ireland and asserted Irish independence. Their compact is considered to mark the birth of modern Irish Republicanism. They sought to place Catholics on a level with Protestants by force of arms and attempted to fight a conventional war in response to atrocities enacted by the government's paramilitary forces. Biased English accounts clung to the standard narrative, presenting the Irish rebels of the eighteenth and nineteenth centuries as 'an aimless and bloodthirsty rabble', not, as would have been more accurate, a downtrodden people with just grievances.

The dramatic demise of the United Irishmen in 1798, a momentous, ill-judged and mainly one-sided year of battles, lies outside the scope of this narrative, but it should be noted that against better disciplined troops, the poorly equipped rebels stood no chance. At the first battle of the war – fittingly, perhaps, fought on the Hill of Tara in Meath – just three companies of Scottish Fencibles, a handful of yeomanry, flanking cavalry and a single battalion gun proved sufficient to crush a 4,000-strong Irish rebel army.

Historians now sometimes draw a direct line from the Jacobites to later rebellious groups – not just to the United Irishmen but also to others like the Whiteboys, Rightboys, Destroyers, Defenders and Rockites, cliques who took things into their own hands and risked summary execution to oppose injustice. When compared to either the Jacobites or United Irishmen the aims of the Whiteboys and their ilk were however more 'conservative, defensive, regional and episodic', much like other popular movements in pre-industrialised Europe. Debt collectors, landlords and planters were their main targets, not the State itself; many young men up in arms against the ruling class continued to espouse a deep loyalty to the Crown. Named for their white smocks, the Whiteboys were radicalised by agrarian issues: rack-rents, tithes, excessive priestly demands and evictions. They were at their height during the first quarter of the nineteenth century. Men with clandestine names like Captain Moonlight, Captain Steel and Captain Right became their leaders. The English Prime Minister at the time highlighted to parliament the dangers of famine resulting from their depredations. The *Dublin Journal* reported much of the south-east of Tipperary for a time falling under their sway. In Ireland, fear that Light Dragoons sent over by the government would fail to discriminate between the innocent and the guilty led to the flight of many young men and women from counties Cork and Limerick. Houses lay empty or were occupied only by older men, women and young children. At Cappoquin, co. Waterford, the Whiteboys marched in large numbers past the military barracks playing the Jacobite air, 'the lad with the white cockade'. Open displays of defiance erupted. Police stations, barracks and a number of large houses were attacked and burned. Frequent meetings of insurgents were reported. At the Battle of Keimaneigh (the 'pass of the gap of the deer') in the Caha Mountains of Cork, three local Whiteboys and a member of the Crown forces died in a famous shoot-out which made headline news in 1822. A fourth Whiteboy, and others suspected of supporting him, were later hanged. At a memorial service at Keimaneigh in 1999, where plaques to the dead were laid at the end of a century of intermittent violence in Ireland, which included the Easter Rising of 1916, the Irish Civil War and later internecine strife in Ulster, an Irish orator spoke of how those gathered should never forget 'the rock from which we were hewn' or 'the quarry from which we were cut'.

SOURCES AND FURTHER READING

Internet sources

Annals of Clonmacnois [archive.org/stream/annalsofclonmacnoomage]

Annals of Connaught [www.ucc.ie/celt/published/T100011/]

Annals of the Four Masters [www.ucc.ie/celt/online/T100005A/]

Annals of Inisfallen [www.ucc.ie/celt/published/T100004/]

Annals of Ireland [www.ucc.ie/celt/published/T100017/]

Annals of Loch Ce [www.ucc.ie/celt/published/T100010A/]

Annals of Tigernach [www.ucc.ie/celt/published/G100002/]

Annals of Ulster [http://www.ucc.ie/celt/online/T100001A/]

Oxford Dictionary of National Biography [www.oxforddnb.com/]

Triumphs of Turlough [www.ucc.ie/celt/published/T100062/]

Printed sources and further reading

Adams, Max, *The King in the North* (Head of Zeus, 2013)

Aitchison, Nick, *The Picts and Scots at War* (Stroud: Sutton Publishing, 2003)

Arnold, C., Globe: *Life in Shakespeare's London* (Simon and Schuster, 2015)

Asbridge, T., *The Greatest Knight* (Simon and Schuster, 2015)

Bardon, J., *The Plantation of Ulster* (Dublin: Gill & MacMillan, 2011)

Bede, *Ecclesiastical History of the English People* (Penguin Classics, 1990)

Bennett, M., *Richard II and the Revolution of 1399* (Stroud: Sutton Publishing, 1999)

Bennett, M., *Lambert Simnel and the Battle of Stoke* (New York: St Martin's Press, 1987)

Borman, Tracy, *Thomas Cromwell* (Hodder & Stoughton, 2015)

Brady, C., 'The Captain's Games: Army and Society in Elizabethan Ireland', in *A Military History of Ireland*, ed. T. Bartlett and K. Jeffrey (Cambridge: 1996)

Brooks, Richard, *Cassell's Battlefields of Britain & Ireland* (Weidenfeld and Nicholson, 2005)

Brooks, Richard, *The Knight who saved England* (Oxford: Osprey Publishing, 2014)

Cahill, T., *How the Irish saved civilization* (Hodder and Stoughton, 1995)

Canny, Nicholas, *Making Ireland British* (Oxford: 2001)

Charles Edwards, T. M., 'Irish Warfare before 1100', in *A Military History of Ireland*, op. cit.

Childs, J., 'The Williamite War, 1689–1691', in *A Military History of Ireland*, op. cit.

Church, S., *King John, England, Magna Carta and the making of a Tyrant* (MacMillan, 2015)

Clark, A., *The Old English in Ireland 1625–42* (London: 1968)

Connelly, S. J., 'Eighteenth-Century Ireland, Colony or Ancien Regime?', in *The making of Modern Irish History*, ed. D. George Boyce and Alan O' Day (London & New York, Routledge, 1996)

Cooper, J., *The Queen's Agent: Francis Walsingham at the court of Elizabeth I* (Faber and Faber, 2011)

Cowan, E. J., *For Freedom Alone, the Declaration of Arbroath 1320* (Edinburgh: Birlinn, 2008)

Curtis, Edmund, *A History of Ireland* (Methuen, 1950)

Davies, G., *The Early Stuarts, 1603–1660*, (Oxford University Press, 1959)

Davies, Wendy (ed.), *From the Vikings to the Normans* (Oxford, 2003)

De Bedoyere, Guy, *Defying Rome* (Stroud: Tempus Publishing, 2003)

Doherty, R., *The Siege of Derry 1689* (Stroud: Spellmount, 2010)

Duffy, Christopher, *The '45* (Cassell, 2003)

Duffy, Sean, *Brian Boru and the Battle of Clontarf* (Dublin: Gill & MacMillan, 2014)

Duffy, Sean, 'King John's Expedition to Ireland 1210, the Evidence Reconsidered', *Irish Historical Studies* 30 (1996)

Elliot, M., *Wolfe Tone, Prophet of Irish Independence* (Yale University, 1989)

Ellis, P. B, *Hell or Connaught: The Cromwellian Colonisation of Ireland, 1652–1660* (Belfast: The Blackstaff Press, 1988)

Ellis, S. G., *Ireland in the Age of the Tudors* (Harlow: Longman, 1998)

Ellis, S. G., 'The Tudors and the Origins of the modern Irish State: A Standing Army', in *A Military History of Ireland*, op. cit.

Falls, Cyril, *Elizabeth's Irish Wars* (Methuen, 1970)

Fanning, Ronan, *Eamon de Valera: A Will to Power* (Faber & Faber, 2015)

Flanagan, Marie Therese, *Irish Society, Anglo-Norman settlers, Angevin Kingship* (Oxford: Clarendon Press, 1989)

Flanagan, Marie Therese, 'Irish and Anglo-Norman Warfare in Twelfth-Century Ireland', in *A Military History of Ireland*, op. cit.

Foster R. F., *Modern Ireland, 1600–1972* (Penguin, 1989)

Frame, Robin, 'The Defence of the English Lordship, 1250–1450', in *A Military History of Ireland*, op. cit.

Fraser, Antonia, *Cromwell, Our Chief of Men* (Weidenfeld and Nicolson, 1973)

Gillingham, John, 'War and Chivalry in the History of William the Marshal', published in *Anglo-Norman Warfare*, ed., Matthew Strickland (Woodbridge: The Boydell Press, 1992)

Gillingham, John, *Conquests, Catastrophe and Recovery, Britain & Ireland 1066–1485* (Vintage, 2014)

Hanna, J. W., 'The Battle of Magh Rath, its true site determined', *Ulster Journal of Archaeology*, first series, volume 4 (1856)

Harbison, Peter, *Guide to the National Monuments in the Republic of Ireland* (Dublin: Gill and MacMillan, 1970)

Hayes-McCoy, G. A., *Irish Battles: A Military History of Ireland* (Dublin: The Appletree Press, 1969)

Hill, G., 'Shane O'Neill's expedition against the Antrim Scots 1565', *Ulster Journal of Archaeology* (1861)

Heather, Peter, *Empire and Barbarians* (Pan Books, 2009)

Hegarty, Neil, *The Story of Ireland* (BBC Books, 2012)

Henthorn, James, ed. *Cogadh Gaedhel Re Gallaibh* (Ulan Press, 2012)

Higgins, C., *Under another Sky, Journeys in Roman Britain* (Jonathan Cape, 2013)

Hutchinson, R., *The Spanish Armada* (Weidenfeld and Nicolson, 2013)

Jacob, E. F., *The Fifteenth Century* (Oxford: 1961)

James, Jeffrey, *Swordsmen of the King* (Eastwood: Partizan Press, 2015)

Kinross, John, *The Boyne and Aughrim, the War of the Two Kings* (Windrush Press, 1997)

Laing, Lloyd & Jenny, *The Picts and Scots* (Stroud: Alan Sutton, 1993)

Lenihan, Padraig, *The Battle of the Boyne* (Stroud: Tempus, 2005)

Levene, M. & Roberts P., eds., *The Massacre in History* (New York & Oxford: Berghahn, 1999)

Loades, David, *Thomas Cromwell, Servant to Henry VIII* (Stroud: Amberley, 2013)

Lydon, J. F., 'The Braganstown Massacre, 1329', *Louth Archaeological Journal* XIX (1977)

Mac Carthaigh, P., 'Ireland versus England: The First Battle, Clashacrow', *Old Kilkenny Review* 24 (1972)

McKisack, May, *The Fourteenth Century* (Oxford: The Clarendon Press, 1959)

Magnussen, M., *Njal's Saga* (Penguin, 1987)

Marsden, John, *The Fury of the Northmen* (Kyle Cathie, 1996)

Miller, J., *James II, A Study in Kingship* (Methuen, 1989)

O'Siochru, M., *God's Executioner*, (Faber and Faber, 2008)

Ohlmeyer, J. H., 'The Wars of Religion, 1603-1660', in *A Military History of Ireland*, op. cit.

Penman, M. A., *The MacDonald Lordship and the Bruce Dynasty, c.1306–c.1371* (Stirling: 2014)

Poole, A. L., *Domesday Book to Magna Carta* (Oxford: 1955)

Powicke, M., *The Thirteenth Century, 1216–1307* (Oxford: 1962)

Reagan Butler, R., *Warriors of the Pale: An Irish Saga* (Spellmount, 2006)

Roberts, Alice, *The Celts: Search for a Civilization* (Heron Books, 2015)

Roche, Richard, *The Norman Invasion of Ireland* (Dublin: Anvil Books, 1970)

Ryan, Rev J., 'The Battle of Clontarf', *The Journal of the Royal Society of Antiquaries of Ireland* (1938)

Ryder, Ian, *An English Army for Ireland* (Eastwood: Partizan Press, 1987)

Simms, Katherine, 'Gaelic Warfare in the Middle Ages', in *A Military History of Ireland*, op. cit.

Somerset Fry, P. & F., *A History of Ireland* (New York: Barnes and Noble, 1993)

Tacitus, *The Agricola and the Germania* (Penguin Classics, 2009)

Walker, D., *The Normans in Britain* (Blackwell, 1995)

Warren, W. L., *King John* (Yale, 1997)

Wauchope, Piers, *Patrick Sarsfield and the Williamite war* (Dublin: 1992)

Webster, B., *Medieval Scotland, the making of an identity* (MacMillan Press, 1997)

Weir, M., *Breifne, from Chieftain to Landlord* (Reading: Nonsuch Publishing, 2009)

Whittock, Martyn, *Celtic Myths and Legends* (Robinson, 2013)

Zinsser, Hans, *Rats, lice and history* (New York: Little, Brown, 1935)

INDEX